CUMINGS

The Carter Presidency
and Beyond
Power and Politics in the 1980s

Laurence H. Shoup

Foreword by
Richard A. Falk

Ramparts Press

Palo Alto, California 94303

Library of Congress Cataloging in Publication Data

Shoup, Laurence H
  The Carter Presidency, and beyond.

  Includes bibliographical references and index.
  1. United States — Politics and government — 1977-
2. United States — Foreign relations — 1977-
3. Carter, Jimmy, 1924-   4. Presidents — United States —
Election — 1976.   5. Presidents — United States — Election
— 1980.   I. Title.
E872.S55   973.926'092'4   79-22593

ISBN 0-87867-075-0

Published by Ramparts Press, Palo Alto, California 94303.

Library of Congress Catalog Card Number 79-2710
ISBN 0-87867-075-0

First printing January 1980

Printed in the United States of America.

Contents

Foreword

The central mystery of American politics is the persisting demobilization of the electorate. How is it achieved? by whom? for what ends? with what instrumentalities? Presidential politics illustrates this climate of demobilization. Over and over again the American electorate is given a choice between centrist and right centrist candidates for the presidency.

After all, the United States has the trappings of democratic process. Furthermore, a serious mood of public discontent has emerged — anger with the price spiral and a tax system abusive of lower and middle income groups, the approach to national security that keeps alive threats of mass extinction and is hugely wasteful, and an energy policy that is dangerous, regressive, as well as being largely shaped by the whims of the oil companies (in concert, of course, with their colleagues in the corporate/banking stratosphere).

It seems strange that this combination of democratic process and public discontent doesn't translate itself into a radical mass movement of some kind. By and large, however, disadvantaged groups seem listless; even labor has not acted to protect its position in the economic and political order. Rightist discontent, although better organized, has also been largely marginalized. In the end, political competition at the presidential level is a bland affair, nothing of much consequence is at stake. Hence, a focus on image and personality rather than on ideology is to be expected.

Intellectuals cooperate in sustaining this demobilized political climate. Overwhelmingly, respected scholarship is oriented toward an audience of apolitical experts. Evident in this emphasis is a tacit conspiracy of silence about the role and character of the American ruling class. A central feature of ruling class objectives is to take the political center for granted as *the* realm of reason and responsibility. Such a position presupposes discrediting the left, and to a lesser degree, the far right. Such a centrist politics enables class privilege to persist without serious challenge. Even the right, by its overt defense of privilege, would threaten the ruling class, both by its style and, even more so, by its tendency to give credibility to a left challenge.

Why have our leading intellectuals been so effectively coopted? Why, for instance, have they subscribed to the pernicious myth that the United States is a country without a ruling class? This question haunts the political conscience of progressive Americans at the present time when it is becoming increasingly evident that the center cannot hold. Of course, all along at the margins there have existed a band of radical critics who have broken ranks with their colleagues to report on the existence and machinations of the ruling class. Among these critics, the work of William Appleman Williams, C. Wright Mills, Herbert Marcuse, Gabriel Kolko, G. William Domhoff, Noam Chomsky, and now Laurence Shoup particularly stands out. Even here, it must be noted, the influence of the ruling class upon the media and the academy has been felt, denying these writers the attention and stature (and, sometimes, even the publisher) that is their due. Here, too, the influence of the ruling class has effectively denied this body of work its proper stature in the study of American politics.

Laurence Shoup's earlier exposé (in collaboration with William Minter) of the class and institutional basis of American foreign policy in *Imperial Brain Trust* stands as a landmark of independent, pioneering scholarship. And now in *The Carter Presidency and Beyond* he brilliantly depicts and documents the essential anti-democratic closure of American politics that follows from the actions and worldview of its ruling class. Impressively, Shoup rests this assessment upon a concretely identifiable ruling class that acts through particular ideological mechanisms to exert pervasive, largely subliminal, influence over the governing processes at work in this country.

In Marxist terminology, the contradictions in American society have been rapidly sharpening during recent years: As the poor get squeezed, oil companies report record profits; as social services for the disadvantaged are cut back, lavish increases in the military budget are agreed upon; as the menace of petrochemical complexes and nuclear energy grow manifest, ways to accelerate the issuance of reactor licenses and reduce the burdens of environmental regulation are officially advocated. In these circumstances, it is difficult to act as if nothing fundamental is wrong with the way in which the American political system is performing.

The pretense that no ruling class exists in the United States is beginning to break down. Important limitations on tactics exist for a ruling class that seeks to convince the public (and possibly even its own members) that it doesn't exist. It requires subtle forms of manipulation that operate indirectly through the existence of authoritative screening procedures to legitimate or discredit individuals seeking political power, as well as to position ruling class members or their trusted agents in such a way as to assure that they will be "freely" chosen, on grounds of merit, for top policy-making roles. A deep economic crisis tests the composure of the American ruling class. Backstage its leaders grow restive and quarrelsome and become dissatisfied with their preferred strategy of indirection. Once on stage, however, the inhibition on academic and media commentary erodes, although slowly and tentatively. Perhaps during 1980 we will have reached a sufficient level of political consciousness so that Laurence Shoup's book can receive the wide audience its message warrants.

The public formation of the Trilateral Commission in 1973 was virtually "a coming out party" for the ruling class. It reflected a conviction of these leaders that their indirect and covert style of rule was insufficient to meet the new agenda of challenge in the leading capitalist countries of the world. Accordingly, it had become necessary for the American ruling class to exert a direct influence upon the governing process, and to do so in the spirit of a transnational ruling class concerned about keeping world capitalism healthy. The main immediate threat, I believe, prompting the formation of the Trilateral Commission was the fear that growing tensions among the capitalist governments of North America, Western Europe and Japan over the division of markets, access to raw materials, and the framework of trade and investment would produce an era of destructive competition, economic nationalism, and possibly war. In the background, also, was a growing concern about the Third World, centering around vulnerability to OPEC pressures, but extending to a desire to fend off calls for a new international economic order. To offset the growing solidarity of the Third World in these circumstances, the ruling class insisted on the importance of organizing greater solidarity among elites in the advanced industrial countries.

Yet, significantly, the Trilateralists moved quickly from their avowed "managerial" preoccupations about the world economy to proclaim, as well, "a crisis of democracy" at home. This alleged crisis consisted of a variety of unruly activist demands for reform in the political arena that were undermining the ideological coherence required to reconcile mature-to-senile capitalism with the existence of democratic procedure. Further damage was being done, according to the Trilateral Commission, by the refusal of "value-oriented intellectuals" to shut up and play along with the system in the manner of their opposite number, the good guys, who are aptly labeled "technocratic and policy-oriented intellectuals." Democracy is the preferred political form of governanace for the ruling elite so long as change-oriented groups don't exercise their democratic rights in such a vigorous way that the basic theorisms of capitalism are drawn into question. It seems clear that if a conflict breaks out between saving capitalism and upholding liberal ideology, the ruling class will compromise the latter to whatever extent seems necessary. This commitment to "stability" in defiance of popular demands overseas has consistently led the United States in recent decades to intervene in foreign societies on behalf of anti-democratic, rightist elites and regimes. And now, with the quickening of discontent at home, there is a similar conviction taking shape that the domestic requirements of capitalism call for the reining in of democratic practice. In this regard, the Brazilian and Indonesian generals provide us with an unsavory image of what we can look forward to in the United States itself if, as is almost certain, the world economic crisis deepens, and the Trilateralist ideologues like Zbigniew Brzezinski or Samuel Huntington continue to call the tune.

Let us be clear. The American ruling class would prefer not to end up with militarized governance. It prefers a moderate politics that rests on the consent (or acquiescence) of the citizenry. It is only if this consent is militantly withdrawn and cannot be easily reestablished, as seemed to be happening in the late 1960s, that more drastic means are reluctantly proposed. Similarly, abroad. Counterinsurgency warfare, CIA covert operations and interventionary diplomacy are options of last resort, undertaken because liberal democratic fixes lack a sufficient stabilizing capacity in particular situations. Chile is illustrative. United States security managers preferred a reformist Frei to a repressive Pinochet, but in 1970-73 facilitated Pinochet's coup as an antidote to Allende's radicalism.

Laurence Shoup gives us a clear, coherent account of ruling class politics as it has related to Jimmy Carter's candidacy and presidency. The casting of Carter as a presidential candidate is vividly explicated, as is the degree to which Carter has delivered, as expected, while in the White House. Shoup backs up this analysis of Carter's policies with an illuminating depiction of Carter's top appointments. He notes, of course, the high density of Trilateral Commission members in cabinet and sub-cabinet posts.

In the background is the haunting question of why Americans put up with this kind of political hype. Part of the answer, as Shoup effectively shows, is a consequence of the complicity of big-time media, which polices the boundaries of what is responsible and reasonable when it comes to interpreting the news or assessing an individual's qualifications for high political office. Closely related to this is the apolitical myths of public service disseminated so effectively by power-wielders. *White House Years* by Henry Kissinger can be used as a monumental illustration of this technique. Kissinger would have us believe that foreign policy is hammered out by dedicated public servants, differing from "ordinary" Americans only in their greater capacity to discern the national interest. Rather than inquire into possible class bias, Kissinger exalts, without qualification, the American aristocracy: "Dean Acheson, David K.E. Bruce, Ellsworth Bunker, Averall Harriman, John McCloy, Robert Lovett, Douglas Dillon, among others, represented a unique pool of talent — an aristocracy dedicated to the service of this nation on behalf of principles beyond partisanship." Of course, and it is part of the argument, the list is non-partisan in the sense of party politics, but is extremely partisan when it comes to economic affiliations and ruling class politics. Each of these individuals is tied by family and profession to the world of high finance. Kissinger's refusal to acknowledge such forms of partisanship is partly what makes him such an exemplary instrument of the ruling class.

Reading Shoup is, if nothing else, an antidote to the commercial blitz associated with Kissinger's account of how national policy emerges from government. But it is much more than this. Shoup, without jargon or dogmatism, clearly depicts the structure of the American political system at the present time. Without his kind of structural account it is impossible to grasp the constraints on the nominating, electing, and governing process or to understand why the relative idealism of a liberal presidential campaign is discarded so soon after ascent to high office. This disillusioning realization has generally nothing to do with sincerity of the particular politician. In the pre-nominating phase a candidate becomes credible to the extent that he demonstrates capacity and willingness to govern in a manner responsive to ruling class requirements. During the post-nominating campaign stage a candidate has some limited discretion to project an image that arouses mass enthusiasm, and is then free to advocate positions that are relatively unpopular with the ruling class. Indeed, such advocacy is often necessary for Democratic Party candidates who must generate left-liberal backing to get elected. Once elected, however, the noose tightens again, as capacity to govern depends on a renewed display of responsiveness to ruling class priorities.

Shoup also persuasively shows that the dominant sector of the ruling classes should not be confused with the reactionary outlook of the political right. No, indeed, the ruling class is itself attacked from the right as tool of the Communists and the like. The right proposes a set of policies that promote the interests and values of national capitalism, favoring protectionism, low taxes, the elimination of welfare programs, balanced federal budgets, and old-style nationalism. These policies are not compatible with the dynamic, internationalist sector of corporate and banking leadership that seeks to maximize trade and investment possibilities, envisioning as their ideal the entire world organized as a single integrated market.

A hopeful future for America, and for the world, depends on the rapid emergence of a left politics capable of challenging ruling class politics. Whether such a new political formation is being prefigured in the struggle against nuclear power is one of the prime questions of the 1980s. Whether such a challenge can be mounted partly depends on the capacity of the anti-nuclear movement to broaden its appeal to become a mass movement with significant rank-and-file labor and minority support. Laurence Shoup's book represents, then, an indispensable guide for all those committed to a serious program of progressive political change in the United States, a commitment that itself expresses the urgent need for some radical departures from orthodoxy in both domestic and foreign policy.

— Richard A. Falk
Director, Center of International
Studies, Princeton University

Preface

This book is in many respects an outgrowth of my first book, *Imperial Brain Trust: The Council on Foreign Relations and United States Foreign Policy* (co-authored with William Minter), published by Monthly Review Press in 1977. While studying the Council and the related private policy-planning organizations of what is usually labeled the "Eastern Establishment," I noted at an early date the involvement, and thus the likely importance, of Jimmy Carter. This enabled me to predict during 1975 that Carter's candidacy was a serious one that had the potential to gain power. Once Carter had been elected President, I decided to do an in-depth study of exactly how he rose from a fairly obscure governor to President in less than two years, and the role of Eastern Establishment organizations in his rise to power.

Once I had finished a short manuscript on this topic, I received interest and encouragement from the publisher and editor of Ramparts Press. They suggested I expand the book to include not only the origins of the Carter presidency, but also his administration's policies. I have tried to show how these policies reflect the priorities of the corporate leaders who actually put Carter in office and not the constituency which voted for him, as well as to offer a perspective on the future.

The result is *The Carter Presidency and Beyond*, an attempt to go beyond the more common focus on personalities in political reporting and delve into the actual structural roots of political power in modern America, using the Carter presidency as a case study.

I would like to thank Laurence Moore, who published this book, and Russell Stetler, who edited the manuscript. Their teamwork in making suggestions, offering criticism and encouragement made the book possible. Despite actively pursuing her own career in archeology, my wife, Suzanne Baker Shoup, took time out to make numerous valuable suggestions and also typed much of the manuscript. Others who helped in some way with this effort include G. William Domhoff, William Minter, Benjamin Smith, S. Dan Schwartz, and Pauline Jaenke Condrick, who encouraged me to begin. None of the above can, of course, be held responsible for any errors or shortcomings which this work may have. Finally, I want to thank my son Daniel David, almost three years old now, who cheerfully accepted the frequent fact that, as he put it, "Daddy's writing a book on Jimmy Carter," and waited patiently for a section or page to be completed before getting some attention from his father.

Laurence H. Shoup

Introduction

This is a book about the real sources of political power in the United States. Who the real power wielders of the United States are and how they operate both behind the scenes and openly in the media are explored by means of a concrete case study of Jimmy Carter's political roots, presidency and 1980 election prospects.

Carter's rise to power is usually described with superlatives — "incredible," "remarkable," "amazing," "extraordinary," "phenomenal," "the number one success story of our time," "the political miracle of the century." How and why Carter succeeded in gaining the 1976 Democratic nomination and the presidency is indeed an important and fascinating story.

Most political writers have explained Carter's rise to power as a kind of Horatio Alger story. Martin Schram's *Running for President* and Jules Witcover's *Marathon* are the two most widely acclaimed books on the 1976 campaign. They argue that it was Carter's attractive personality, hard campaigning and talent that gained him the presidency.[1] Schram states that the "essential factors" explaining Carter's nomination were his and his advisers' success at grassroots campaigning, skill in organization, knack to make the right moves at the right moments and ability to formulate popular positions on the issues.[2] Witcover argues that Carter, without fame, much money or established political support was still able to win with the deft use of the resources he had — time, determination, intelligence, an attractive family, a superb sense of timing and an ability to attract other able people.[3]

It is clear that Jimmy Carter and his staff did have, to some degree, the qualities which Schram, Witcover and other writers stress. Carter was indeed an excellent salesman for himself. Yet such an individualistic approach — focusing on the personal characteristics of candidates — is only one part of a satisfactory explanation of a leader's rise to power. Such a narrow approach cannot explain why other candidates, and their staffs, who had roughly similar qualities, failed where Carter succeeded. The whole truth demands something more than a focus on the individual candidates — it requires an understanding of the structure of power in America. How does a candidate make contact with and become acceptable to the key power centers of this society and how does their support give the candidate the financial wherewithal and necessary favorable coverage in the mass communications media to become President? And how does a President successfully rule the United States and its de facto empire?

To answer these questions we need to understand that there are two separate levels of political process operating in the American political system. The first, which receives greater attention in the news media and academic publications is best labeled the "party politics" level. This is the familiar world of political bosses and party elites, of advertising agencies merchandising a candidate to the voters, and the carnival-like atmosphere of "grass roots" campaigning in primaries and general elections. The second level, usually ignored — at least partly because it takes place behind the scenes — is actually more important than the first. It is best called the "ruling class" level of American politics. This term refers to the ways in which power brokers representing the upper class can and do control the political process.[4] This level includes the world of large-scale fund-raising from wealthy "fat-cats," the networks of influential people developed by exclusive private clubs and policy-planning groups, and the media's merchandising of favored candidates through manipulation of the definition of "news." The two levels of politics are, of course, interconnected and always interact in some fashion — a successful politician has contacts with both realms and attempts to reconcile them — but they do represent different traditions, constituencies and purposes and thus are conceptually distinct. The ruling class level of American politics is the central focus of the case study presented here. This analysis will show how a small group of wealthy and powerful people — members of the corporate upper class — shaped the 1976 presidential selection process, helped a relatively obscure former Governor of Georgia gain power, then molded his administration, and are already shaping the candidates and issues for the 1980 election.

It is an accepted fact that major party presidential *nominations* are "the most critical stage of the entire process of presidential choice," because it is at this stage that alternatives are excluded and the voters' choices narrowed to only two individuals.[5] The two or three years before the primaries begin and, depending on circumstances, the primaries themselves, are crucial to the nominating process. During the pre-primary period, labeled the "invisible primary" by some, the mass communications media, political financiers, pollsters, polls and party leaders produce an unofficial nominee or at most several "viable," "serious" candidates, acceptable to the powerful and likely to be able to lead the people.[6] Part I of this study will therefore examine the five-year period prior to March 1976. By late March Carter was so high in the public opinion polls and was gathering support so rapidly that he had virtually cinched the nomination.

During this early period two things were essential to the

success of candidate Carter. First, adequate financing was needed to hire a staff, travel, disseminate campaign literature, buy advertisements — in short, supply all the necessities of a modern political campaign. Second, favorable coverage from the mass communications media — especially the elite of both the press and broadcast media — was absolutely vital. As candidate Robert Dole expressed this fact, "the press in effect decides who the candidates are," and as Keech and Matthews, two authorities in this field, put it: "if the mass communications media do not pay attention to a person, he has no chance of becoming president."[7] Media coverage, or the lack of it, also plays a major role in raising money, since journalists and media commentators can and do label a candidate a "winner" or "loser," "serious" or not, "viable" or not, and political financiers, like voters, take notice of these appraisals. Favorable media coverage was especially crucial to Carter since he was one of the least known candidates in the field.

Part I will cover all these areas. Chapter one recounts Carter's origins and his early support from the upper class of Atlanta, Georgia — and the campaign funding it supplied. Chapter two relates how the Atlanta establishment put Carter in touch with the "Eastern Establishment," the locus of national power.[8] This contact led to Carter's early membership in the exclusive Trilateral Commission, an organization dominated by leaders of the Eastern Establishment. Chapter three gives detailed information and analysis on how and why major mass communications corporations helped create a positive public image for candidate Carter.

Once in office, any President — other than one who is a revolutionary intent on redesigning society — needs the cooperation of the economic powers that be in order to rule the nation. In the long run, he can only obtain this cooperation by pleasing these existing powers through his appointments and policies. Otherwise the large corporations and banks which dominate the economy will lack confidence and withhold the investment needed to maintain the economy on an even keel. Part II's focus then is on how Carter's foreign (chapter four) and domestic (chapter five) policies as President conform to the wishes of the top corporate leaders who put him in office. It also examines why these policies are not in the interests of the great majority of the American people. The final chapter discusses in depth the evolving shape of the 1980 presidential election campaign, the key candidates, their support groups, and the President's strategy to remain in the White House for another four years.

Notes

1. Martin Schram, *Running for President: A Journal of the Carter Campaign* (New York: Pocket Books, 1978); Jules Witcover, *Marathon: The Pursuit of the Presidency 1972-1976* (New York: Viking, 1977).

2. Schram, *Running for President*, p. 9.

3. Witcover, *Marathon*, p. 647.

4. The terms "ruling class," "corporate upper class," "upper class," and "capitalist class" refer to the political, economic and social role of the roughly 1-2% of American families who stand at the top of this nation's wealth pyramid, interact and intermarry, are listed in the *Social Register* and other exclusive directories, attend private schools, belong to restrictive social clubs, control the most important private policy-planning organizations and direct the dominant corporations of the United States. Basic works on this class and its role include several books by G. William Domhoff: *Who Rules America?* (Englewood Cliffs, New Jersey: Prentice-Hall, 1967); *The Higher Circles: The Governing Class in America* (New York: Random House, 1970); *Fat Cats and Democrats* (Englewood Cliffs, New Jersey: Prentice-Hall, 1972); *The Bohemian Grove and Other Retreats* (New York: Harper and Row, 1974); *Who Really Rules? New Haven and Community Power Reexamined* (Santa Monica, California: Goodyear, 1977); and *The Powers That Be: State and Ruling Class in Corporate America* (New York: Random House, 1979), and works by Paul Sweezy, *The Present as History* (New York: Monthly Review, 1953); E. Bigby Baltzell, *Philadelphia Gentlemen* (New York: Free Press, 1958); Ferdinand Lundberg, *The Rich and the Super-Rich* (New York: Lyle Stuart, 1968); James Weinstein, *The Corporate Ideal in the Liberal State* (Boston: Beacon, 1968); S. Menshikov, *Millionaires and Managers,* (Moscow: Progress Publishers, 1969); and Laurence H. Shoup and William Minter, *Imperial Brain Trust: The Council on Foreign Relations and United States Foreign Policy* (New York: Monthly Review, 1977).

5. James D. Barber (ed.), *Choosing the President* (Englewood Cliffs, New Jersey: Prentice-Hall, 1974), p. 36.

6. See William R. Keech and Donald R. Matthews, *The Party's Choice* (Washington, D.C.: The Brookings Institution, 1976), vii. p. 1; and Arthur T. Hadley, *The Invisible Primary: The Inside Story of the Other Presidential Race: The Making of the Candidate* (Englewood Cliffs, New Jersey, Prentice-Hall, 1976).

7. *San Francisco Sunday Examiner and Chronicle Sunday Punch* June 17, 1979, p. 4; Keech and Matthews, *The Party's Choice*, pp. 9-10.

8. The term "Eastern Establishment" refers to both the leaders of the upper-class families of the northeast coast of the United States and the key institutions they control. These families are centered in New York City especially, but also in Boston, Philadelphia, and Washington, D.C. They control a complex of institutions which are dominant in the political, economic and social life of America — leading financial, industrial and media corporations, law firms, policy-planning organizations, exclusive clubs, top foundations and elite universities.

Part I

The Making of President Carter

1

Carter and the Atlanta Establishment

Atlanta, Georgia, is the financial, trade, transportation and communication center of the southeastern United States. It is also the cultural focus of this section of the country, a nationally oriented city with cosmopolitan tastes. The city has grown very rapidly during the past twenty-five years, as Georgia has transformed itself from a primarily rural, agricultural state to an urban one dominated by finance and industry, with "agribusiness" in an important, but secondary position. During this period of growth the local upper class which dominates Atlanta's economy and society — made famous in a detailed study of its power structure by sociologist Floyd Hunter — has prospered economically and increased its political influence and contacts both statewide and on a national scale.[1] The more liberal, cosmopolitan upper class of Atlanta was in a comparatively good position to take advantage of the progressive trends of the 1960s — voting rights for blacks, the decline in vote stealing in rural areas, and Supreme Court decisions like *Baker* v. *Carr*, which ended indirect voting systems favoring rural over urban areas. By contrast the more conservative local gentry of

Georgia, whose influence was based on racism and the near feudal control of rural areas, found their power ebbing as the 1960s progressed.

Jimmy Carter of Plains, in Sumter County, southeast Georgia, was born into one of these local gentry families, historically conservative and racist, yet having a paternalistic, "noblesse oblige" feeling towards those they control in their local area. His father was in the old mold, a "baron in a feudal situation."[2] For whatever reasons, among them the influence of his mother, Carter grew up a racial moderate, even a liberal by Georgia standards, and a forward-looking innovative capitalist and agribusinessman. The Carter family was well-to-do even in Jimmy's youth. It had large landholdings — about four thousand acres — and local business interests, and at one time employed three hundred black workers.[3] Later, when presidential candidate Carter was stressing his "humble" beginnings to conform to the Horatio Alger myth of American politics, it irritated his mother who, her pride hurt by the gross exaggeration, said: "he makes us sound so poor you want to get out a hat and take up a collection."[4] By the mid-1970s the financial holdings of the Carter family — Jimmy, his mother Lillian, brother Billy and their wives — were estimated at about $5 million, including Carter's peanut business, over three thousand acres of land, ten lots in Plains, and three homes, as well as stockholdings in Coca-Cola and other companies. Jimmy was the principal owner in the Carter family property, holding about 60 percent of the peanut warehouse stock, for example.[5] This wealth, while certainly not stupendous by national standards, gave Carter the freedom to develop his political career full time and provided substantial amounts of cash at crucial moments in his races for both the Georgia governorship and the presidency. In his 1966 campaign for governor, for example, he spent $60,000 of his own money.[6] In the presidential campaign he spent over $30,000 of his own and family funds during the first nine months of 1975 alone. Carter also borrowed heavily in 1976, including $100,000 against his personal assets.[7]

This was a "potent factor" in his rise to power, said the *New York Times*, since most other Democratic candidates did not have access to such sums.[8]

Carter's first close contact with the Atlanta Establishment came in 1962 when he ran for the state senate. Carter appeared to have lost the election, when he heard about possible vote fraud in one part of his district controlled by rural machine politicians of the old school. With the help of an *Atlanta Journal* reporter and lawyer Charles Kirbo of King and Spalding, the city's (and state's) best-connected law firm, Carter was able to appeal and win the election.[9] Once in office Carter solidified contacts with the capital's higher circles. Kirbo became a close friend and gave Carter access to some of the main power people of Atlanta. An unsuccessful campaign for governor followed in 1966. It was a premature effort, as Carter at this point lacked a statewide power base.

Following his defeat, Carter used his ample free time to make speeches and shake hands around the state, attracting media coverage and building up the voter support necessary for a winning campaign. When he ran in the 1970 primary, however, only a part of the Atlanta Establishment was behind him. The liberal Cox-Chambers newspaper and television empire (the two biggest Atlanta newspapers and the largest statewide television network, an NBC affiliate) strongly favored former governor Carl Sanders and portrayed Carter as "an ignorant and bigoted redneck peanut farmer," leading to an angry and ill-tempered Carter attack on the media.[10] Carter, however, got strong support from a more conservative group of powerful Atlantans — bankers, corporation lawyers, business executives and contractors — the inner circle of which was to provide the core of his financial support in his presidential campaign as well.

Prominent individuals contributed heavily to Carter's campaign and signed notes for bank loans to keep the campaign going. These men included Charles Kirbo, a senior partner in the King and Spalding law firm, Atlanta's "most prestigious" and one of the wealthiest, with clients like Coca-Cola, General Motors, Cox Enterprises (owners of the Cox-Chambers media empire), Rich's Department Stores (biggest in Atlanta), Prudential Insurance, and the Trust Company of Georgia, the state's third largest banking institution, and widely known as the "Coca Cola bank."[11] King and Spalding lawyers sit on the boards of many corporations and as individuals "have traditionally been pillars of the local establishment. Many of them belong to the Piedmont Driving Club and Capital City Club."[12] Membership in these exclusive social clubs is a major index of upper-class standing. To join requires not only acceptance by a membership committee, but also an initiation fee of $5000.[13]

Another important Carter supporter was Philip H. Alston, Jr., a senior partner in the law firm of Alston, Miller and Gaines, whose clients include Chrysler, Aetna Life, E. I. duPont de Nemours, Eastman Kodak, Sears Roebuck, Equitable Life, the Atlanta Braves, Citizens and Southern National Bank, and other big corporations. Alston has "wide business contacts," says *Business Week*.[14] He and his family gave thousands to Carter's campaign and raised thousands more from friends and business associates.[15] The Alston law firm is also part of the social and economic elite of the city. Called "well-bred" by *Newsweek*, Alston himself is a past president of the Piedmont Driving Club, the most prestigious in the city.[16]

David Gambrell and his father E. Smythe Gambrell were also early Carter supporters. David was a Carter fund-raiser and strategist in 1966 and campaign treasurer in 1970. Wealthy and socially prominent, the Gambrells contributed thousands of dollars to both campaigns. David is a member of the Piedmont Driving Club, and the elder Gambrell is a former president of the American Bar Association and Georgia State Chamber of Commerce. His law firm represents corporations like Eastern Airlines, Greyhound, Allstate Insurance, Travelers Insurance, Olin-Mathieson, Uniroyal, Cummins Engine, RCA, Continental Can, and others.[17]

While these early Carter backers came from Atlanta's white, gentile power structure of big bankers, businessmen, and lawyers, another key supporter, Robert Lipshutz, represents a different sector of Atlanta society. He is a major leader of the reform wing of the city's Jewish community. Lipshutz's law firm represents the smaller local businesses — real estate, small banks, credit unions, co-ops, and so on — rather than the national and multinational corporations represented by the law firms mentioned above.[18] As could be expected, Lipshutz's income was roughly half that of Kirbo, Alston, and the Gambrells. Informed estimates of Lipshutz's income in the mid-1970s were around $70 to $80,000 a year, whereas Kirbo's was about $200,000.[19] Lipshutz gave Carter's 1970 campaign at least $6000.[20]

There were others helpful to Carter in both the 1966 and 1970 campaigns, such as Gainesville attorney William Gunther and a group of individuals — Bert Lance, James B. Langford, and others — who owned the National Bank of Calhoun, Georgia. But the Atlanta group was "at the center of his backing."[21] Without them Carter would have had much less support, financially and otherwise, and might well have lost, ending his political career. These men, with their wide contacts, brought in other supporters, accounting for a large percentage of the nearly $700,000 which Carter raised for his 1970 governor's campaign.

It was also through these influential Atlantans that Carter "first came to the attention of Anne Cox Chambers," wife of the chairman of the Cox Broadcasting Company.[22] This corporate group, controlled by the Cox-Chambers families, owns the two major newspapers of Atlanta as well as a radio and television station. Their media collectively reach over 80 percent of the state's households and are thus by far the most important media group in Georgia (the second group reaches only 17 percent of the state's audience).[23] Mrs. Chambers and her husband, Robert, who hold key positions in the company, opposed Carter in the primary, but once he became the Democratic nominee gave $26,500 to Carter's 1970 general election campaign, the largest personal contribution Carter received.[24]

Kirbo and the others also introduced Carter to J. Paul Austin, chairman of Coca-Cola and a board member of New York multinationals like Morgan Guaranty Trust bank and General Electric. Austin gave $2500 to Carter's 1970 campaign and other Coca-Cola executives gave lesser amounts of money or free time to Carter's efforts.[25]

In contrast to the financial support given Carter by Atlanta's corporate lawyers and their clients, only one large contribution — of $500 — came from a labor union.[26] Labor's role in Carter's 1970 victory was nearly nonexistent.

Why did these wealthy and socially prominent individuals choose to support Jimmy Carter, an obscure land owner and agribusinessman from Plains, for governor? The answer lies in the problem faced by the rich in a state where a large percentage of voters have a populist consciousness and a natural distrust and resentment of the wealthy and powerful. The corporate leaders of the Atlanta Establishment look for candidates who can command a large populist following while remaining sympathetic to corporate interests. Jimmy Carter was a man who could convincingly speak the language of the mass of voters, yet represent business interests once in office. He was very ambitious; had a talent for being all things to all people; projected charm and idealism; and was attractive, intelligent, and conscientious. Most importantly, he was part of the establishment in his political and economic views. He could be trusted not to rock the boat to any significant extent. For all his expressions of Christianity, he ran a hardheaded multi-million-dollar business operation which paid its workers non-union hourly wages near the minimum. One of Carter's peanut factory employees, for example, was found in 1976 to be making $2.54 an hour, with no additional pay for overtime, after five years of service.[27] This kind of non-union, low-wage business operation is typical for the South, and Carter was simply paying the going rates. Nevertheless, sharp business practices were something which other business-men could relate to and, partly as a result, Carter later had an edge over other Democratic presidential candidates when talking to business groups. As *The Economist* of London put it: "his proven skills as a manager win him a good hearing on Wall Street."[28]

Once in the governor's mansion, Carter used his political, economic and social power, as well as his considerable charm, to win over completely many of the remaining wealthy Atlantans who had held back during his campaign. He attempted to build a machine by appointing his supporters to state and Democratic party offices. Kirbo became the state's Democratic party chairman; David Gambrell was appointed to the United States Senate when Senator Richard B. Russell died; Philip Alston was named to the University of Georgia Board of Regents; William Gunther was appointed to the Georgia Supreme Court; and Bert Lance became director of the State Highway Department. Lance's post was a good place for an aspiring state-level politician to be stationed, since road contractors depend on the state for business and make up a pool of available campaign contributions. In his 1970 campaign, Carter received about $70,000 in contributions from special interest groups which did business with the state.[29]

Carter was successful in becoming "extremely popular" with most wealthy Atlantans, broadening his potential base for higher office.[30] He and his close advisers had decided by 1972 that the higher office was to be the presidency. The possibility had been raised in 1971, but was apparently not seriously considered until after the 1972 Democratic convention. Carter's remaining two years as governor were devoted to establishing a good record to run on; making nationwide contacts with economic, media, and political leaders; collecting lists for fundraising; and planning the campaign in detail.

This same group of Atlanta Establishment figures donated the essential early money during 1975 and early 1976 which propelled Carter into the presidential race. A certain minimum of financial support is necessary to set up a campaign staff, conduct a national delegate drive, enter primaries, and so on. This money, for Carter and all the candidates, comes from a small segment of the population. Several studies have shown that only about 10 percent of the population contributes to presidential campaigns.[31] An even smaller group, the wealthy "fat cats," less than 1 percent of the population, provide the decisive money. It was criticism of the major role of these fat cats which led to the 1974 campaign reform act. A $1000 *per person* contribution limit was established for the primary and general election campaigns with "organizations" limited to $5000. Federal matching funds were offered to candidates after January 1, 1976 based on fundraising during 1975 if a candidate raised $5000 in $250 or smaller contributions in at least twenty states. Maximum spending amounts per state and overall were set and stricter reporting rules were also established. This law had certain important effects, at least some of which were apparently unforeseen. First of all, since the law allowed a candidate to spend as much of his own money as he wished, candidates who were personally wealthy had an advantage. Second, the new laws tended to favor candidates with state-level patronage systems, especially governors, who receive campaign contributions from political appointees and others who are dependent upon government largesse. Finally, since maximum-spending limits were set for each state, little-known candidates could not become well known by an expensive overnight media blitz. This had an additional effect: the already great powers of the mass communications media in making or breaking a candidate with free media coverage, especially a little-known one like Carter, were increased.[32]

Since the law placed a spending limit far beyond the means of the average American, it did little to curb the power of the upper class, which could still contribute $1000, or the groups just below the upper class in the social structure, such as doctors, lawyers or small businessmen, who could contribute a like amount. Thus the campaign-spending law actually reformed little. It continued to favor wealthy, middle-of-the-road candidates who could get free media support. However, the new campaign-funding rules did make it easier for a governor with a solid financial base in his own state to compete for the presidency, a fact which helped Jimmy Carter.

Before discussing direct campaign contributions, the ones which show up on official reports by the campaign treasurer, we will consider briefly a form of indirect contribution which was especially important to the Carter candidacy. In the early period of his campaign, during 1972, 1973, and 1974, while he was governor and had decided to run for President but had not officially announced, Carter spent much time making national contacts and traveling abroad to foster an image of competence in foreign policy. While governor, Carter depended for a good deal of his transportation on free rides on the executive jets of major Georgia corporations. Coca-Cola's airplanes have been most often mentioned in this regard. Coke jets took Carter to "several" national and southern governors' conferences, on at least one three-week Latin American trip, and "may" have been used to fly Carter to Washington D.C. and other cities.[33] On his overseas travel Carter also depended on Coca-Cola executives to pick him up at airports and escort him around.[34]

Coca-Cola has a tradition of interest in President making. While studying the Atlanta Establishment in the early 1950s, sociologist Floyd Hunter was informed that leaders of Coca-Cola were "among the men who had urged General Eisenhower to take his post-war European assignment as an aid in grooming him for the presidency."[35]

Carter was very complimentary about Coke's contribution to his state and his own enlightenment, saying in 1974 that ". . . we have our own built-in State Department in the Coca-Cola Company. They provide me ahead of time with. . . penetrating analyses of what the country is, what its problems are, who its leaders are, and when I arrive there, provide me with an introduction to the leaders of that country. . . . "[36] This kind of intimate relationship with the Coca-Cola Company and its executives also had advantages in campaign fundraising. During 1974 when the first of Carter's presidential campaign money was raised, Coca-Cola's employees provided the biggest single contribution — $3000.[37]

The history of Carter's prenomination fundraising efforts has two basic periods. The first is best described as the "pre-bandwagon" period, from late 1974 to the end of 1975. During this time, when only true believers in Carter and those willing to gamble on a longshot invested in the campaign, Carter raised almost $1 million.[38] This early money was the hardest to collect of all campaign money. During 1974-75, Carter stood fourth in fundraising, collecting substantially less than Wallace, Jackson, and Bentsen, about the same as Udall, and substantially more than Harris, Shriver, Bayh, and Shapp.[39]

What could be called the "bandwagon" period extended from January to July 1976. As the campaign progressed month by month, a higher and higher percentage of Carter's campaign donations came from outside Georgia and from the politically expedient — those who wanted to be with the winner whoever he was. At the same time financial support dropped sharply for other Democratic candidates who gave up the race one by one. Carter raised by far the greatest amount of his funding during this bandwagon period — about $10.5 million, including $3.4 million in public funds.

Carter was the most successful Democratic fundraiser and greatest spender during the prenomination period — $11.4 million to $7.9 million for Wallace and $6.2 million for Udall.[40] Carter got by far the largest percentage of his money from donations over $101. The figure that the Federal Election Commission (FEC) gives in its report is 61 percent, but this is greatly *understated*, since the same person could give many $100 donations and have all of them count in the under $101 category for accounting purposes. In contrast to the FEC's figure of 39 percent of Carter's total contributions in the $100 or under range, 89 percent of Wallace's, 85 percent of Harris's, and 73 percent of Udall's were under $100.[41]

In studying how a president is actually chosen, the early or "pre-bandwagon" period is obviously crucial. It is during this early period that a candidate lays the groundwork for future success or failure and obtains the money which allows him to get into the race as a "serious" candidate. As campaign finance expert Alexander Heard put it, ". . . money probably has its greatest impact on the choice of public officials in the shadow land of our politics where it is decided who will be a candidate for a party's nomination and who will not. A 'choke point' exists where vital financial encouragement can be extended or withheld."[42] Where then did Carter's campaign funding come from during this crucial early time of 1974 through 1975?

As could be expected, Georgia and the South dominated Carter's fundraising efforts during 1974 and 1975. Georgia alone supplied over two-thirds of the money Carter collected during 1974 and the first months of 1975.[43] The percentage from Georgia dropped as the year progressed, reaching just under 50 percent by summer and remaining at that figure for the rest of 1975. During the first months of 1976, with the bandwagon effect under way, the percentage of campaign funds coming from Georgia dropped to less than 30 percent and continued to slide downward as money poured in from around the country following Carter's primary victories.[44] Georgia contributors continued to give at a high rate, but amounts coming from other parts of the country were so great that Georgia's percentage of the total was much smaller.

The bulk of the approximately $1 million Carter raised during 1974 and 1975 came from two sources — the Atlanta Establishment, which directly or indirectly through their business contacts supplied the majority of the Georgia contributions, and a few "fat cats" around the country who organized gatherings of their wealthy friends to collect money for Carter. Atlanta's upper class had moved behind Carter in concert once he declared for the presidency.

One authority on Georgia campaign finance pointed out

that the state has a "narrow base of available political money," the key sources being banks, the wealthy, and special interests.[45] The role of banks and the wealthy was especially important in the Carter campaign. As this is being written in the summer of 1979, charges have been made about improprieties, if not illegalities, in the financing of the Carter presidential campaign. The controversy centers around the role of the National Bank of Georgia — headed in 1975 and 1976 by close Carter friend and political ally Bert Lance — in loans to both the Carter peanut warehouse and Carter friend Gerald Rafshoon's advertising company of Atlanta, which ran Carter's advertising campaign. Lance's bank loaned Carter's warehouse about $1 million during 1975 and 1976, making this relatively small peanut operation one of the bank's biggest borrowers. Lance's bank also loaned the Rafshoon agency $155,000 in mid-April, 1976, secured by the agencies' accounts receivable, including receivables from a Carter campaign organization that was over a million dollars in debt.[46] In terms of the size, volume and profits of both the Carter warehouse and the Rafshoon agency, and since a good part of Rafshoon's receivables were due from a highly risky political venture, neither of these loans made sense in terms of the normal business goal of maximization of profit.[47] The picture is further complicated and darkened by the fact that the Carter peanut warehouse reportedly was at times delinquent in making payments on the loan and Billy Carter is known to have deposited about $500,000 from the Carter warehouse accounts at the National Bank of Georgia into his personal bank account at the peak of the presidential primary season during March, 1976 and withdrawn the money shortly thereafter.[48] Yet another suspicious aspect is that the Rafshoon agency carried a debt, owed it by the Carter campaign, ranging from $176,000 to $645,997 during the key primary months of February-April, 1976. It is as yet unclear where Rafshoon got the money to extend such large sums to Carter. He says the Lance loan, credit from suppliers, and deferring profit taking account for it.[49] Since the Rafshoon agency's profits for 1976 have been estimated at only $70,000 and credit from suppliers would have had to come from major media outlets (which would itself have been an illegal corporate campaign contribution) there is justified skepticism about Rafshoon's explanation. The more probable explanation is that Billy Carter's withdrawal of $500,000 from the peanut warehouse account found its way into Rafshoon's hands. This would also explain why Billy Carter reportedly took the fifth amendment before a federal grand jury investigating the whole matter in October 1978.

Viewed from any perspective, several aspects of these arrangements appear to amount to illegal corporate campaign contributions and Lance's recent indictment on charges which include misappropriation of bank funds seems to confirm the suspicion that many of his business dealings had unethical and perhaps illegal aspects. To cite one specific example, Lance's National Bank of Georgia loan to the Rafshoon advertising agency and Rafshoon's extension of large amounts of credit to the Carter campaign both amount to de-facto illegal corporate campaign contributions, since Lance's loan in effect allowed Rafshoon to give the Carter campaign credit in a business where the standard industry practice is "cash in advance."[50]

More fundamentally, since Jimmy Carter personally contributed at least $30,000 (and other family members thousands more) and almost two years of his time to his own campaign, money which must have come at least partly from the peanut warehouse, it is evident that one cannot separate the credits given the warehouse by Lance's bank from the financing of the presidential campaign. Carter's personal fortune, partly achieved and maintained through his contacts with Lance and other wealthy, well-connected and credit-worthy men clearly played a key role in the campaign. The central point then, more important than the specific machinations of this or any other campaign, is the fact that the entire structure of political finance at the highest levels heavily favors a specific class of people, those with a high level of assets and connections to bankers or the rich. In short, the upper class controls the bulk of campaign contributions, and this is especially true in Georgia, which is a state without strong labor unions. Economically and socially, Atlanta dominates Georgia, and Carter "had become extremely popular" with upper class Atlantans.[51] They became the big benefactors of his early presidential campaign. The nature of this group can be illustrated by listing a few of the prominent Atlantans who gave at least $750 to Carter during 1974 and 1975. In addition to the core group composed of people like Kirbo, Alston, the Gambrells, Lance, and Lipschutz who have been previously mentioned were:

Ivan Allen, Jr. — called the "quintessential northside (of Atlanta) 'silk-stocking' politician,"[52] Allen owns his own business and is also director of Rich's Department Store, Equitable Life Insurance, Southern Bell, Cox Broadcasting, and the Atlanta Braves. He is a member of the exclusive Piedmont Driving Club.

William C. Bartholomay — Chairman of the Atlanta Braves, Bartholomay is a member of the Chicago *Social Register*, the exclusive New York Links Club, the Metropolitan Club of Washington, D.C., and the Piedmont Driving Club. His wife is Gail Dillingham of Hawaii, the daughter of Lowell Dillingham, one of that state's biggest businessmen.

Robert and Anne Chambers — Anne Cox Chambers is the daughter of James M. Cox, former governor of Ohio and Democratic presidential nominee in 1920. Together the Chambers chair both the Cox Broadcasting Company and the Atlanta Newspapers Company. Anne also sits on the board of the Fulton National Bank of Atlanta, and Robert is a member of the Piedmont Driving Club.

Alex P. Gaines — A law partner of Philip H. Alston, Gaines is a director of local corporations, a member of the Atlanta Chamber of Commerce and a member of the Piedmont Driving and Commerce Clubs.

John Izard — A Yale graduate, Izard is a senior member of the King and Spalding law firm.

Gordon Jones — President of Fulton National Bank of Atlanta and a director of many local corporations.

Richard L. Kattel — Chairman of Citizens and Southern National Bank of Atlanta, the largest bank in the southeastern United States. Educated at Harvard, Kattel is a director of several local corporations and a member of the U.S. Chamber of Commerce.

J. Mack Robinson — Chairman of Dixie Finance Company and a director of the First National Bank of Atlanta.

It is clear that the core of Carter's supporters were some of the wealthiest and most prestigious capitalists and social leaders of Atlanta, with incomes near or above $100,000 and wealth levels many times that figure, putting them easily in the top one half of 1 percent of the population in those categories. They are part of that top 1 percent of wealth holders who control about 50 percent of America's corporate stock and 25 percent of all wealth in this nation.

Carter also drew contributions from the next stratum of the population, especially the owners of smaller businesses (real estate, local banks, contractors, small industry, insurance, retailers, developers), professionals, especially doctors and lawyers representing smaller local businesses, as well as some of the wealthier educators, public officials, and farmers. A review of Carter's reports to the Federal Election Commission covering 1975 makes it clear that this group of smaller owners and white-collar workers usually referred to as the "new middle class" or "upper middle class" (that 10 percent or so of the population making over $23,000 — 1975 figures) contributed significant amounts of money to Carter's campaign.[53] Strikingly absent from the lists of Carter contributors in 1974 and 1975 were labor unions or other blue-collar working-class sources of money. They simply did not give significant amounts to the Carter candidacy during this crucial early period.

Before concluding this chapter, we should mention Carter's fundraising techniques, which concentrated on getting big contributions, especially in the early stages of the campaign. Carter's strategy began with an attempt to collect large contributions or loans from those he called "prosperous Georgians" whom he had appointed to office while governor.[54] In his important memorandum of November 4, 1972 outlining the future course of the campaign, Hamilton Jordan, Carter's campaign manager, stressed the need to find a rich man who "has guts and knows how to put the squeeze on fat cats."[55] The campaign's early stages were marked by this approach, which was broadened during 1975 to fundraising through receptions, dinners, telethons, concerts, and direct mailings. By August 1975 receptions and dinners at a certain amount per plate were providing the largest amount of money, followed by direct mailings.[56] By the end of 1975 a grand total of about three thousand people, mostly Georgians, had given $100 or more to the Carter campaign.[57] This small group put him in the race. To achieve the presidency, however, something more than support from within Georgia and the Atlanta Establishment was required. National level leaders had to be involved.

Notes

1. Floyd Hunter, *Community Power Structure* (Chapel Hill, North Carolina: University of North Carolina Press, 1953).

2. *Newsweek*, September 13, 1976, p. 30.

3. Ibid., p. 25.

4. Ibid. Carter, when pressed, admitted that as a youth, "I had almost everything that I could have needed." *Collier's Encyclopedia 1977* (New York, 1977), V, p. 486A.

5. *Washington Post*, August 19, 1976, p. A4; *New York Times*, May 26, 1976, pp. 1, 15.

6. *New York Times*, May 26, 1976, p. 15.

7. Report of Committee for Jimmy Carter to the Federal Elections Commission, October 10, 1975, Schedule A: p. 46; Jules Witcover, *Marathon: The Pursuit of the Presidency 1972-1976* (New York: Viking, 1977), p. 300.

8. *New York Times*, May 26, 1976, p. 1.

9. Jimmy Carter, *Why Not the Best?* (Nashville, Tennessee: Broadman, 1975), pp. 82-84.

10. Ibid., pp. 102-103.

11. *San Francisco Chronicle*, December 27, 1976, p. 8; *Atlanta Constitution*, May 29, 1976, p. 2A.

12. *San Francisco Chronicle*, December 27, 1976, p. 8.

13. Ibid., December 22, 1976, p. 7.

14. Martindale-Hubbell Law Directory (New York, 1976), Vol. II, p. 862B; *Business Week*, July 19, 1976, pp. 20-21.

15. *Atlanta Constitution*, May 29, 1976, p. 2A.

16. *Newsweek*, September 13, 1976, p. 24.

17. Martindale-Hubbell Law Directory (New York, 1976), Vol. II, pp. 893B-894B.

18. Ibid., p. 946B; *San Francisco Chronicle*, January 1, 1977, p. 32; *Business Week*, July 19, 1976, p. 21.

19. *Newsweek*, January 24, 1977, p. 24; *Parade, The Sunday Newspaper Magazine*, August 7, 1977, p. 4.

20. *Atlanta Constitution*, October 18, 1976, p. 13A.

21. *New York Times*, October 22, 1976, p. A16.

22. Ibid.

23. Martin H. Seiden, *Who Controls the Mass Media?* (New York: Basic Books, 1975), p. 57. In 1972 the Cox-Chambers families held 100% of capital stock and 56% of common stock in Cox Broadcasting. See *Moody's Industrial Manual* (New York: 1976), Vol. II, pp. 1033-1034.

24. *Atlanta Constitution*, October 18, 1976, p. 1A.

25. Ibid., pp. 12-13A.

26. *New York Times*, October 22, 1976, p. A16.

27. *San Francisco Sunday Examiner and Chronicle*, March 28, 1976, p. A13.

28. *The Economist*, April 17, 1976, p. 32.

29. *New York Times*, October 22, 1976, p. A16.

30. Howell Raines, "Georgia: The Politics of Campaign Reform" in Herbert E. Alexander (ed.), *Campaign Money: Reform and Reality in the States* (New York: Free Press, 1976), pp. 210-21

31. David W. Adamany and George E. Agree, *Political Money: A Strategy for Campaign Financing in America* (Baltimore: Johns Hopkins University Press, 1975), p. 35; Nelson W. Polsby and Aaron Wildavsky, *Presidential Elections: Strategies of American Electoral Politics* (New York: Scribner, 1976), p. 52.

32. Although this latter generalization is qualified by the fact that the spending limits were fairly high.

33. *New York Times*, April 1, 1976, p. 20.

34. *Newsweek*, February 7, 1977, p. 57.

35. Floyd Hunter, *Top Leadership U.S.A.* (Chapel Hill, North Carolina: University of North Carolina Press, 1959), p. 3.

36. Robert W. Turner, *I'll Never Lie to You: Jimmy Carter in His Own Words* (New York: Ballantine, 1976), p. 36.

37. *Atlanta Constitution*, January 1, 1975, p. 3A.

38. Report of Committee for Jimmy Carter to the Federal Elections Commission, November 8, 1976; *Time*, February 9, 1976, p. 13; *Atlanta Constitution*, January 30, 1976, p. 2A and June 17, 1976, p. 1A.

39. *Time*, February 9, 1976, p. 13; *Washington Post*, July 16, 1975, p. A4.

40. Federal Election Commission, *FEC Disclosure Series No. 7: Presidential Campaign Receipts and Expenditures* (Washington D.C.: 1977), p. 11.

41. Ibid., p. 12.

42. Alexander Heard, *The Costs of Democracy* (Chapel Hill: University of North Carolina Press, 1960), p. 34.

43. Computed from *Atlanta Constitution*, January 1, 1975, p. 3A and Report of Committee for Jimmy Carter to the Federal Election Commission covering period January 1, 1975 to February 28, 1975. These figures refer to *itemized* contributions (those over $101 or adding up to that sum during one year) since unitemized contributions are unavailable.

44. Computed from Reports of Committee for Jimmy Carter to the Federal Election Committee.

45. Raines, "Georgia: The Politics of Campaign Reform," p. 194.

46. See the comprehensive article by Peter Peckarsky in *The Nation*, May 19, 1979, p. 567.

47. Ibid., pp. 565, 571.

48. Ibid., pp. 565-566.

49. Ibid., p. 567.

50. Ibid., pp. 566-567.

51. Raines, "Georgia: The Politics of Campaign Reform," pp. 210-211.

52. Ibid., p. 209.

53. For recent figures on income distribution see the analysis of 1975 Internal Revenue Service statistics done by the Tax Foundation Inc. of New York City, reported in *San Francisco Sunday Examiner and Chronicle*, September 25, 1977, p. A13.

54. *New York Times*, December 28, 1974, p. 29.

55. Kandy Stroud, *How Jimmy Won: The Victory Campaign from Plains to the White House* (New York: Morrow 1977), p. 185.

56. *Atlanta Constitution*, August 9, 1975, p. 5A.

57. *New York Times*, December 15, 1975, p. 40.

2

Carter's Trilateral Connection

Carter's Atlanta backers included some of the most powerful figures of that city and the southeastern United States, but most of them were part of the local, not the national, establishment. The heart of the national power structure is still that complex of economic, social, and political institutions centered in New York and labeled, for the sake of convenience, the "Eastern Establishment." This interlocking web of Wall Street commercial and investment banks, prestigious law firms and leading industrial corporations still stands at the top of the pyramid of American capitalism. The heads of these institutions meet and intermingle not only as directors of each others companies, but also socially in upper class "gentlemen's" clubs like the Links and Century. These men control the elite universities of America as trustees, fund-raisers, and officers of Harvard, Yale, Princeton, Columbia, the University of Chicago and others. While the government implements public policy, it is these individuals who formulate it in private planning and discussion organizations, the most important of which are the Council on Foreign Relations, Committee for Economic Development, Business Council, Business Roundtable, Conference Board, Atlantic Council, the Brookings Institution, and more recently, the Trilateral Commission and the Committee on the Present Danger. The normal functioning of these policy-planning organizations involves not only the advance planning of America's foreign and domestic policies, but also the selection and training of individuals who then enter the government to implement those policies. Through their media outlets, they publicize and advance the careers of favored politicians and create the climate of opinion within the country which aids in the implementation of their policies.[1]

This Eastern Establishment makes up the core of the American ruling class. As a class, it amounts to only ½ of 1 percent of the population, but it directly *owns* about 22 percent of all personally held wealth.[2] This class *controls* a far greater percentage of American wealth because a small percentage of the total stock of a publicly held corporation may give that owner effective control. This core of the ruling class is made up of the biggest, most internationally oriented corporations, especially banks, the oldest wealthy families like the Rockefellers, the centrist wings of both major parties, the major private policy-planning groups mentioned above, the most exclusive private clubs, the oldest, most prestigious universities, and the largest foundations and law firms. It is strongest in the Northeast and Midwest and its policy perspective is to look out for its general interests as a class rather than the more specific interests of one sector of the economy. This elite supports Keynesian economic policies, accepts some aspects of the welfare state, and has tolerated unions — although this appears to be changing — as a stabilizing force within the working class. It is interventionist and internationalist in foreign policy. Its political control is centered in the executive branch of the Federal government, but it also has strong influence in Congress.

The other, weaker, sector of the American ruling class is represented by smaller, more domestically-oriented corporations, newer wealth, the right wing of the Republican and Democratic

parties, private policy-planning organizations like the National
Association of Manufacturers, the American Conservative
Union, Chamber of Commerce, and American Security Council.
Geographically this second sector of the ruling class is stronger in
the South and West and politically is more influential in
Congress, making up the core of the Republican-Southern
Democrat Conservative Coalition which has controlled the
Congress, with rare interruptions, since 1876. It tends to be
more nationalistic in foreign policy and to have a more
narrowly special-interest focus at home. It is for balanced
budgets, "free enterprise" and a union-free environment.[3]

Our main focus here is the Eastern Establishment or big
bourgeoisie, the dominant sector of the American ruling class,
because Jimmy Carter allied himself with this strongest power
group. It has counterparts in every major city in the United
States — persons having close economic, social, political, or
personal ties with the dominant individuals and institutions of
New York. Atlanta is one of those cities. Many of Atlanta's
leaders are linked with the Eastern Establishment by interlocking directorships, friendships, or family alliances cemented
by intermarriage or common ownership of large property.
These connections became important for Jimmy Carter because
they provided entree into and, ultimately, acceptability from
the highest levels of the northeastern power structure as per-
sonified by Chase Manhattan Bank chairman David Rockefeller.

The several ways in which an obscure but attractive and
ambitious politician like Carter became allied with leading
power wielders like Rockefeller illustrate the manifold economic,
social, and political ties uniting the upper class in America
across regional, religious, and special-interest lines. Several of
Carter's early support group in Atlanta — Gambrell, Kirbo,
and Austin — have close links with either the Rockefeller
family or the broader Eastern Establishment. The Gambrell
family is a major stockholder in Eastern Airlines, where Laurence
Rockefeller is the single biggest individual stockholder. The
elder Gambrell is on that corporation's board of directors,

and his law firm is general counsel for Eastern.[4] The trust department of the Rockefeller family bank, Chase Manhattan, holds the largest single block of Eastern's stock. Chase is also the chief lender to the airline. Laurence Rockefeller or his representative — Harper Woodward — has long been on the Eastern board with Gambrell.[5]

Carter's second tie with the Eastern Establishment was through his closest adviser, Charles Kirbo of the King and Spalding law firm. This firm's clients include International Business Machines and Kirbo is a friend of Thomas J. Watson, Jr., former president of IBM and senior member of the founding family which is still a major owner of the company.[6] Watson and his family are important supporters, through membership and large financial contributions, of Eastern Establishment organizations such as the Council on Foreign Relations.[7] Watson is also a friend of David Rockefeller, the Council's current chairman, and during the 1960s, both served on the Board of Directors of the Atlantic Council. Rockefeller and Watson also share membership in the exclusive Links Club.[8]

J. Paul Austin is yet another individual who ties Carter to this power group. Austin, chairman of Atlanta-based Coca-Cola, sits on the board of New York-based firms like J. P. Morgan, Dow Jones, and General Electric. Austin is also a member of the Links Club and, with Rockefeller, belongs to the Business Council. Austin was called Carter's "chief proselytizer" in the business community during 1975 and 1976, and Dun's Review reported in December 1976 that "the influential Austin has spent most of the last year allaying businessmen's fears about a Carter Administration."[9]

Additional contacts between Carter and the Rockefellers and the Eastern upper class came through Dean Rusk, former President of the Rockefeller Foundation, a member of the Council on Foreign Relations, and a director of the Atlantic Council. Rusk began advising Carter not long after he became governor.[10] Another of Carter's Atlanta supporters, Ivan Allen, Jr., was invited in 1974 to join Nelson Rockefeller's Commission on Critical Choices for Americans, joining Gerald Ford, Henry Kissinger, William S. Paley, chairman of CBS, and others on that body. These multiple ties show the interconnectedness of local and national ruling groups and the ways by which local politicians come into contact with the dominant sector of the ruling class.

It is not surprising then to find that by 1971 Carter was meeting with both David Rockefeller and Hedley Donovan, editor-in-chief of *Time* magazine and also a director of the Council on Foreign Relations.[11] *Time* had a cover story on Carter and the "New South" in May 1971, the first national media attention given Carter.[12] Following the *Time* story Carter met with Donovan, who introduced him to George S. Franklin, a Rockefeller in-law who was then Executive Director of the Council on Foreign Relations.[13] Through one or more of these connections, Carter became known to David Rockefeller and had lunch with him at the Chase Manhattan Bank in November 1971.[14] Rockefeller, Donovan and Franklin must have been impressed with Jimmy Carter; for in 1973, when they and a few others formed an exclusive new organization called the Trilateral Commission, Rockefeller invited Carter to dine at his London estate and asked him to join the Commission.[15]

The Trilateral Commission is a private international organization composed of wealthy, powerful and well-connected individuals from the advanced capitalist "trilateral" world — North America, Western Europe and Japan. First proposed by Council chairman David Rockefeller in 1972, its membership, constitution, and general policies were finalized by 1973 when about 180 multinational businessmen, corporate lawyers, government officials, academics, labor leaders and officials of private organizations agreed to serve on this commission. The Trilateral Commission is the most recent of a long series of organizations — some constituted on a permanent basis, others (like the Commission) on an ad-hoc one — founded and funded by key sectors of the ruling class to plan solutions to the ideological and programmatic problems facing the capitalist state. The role of such organizations in outlining new strategic directions for the society makes them more important than the government itself. The Trilateral Commissioners were — and still are — a very elite group, members by invitation only, with a majority composed of multinational businessmen and corporate lawyers. All were chosen, directly or indirectly, by Rockefeller from his multitude of contacts in these three areas of the world. One journalist called the Commission "an exclusive association of the Western World's most powerful and influential individuals."[16] *Newsweek* said the Commissioners were "movers and shakers. . . a remarkable cross section of the interlocking establishments of the world's leading industrial nations."[17] The European Commissioners included Giovanni Agnelli, President of Fiat, usually considered the most powerful businessman in Italy; Edmond deRothschild, certainly one of the most powerful in France; John Loudon, chairman of Royal Dutch Shell; plus leading bankers and industrialists and former and current government ministers. Japan's Commissioners include the cream of that country's industry and finance, including the heads of Sony, Datsun, Toyota, Hitachi, Mitsubishi Corporation, Nippon Steel, Sumitomo Bank, the Bank of Tokyo and others.[18]

Exactly how Carter came to be recommended to Rockefeller for membership on the Commission is worth recounting in detail since it illustrates one way in which the national power structure is integrated. In April 1975, at David Rockefeller's request, George Franklin, Zbigniew Brzezinski, Henry Owen, Robert Bowie and Gerard C. Smith — the last four now members of the Carter Administration — were selecting members for the Commission. They wanted to include an internationally oriented politician from the industrializing "New South," preferably a Democratic governor. To help them choose the right man, they drew upon part of their network of contacts in that part of the nation. All of them were leading members of a premier organization of the Eastern Establishment, the Council of Foreign Relations (CFR). The Council has a number of affiliated organizations — called the Committees on Foreign Relations — made up of local leaders in thirty-seven cities around the nation.[19] So Franklin called upon one of the leaders of the Council's Atlanta committee — a group reflecting that city's power structure — to set up an advisory group to recommend possible members for the Trilateral Commission. The group of prominent Atlantans was formed and on April 13, 1973, it recommended Jimmy Carter for membership on the Commission.[20]

Joining Carter on the North American section of the Commission in 1973 were — besides Rockefeller, Franklin, Donovan, Smith and Bowie — men like Brzezinski, a close friend of Rockefeller, who became director of the Commission; Senator Walter Mondale; Wall Street Lawyer and corporate director Cyrus Vance; Bendix Corporation chairman W. Michael Blumenthal; Harold Brown, President of California Institute of Technology and a director of IBM; investment banker Robert V. Roosa; corporate lawyer Warren T. Christopher; management professor Carroll L. Wilson; Hewlett-Packard chairman David Packard; AFL-CIO Secretary-Treasurer Lane Kirkland; Exxon chairman J. K. Jamieson; Bank of America President Alden W. Clausen; Yale University Professor Richard N. Cooper; Sears Roebuck President Arthur M. Wood; UAW President Leonard Woodcock; corporate lawyer Paul C. Warnke; Henry D. Owen, the Brookings Institution's director of foreign policy studies; and J. Paul Austin.[21] The reader will at once notice the large number of leading Carter administration officials — President, Vice President, National Security Adviser, secretaries of State, Treasury, and Defense, and various lesser ministers — drawn from the Commission. The incidence of official representation is especially striking since the U.S. membership in the Commission numbered less than sixty.

The sixteen Commissioners listed above all had various other connections. While many came from outside the East, all except Austin, Clausen, Carter and Wood were members of the Council on Foreign Relations and fully ten were directors of the Council, with Rockefeller and Vance serving as chairman and vice chairman respectively.[22] Thus as a group they can be called a part of the Eastern Establishment.

As of the mid-1970s just five of these men — Rockefeller, Blumenthal, Roosa, Clausen, and Packard — tied the Commission and Council together with the Atlantic Council (Packard is a vice chairman and Blumenthal is a director); the Brookings Institution (Roosa is the chairman); the Business Roundtable (Packard and Rockefeller are policy committee members); Business Council (Packard and Rockefeller are members); Committee for Economic Development (Blumenthal and Packard are trustees); the Conference Board (Clausen is a trustee); and the Committee on the Present Danger (Packard is a co-chairman together with fellow Commissioner Kirkland).[23] Table 2-1 illustrates the dense ties between these organizations and shows that the CFR, CED, Business Council, Atlantic Council, and Brookings are closest to the Commission.

The roughly sixty North American Commissioners are directly tied with an impressive list of large and powerful corporations — ATT, Exxon, Anaconda, Bendix, Coca-Cola, General Electric, IBM, Continental Oil, Texaco, Texas Instruments, Pan American, Kaiser Industries, Lehman Brothers, Bank of America, Chase Manhattan, First National Bank of Chicago, Continental Illinois National Bank, Sears, American Express, and others. Numerous ties also existed with the most exclusive private clubs in the United States like the Links in New York (at least four), Chicago (at least four), Pacific Union and Bohemian Clubs in San Francisco (at least four and seven respectively), Metropolitan in Washington D.C. (at least nine), and others. See Table 2-2. In 1975 and 1976 Trilateral Commissioners also sat on the boards of directors of several key media corporations, a very important fact if one is a candidate seeking attention from the news media. Ownership and control of these corporations are especially concentrated in

Table 2-1
The Trilateral Commission's Policy Planning Interlocks (1975-77)

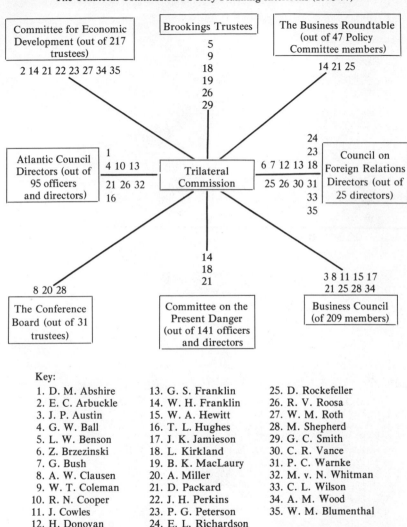

Key:
1. D. M. Abshire
2. E. C. Arbuckle
3. J. P. Austin
4. G. W. Ball
5. L. W. Benson
6. Z. Brzezinski
7. G. Bush
8. A. W. Clausen
9. W. T. Coleman
10. R. N. Cooper
11. J. Cowles
12. H. Donovan
13. G. S. Franklin
14. W. H. Franklin
15. W. A. Hewitt
16. T. L. Hughes
17. J. K. Jamieson
18. L. Kirkland
19. B. K. MacLaury
20. A. Miller
21. D. Packard
22. J. H. Perkins
23. P. G. Peterson
24. E. L. Richardson
25. D. Rockefeller
26. R. V. Roosa
27. W. M. Roth
28. M. Shepherd
29. G. C. Smith
30. C. R. Vance
31. P. C. Warnke
32. M. v. N. Whitman
33. C. L. Wilson
34. A. M. Wood
35. W. M. Blumenthal

Compiled from membership lists and annual reports of these organizations. See appendices. Table adapted from John Treantafelles, "The Trilateral Commission and the Policy Planning Network," Department of Government, California State University Los Angeles, October 1977.

Table 2-2

Club Interlocks with Trilateral Commission Members (1975-77)

Century Association

4 18
7 19
8 22
9 23
10 25
12

Links	3 6 13 15 17 18 19 23	Trilateral Commission	2 5 6 11 14 15 20	Bohemian

1 16
6 21
7 23
10 24
13

Metropolitan

Key:

1. D. M. Abshire	11. W. A. Hewitt	21. G. C. Smith
2. E. C. Arbuckle	12. T. L. Hughes	22. R. A. Taft, Jr.
3. J. P. Austin	13. J. K. Jamieson	23. C. R. Vance
4. R. R. Bowie	14. E. F. Kaiser	24. P. C. Warnke
5. H. Brown	15. D. Packard	25. C. L. Wilson
6. A. W. Clausen	16. J. H. Perkins	
7. L. N. Cutler	17. P. G. Peterson	
8. H. Donovan	18. D. Rockefeller	
9. G. S. Franklin	19. R. V. Roosa	
10. R. N. Gardner	20. W. M. Roth	

This table is adapted from John Treantafelles, "The Trilateral Commission and the Policy Planning Network," Dept. of Government, California State University Los Angeles, October 1977.

the hands of a few families. The Sulzbergers control the *New York Times*; William S. Paley controls CBS; the Luce, Larson, Temple, and Keeler families control *Time*; the Chandler family controls the *Los Angeles Times*; the Graham-Meyer family controls the *Washington Post* and *Newsweek*; and the Bancroft family controls the *Wall Street Journal* (see appendix for details about the ownership and control of these media corporations).

Every one of these powerful means of mass communication — by which the citizens of the United States get the information they need to participate in political life — has a Trilateral Commission-Council on Foreign Relations-Eastern Establishment connection. In the case of the *New York Times* the chairman and president, Arthur Ochs Sulzberger, is a member of CFR. Other directors include Commissioner and early Carter supporter Cyrus Vance, who was also vice chairman and a director of CFR and a Links and Century Club member, CFR member James Reston, CFR member and CED trustee Richard L. Gelb, and CED trustee and Links Club member William F. May. *Time* magazine's directors include two Trilateral Commissioners — editor-in-chief Hedley Donovan (also a CFR director) and corporate lawyer Sol M. Linowitz (a CFR member). Kirbo friend Thomas J. Watson, Jr., of IBM was also a member of *Time*'s board, which includes five other CFR members and several CED trustees and Links Club members. A similar pattern holds for CBS, where eight CFR members and Commissioner Arthur R. Taylor were directors. Paley himself is a long-time active member of the Council and CFR director William A. M. Burden also helps direct CBS. Several CED trustees and members of prestigious clubs also sit on the board. In the case of the *Los Angeles Times* the ties are less close, but even here Harold Brown, a CFR member and Trilateral Commissioner, sat on the board. Similarly, *Washington Post/Newsweek* is tied, although less closely than the *New York Times, Time* and CBS, to this Eastern Establishment network. Katharine Graham, chairperson of the company, is a CED trustee and Arjay Miller, a director, is also a member of the Commission. The *Wall Street Journal* has as a director Carter's friend and fellow Commissioner J. Paul Austin, along with two members of the CFR, a CED trustee, and several members of key clubs. (See Table 2-3.) Almost needless to say, all of these media corporations are heavily interlocked with many other top American corporations. To cite but one example, IBM alone has common board members with every one of the media corporations mentioned above with the exception of CBS. Every one had a direct connection with the Trilateral Commission and CFR.

By becoming a member of the Trilateral Commission, Carter met and became friends with powerful upper class individuals who had contacts and influence where it mattered — in business, the mass communications media, in governments at home and abroad, in universities, in the associations and foundations. Jimmy Carter, the Southern peanut farmer-warehouseman, landowner, and local politician, whom few people outside Georgia had even heard of in 1973, had become part of a group which could help him become President of the United States.

Jimmy Carter was a very active member of the Trilateral Commission, attending all the regional sessions and the first plenary meeting in Japan in May 1975.[24] For his last session Carter paid his air fare and other expenses from campaign funds, then was reimbursed by the Commission. If Carter saw his journey to Japan as a campaign trip, then the Commission's reimbursement represented a campaign contribution of $1323.44.[25] For a period of several years Carter phoned personally to Commission headquarters to keep up with the latest reports, and even passed out its pamphlets in 1974 when he worked with the Democratic National Committee.[26]

Carter and his leading advisers recognized the Commission's importance to his candidacy. Carter said in his autobiography that "service on the Trilateral Commission gave me an excellent opportunity to know national and international leaders in many fields of study concerning foreign affairs."[27] He added that "membership on this Commission has provided me with a splendid learning opportunity. . . "[28] Gerald Rafshoon, Carter's media and advertising specialist, told one reporter that Carter's early Trilateral tie was "most fortunate" for Carter and "critical to his building support where it counted."[29] Rafshoon was no doubt referring to the fact that Carter met "opinion leaders" like Hedley Donovan, *Time*'s editor-in-chief, at Commission meetings.[30] In addition, Carter's entire foreign policy, much of his election strategy, and at least some of his domestic policy has come directly from the Commission and its leading members. The architect of Carter's foreign policy since 1975 has been Zbigniew Brzezinski, the Commission's Director. Brzezinski wrote Carter's major speeches during the campaign, and, as the President's national security adviser, runs foreign policy — with assists from fellow CFR leaders and Trilateral Commissioners like Vance, Brown, Young, and a few others. The watchword for Carter's foreign policy from 1975 on was "clear it with Brzezinski." Carter would always ask when given a memorandum on foreign policy "Has Brzezinski seen this. . . ?"[31]

Less well known than his reliance on the Commission for his foreign policy is the fact that Carter used Commission sources for much of his campaign strategy. Brzezinski stressed as early as 1973 that the 1976 Democratic candidate "will have to emphasize work, the family, religion, and, increasingly, patriotism, if he has any desire to be elected."[32] A Commission publication which appeared in the spring of 1975 seems to have been even more important in setting Carter's campaign strategy. *The Crisis of Democracy: Report on the Governability of Democracies to the Trilateral Commission* was extensively debated at the May 1975 plenary meeting in Japan which Carter attended. It was jointly written by three policy-oriented intellectuals politically close to the Commission's thinking. The section on the United States was written by Samuel P. Huntington, long a friend of Brzezinski and a

Carter adviser during the campaign. After the election, he was hired as coordinator of security planning for the National Security Council at the White House.[33] To become President, Huntington argued, a candidate should cultivate "the appearance of certain general characteristics — honesty, energy, practicality, decisiveness, sincerity, and experience."[34] His next piece of analysis was even more striking. After reviewing the political history of the 1960s and 1970s, Huntington summed up the experience by saying:

> the "outsider" in politics, or the candidate who could make himself or herself appear to be an outsider, had the inside road to political office. In New York in 1974, for instance, four out of five candidates for statewide office endorsed by the state Democratic convention were defeated by the voters in the Democratic primary; the party leaders, it has been aptly said, did not endorse Hugh Carey for governor because he could not win, and he won because they did not endorse him. The lesson of the 1960s was that American political parties were extraordinarily open and extraordinarily vulnerable organizations, in the sense that they could be easily penetrated, and even captured, by highly motivated and well-organized groups with a cause and a candidate.[35]

Needless to say, Carter portrayed himself as an honest, religious, patriotic, family man who, while in reality an "insider," campaigned as an "outsider." As Carter himself expressed it, his campaign did best "whenever we'd project ourselves as the underdog fighting the establishment. . . fighting a valiant battle. . . "[36] And as President, Carter has followed several of Huntington's suggestions on domestic policy, such as tightening control over the Democratic party and lowering expectations about what government can and should do.

One of the Commission's main initial objectives, as stated in its own publications, was to gain governmental influence in each of the three developed capitalist sectors of the world. Only then could plans and policies be put into effect. As a

March 15, 1973, memorandum put it, one of the objectives of the Commission's work would be "to foster understanding and support of Commission recommendations both in governmental and private sectors in the three regions."[37] In choosing members, Rockefeller and other leaders of the Commission stressed the need to find and recruit "men and women of sufficient standing to influence opinion leaders both public and private in favor of the Commission's recommendations."[38] Carter was thus only one of many who Commission leaders felt could be influential in the future. Commission founders also chose other politicians for membership, such as Congressman Wilbur D. Mills; Senators Walter Mondale and Robert Taft Jr.; Governor Daniel J. Evans; former governor William W. Scranton; and Elliot L. Richardson. They were clearly trying to cover as many future possibilities as they could by involving a spectrum of politicians — both Democratic and Republican — in their work. Especially since the Carter Administration took office new political leaders have been invited to join the Commission to replace those going to Washington. These include William E. Brock III, the chairman of the Republican National Committee, and several of the Republican presidential hopefuls for 1980: George Bush, former director of the CIA; Congressman John B. Anderson; and Illinois Governor James R. Thompson. Leading Democrats like Senators Alan Cranston of California, John H. Glenn from Ohio, and John C. Culver of Iowa, as well as Congressman John Brademas and Governor John D. Rockefeller IV of West Virginia are also now Commission members (see Table 2-3). The personalities and issues shaping up for the 1980 election will be covered in detail in Chapter 6.

David Rockefeller called for the formation of the Trilateral Commission in 1972 because the post-World War II alliance system, bringing Western Europe, Japan, and North America together, was under heavy strain from world events and some of the nationalistically oriented Nixon-Kissinger balance of power policies. During the following two years, however, it

Table 2.3   The Trilateral Commission's Political
and Media Interlocks (1973-1978)

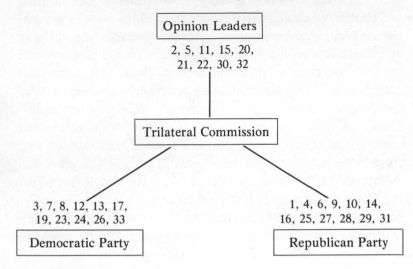

Opinion Leaders

2, 5, 11, 15, 20,
21, 22, 30, 32

Trilateral Commission

3, 7, 8, 12, 13, 17,   1, 4, 6, 9, 10, 14,
19, 23, 24, 26, 33   16, 25, 27, 28, 29, 31

Democratic Party   Republican Party

Key:

1. John B. Anderson, *Congress*
2. J. Paul Austin, *Wall St. Journal*
3. John Brademas, *Congress*
4. William E. Brock III, *Republican National Committee*
5. Harold Brown, *L.A. Times*
6. George Bush, *form. Congressman*
7. Jimmy Carter, *Gov., President*
8. Lawton Childs, *Senate*
9. William S. Cohen, *Senate*
10. Barber B. Conable, *Congress*
11. John Cowles, *Minneapolis Star & Tribune*
12. Alan Cranston, *Senate*
13. John C. Culver, *Senate*
14. John C. Danforth, *Senate*
15. Hedley Donovan, *Time*
16. Daniel J. Evans, *form. Governor*
17. Thomas A. Foley, *Congress*
18. Donald M. Fraser, *former Congressman*

19. John H. Glenn, *Senate*
20. James F. Hoge, *Chicago Sun-Times*
21. Sol M. Linowitz, *Time*
22. Arjay Miller, *Washington Post*
23. Wilber Mills, *form. Congressman*
24. Walter F. Mondale, *former Senator, Vice President*
25. Elliot C. Richardson, *former cabinet officer*
26. John D. Rockefeller IV, *Governor*
27. William V. Roth, *Senate*
28. William W. Scranton, *former Governor*
29. Robert Taft, *former Senator*
30. Arthur R. Taylor, *CBS*
31. James R. Thompson, *Governor*
32. Cyrus Vance, *N.Y. Times*
33. Andrew Young, *Congress, U.N.*

became clear that these strains were global in scope and something more than a mere reinvigoration of the old alliance system was needed. A renovation of the entire international system — the creation of a new world political and economic order — now seemed imperative. Global power shifts, including the rebellion of the Third World against the old order (the Vietnam revolution, the rise of oil power, and the demand in the United Nations for a new world economic order were the most prominent features of this rebellion), trade and other conflicts within the advanced capitalist world, monetary problems, and world inflation and recession all made it evident that the old world order, created during and after World War II, was now inadequate. The Trilateral Commission and the Council on Foreign Relations decided to plan the necessary changes in policies, structures, relationships, rules, and institutions to create a new world order. Such an order, as perceived by these planners, would involve just enough changes domestically and internationally to dampen revolution in the Third World and still be acceptable to the establishments of the trilateral world.[39] In this planning different Commissioners play different roles. For example, Rockefeller has the upper class and multinational corporate contacts, and so can deal with this group of power wielders; Brzezinski has the theoretical perspective; and Carter and other politicians complete the picture by being the liaison to larger publics, both in the Democratic and Republican parties. The politician's role is an implementary one then, as the super salesman of the Trilateral program, reaching larger constituencies at home and abroad.

In addition, Carter appealed to Rockefeller and others because he was an ambitious man, an eager convert very impressed with trilateralism and its leaders. And, as an intelligent, attractive individual with considerable folksy charm, an interesting family, traditional values, and an "outsider's" image, he could win. Once in office, ruling class leaders felt there was a good chance that Carter could, with liberal rhetoric and a reputation for forthrightness, mobilize the constituency needed to implement Trilateral plans for a new world order. As Cyrus Vance put it during the campaign, Carter "has the qualities to bring us together."[40]

Carter's Trilateral-Eastern Establishment connection had concrete, tangible benefits for his presidential campaign. The social, economic and political network of the fifty-odd American Commissioners was a large one, and it brought Carter into touch with key campaign fund-raisers outside Georgia, interest groups which could help him in certain primary and caucus states, and, most important, the owners and leading journalists of the media of mass communication. The relationships between Carter and the media will be left to the next chapter. Here we will show how the Trilateral connection, together in some instances with links to party liberals and the Atlanta Establishment helped him raise money and gain acceptability among businessmen and other important interest groups.

One of Jimmy Carter's key characteristics as a candidate was his "centrist" position — he tried to be all things to all people. Although this approach had its strengths, one of its weaknesses was that the level of commitment among the mass of his supporters was generally not very high. Carter was also charming in small groups, although not an outstanding public speaker. These facts dictated Carter's approach to fundraising outside Georgia after mid-1975. Direct mail solicitation on a mass level — which candidates like McGovern and Wallace had used because of the high level of commitment of their supporters — was not possible. Instead Carter's efforts were centered "on direct, personal solicitation by finance committees set up in various cities around the country."[41] An individual Carter supporter would be asked to have an event, such as a dinner or cocktail party, invite his friends and candidate Carter, and collect contributions. Such small circles of the wealthy or near wealthy provided Carter with an increasing percentage of his campaign funds from the summer of 1975 on, including contributions in enough states to qualify for Federal matching funds. How did such individuals, from

California and New York especially but also from other states, come in contact with and support Carter at an early date? Carter's Trilateral connections, his links with former McGovern supporters, and his Atlanta Establishment ties were the main avenues of influence.

California is a good place to begin to unravel these often complex links. Carter's 1975 fundraising in California was the result of the efforts of two groups of fat-cat contributors. The smaller group was centered around Lew R. Wasserman, chairman of Music Corporation of America. A traditional Democratic fund-raiser, he had given large amounts to Hubert Humphrey's 1968 campaign. The larger group revolved around Max Palevsky, a large stockholder in and former director of Xerox, and Harold Willens, a Los Angeles businessman, both of whom were important supporters of George McGovern in 1972.[42] Palevsky and Willens were introduced to Carter by former McGovern supporters Morris Dees and Marjorie Benson. Carter made a point of cultivating this group of Democrats who represent the importance of the party politics level in the presidential selection process. These liberals — former McGovern supporters — were taken with Carter for two reasons: his recognition of the need for moral leadership and the desire to pose a clear alternative to George Wallace, who was ranked high in public opinion polls in 1974 and 1975 and was seen as a serious threat by non-racist middle-of-the-road and liberal Democrats.[43] As a Southerner, it was felt that Carter could defeat Wallace on his home ground and end this threat "once and for all."[44]

At the same time, Wasserman, Willens and Palevsky, while not members of Eastern Establishment organizations like the Council on Foreign Relations or the Trilateral Commission or of New York clubs like the Links or Century, nevertheless have direct ties with Trilateral Commissioners and others who are major figures in the Eastern Establishment. Wasserman, for example, sits on the Board of Trustees of the California Institute of Technology whose president from 1969 to 1977 was Trilateral Commissioner Harold Brown, now Secretary of Defense. Also on Cal Tech's board are J. Paul Austin, Thomas J. Watson, Jr., and others with Eastern and Trilateral Commission connections.[45]

Palevsky and Willens held a $1000 a couple reception at Palevsky's home in July 1975, raising over $30,000 at a crucial point in Carter's campaign.[46] Both individuals are on the governing board of Common Cause, which also had as a board member Trilateral Commissioner Lucy Wilson Benson, president of the League of Women Voters. Palevsky also sits on the Board of Trustees of the University of Chicago, joining on that board David Rockefeller; Robert O. Anderson, chairman of Atlantic Richfield Company and a director of Chase Manhattan Bank, the Council on Foreign Relations, CBS, and Pan American Airlines; and Trilateral Commissioner Emmett Dedmon, who is Vice President and Editorial Director of Field Enterprises, owners of two newspapers and other corporations in Chicago. These kinds of links made it certain that Carter, Wasserman, Palevsky, and Willens would have mutual friends and meet each other. Carter's charm, policy positions, and strategy as an anti-Wallace Southern candidate could then have a chance to make converts. These connections also illustrate again how closely tied together the American power structure is — many leading liberal Democrats are on the same boards of directors as leading Republicans.

New York campaign contributions also began to become an important supplement to Georgia funds during the second half of 1975 and throughout 1976. The main group of New York Carter backers, individuals who hosted gatherings or served on the Wall Street Committee for Carter, collectively made up an impressive list of socially and economically prominent people.[47] They are connected to each other and socially interact through common membership in various institutions of the Eastern Establishment — elite social clubs, the Council on Foreign Relations, or corporate boards of directors. These men and their positions as of 1976 included:

Roger C. Altman of Lehman Brothers investment banking firm, whose chairman, Peter G. Peterson, is a member of the Commission and director of the CFR.

John Bowles, a banker and member of the Metropolitan Club, which has Trilateral Commissioners and numerous CFR leaders as members. Bowles first met Carter through a close friend who was a lawyer with the Alston, Miller and Gaines law firm in Atlanta.[48]

C. Douglas Dillon, head of U.S. and Foreign Securities Corporation, a director of the Council on Foreign Relations, a trustee of the CED, Brookings, and Business Council, a member of the Chase Manhattan Bank's international advisory board, a member of the Links and Century Clubs, and a former trustee of the Rockefeller Foundation.

Henry Luce III, a director of *Time* magazine (which has two Trilateral Commissioners as directors) and a member of the Yale and University Clubs (which have other Commissioners as members).

Howard Samuels, Baggies tycoon and Democratic party official.

Theodore C. Sorenson, a corporate lawyer and active member of the CFR (which has thirty-six members and ten directors of the Trilateral Commission).

Cyrus Vance, a director of several leading corporations, including the *New York Times*, member of the Commission, and a vice chairman and director of the Council on Foreign Relations.

Many of Carter's over-$500 contributors during this early period shared similar connections and also included many traditional Democratic and liberal fat cats — men like corporate lawyer Thomas K. Finletter; San Francisco landlord Melvin M. Swig; investment company executive Robert K. Lipton; corporate director Walter N. Rothschild; Jr., Howard M. Stein, chairman of Dreyfus Corporation; William W. Wolbach, president of The Boston Corporation; investment banker Herbert A. Allen; Iowa businessman David Garst; corporate lawyer Francis T. P. Plimpton; Edgar Bronfman, head of Seagram Distillery Company; Charles Benton, President of Films, Inc.; Daniel R. Noyes, heir to the Lilly Drug fortune; and Arthur G. Cohen, chairman of giant Arlen Realty in New York.[48] Carter was thus acceptable to and derived early support from many wealthy individuals. These and other businessmen spoke well of him during the campaign.

As Carter's campaign took off in early 1976, another group of business leaders from around the nation — individuals not connected with the higher circles represented by the Trilateral Commission and the New York establishment — were apprehensive about a potential president about whom they knew little or nothing. These businessmen "flooded" Atlanta businessmen with calls about Carter. The Atlanta Establishment responded favorably. Almost to "a man, the local businessmen spread the word that Carter, while not always pro-business, was in their judgment trustworthy and an efficient administrator."[49] Carter supporter Ivan Allen III said, "there was a pretty general discussion in the business community throughout the country with those of us in Atlanta about the kind of job he (Carter) had done as governor."[50] The men who responded favorably were those well-connected individuals mentioned previously plus Delta Airlines chief William Thomas Beebe, Southern Railways president William Graham Clayton, Jr., Georgia Theaters head John H. Stembler, Rich's Department Store chairman Harold Brockey, and others.[51] The *Atlanta Constitution* said, "the Atlanta power structure has rendered a Democratic presidential candidate. . . palatable to many Republican businessmen."[52]

Carter's early campaign during 1975 and the first months of 1976 was marked by a general lack of support from one of the mainstays of the Democratic Party, organized labor, most of which was behind Henry Jackson, Hubert Humphrey, Fred Harris, or Birch Bayh. The one exception to this generalization was the United Auto Workers, one of the largest and most progressive unions in the nation. The UAW played an important role in Carter's victories in several early caucus or primary states — Iowa in January and Florida in March 1976 stand out in particular. One important source for this support was Leonard Woodcock, the UAW's president at the time and an "informal" Carter supporter.[53] Woodcock was also one of the only three U.S. labor leaders on the Trilateral Commission. When Woodcock announced his formal backing of Carter in early May 1976, he stated that "I had made up my mind a long time ago to be for Governor Carter."[54]

It is interesting to speculate as to why the United Auto Workers, one of the most liberal unions in the nation, supported Carter over more liberal and pro-labor candidates like Bayh, Harris, or Morris Udall. Part of the reason was the belief that Carter could defeat George Wallace in the South and end the Wallace threat within the Democratic party. Woodcock, like other liberal Democrats, feared Wallace's potential and backed Carter early in the campaign as a tactical maneuver to defeat the Alabama governor.[55] But Woodcock's personal ties to Carter through their joint membership in the Trilateral Commission must also have played an important role.

The UAW's support was instrumental in Carter's win in Iowa. With both Woodcock and the state's retired UAW president behind Carter, the rest of the union's state leadership swung behind him and "packed" the caucuses with its members.[56]

In Illinois and Florida the auto workers union also were important in Carter's victories. In Illinois one of the union's regional directors ran as a Carter delegate. The Citizen's Action Program, the political arm of the UAW in Florida endorsed Carter in November 1975 and Woodcock campaigned for Carter in that state.[57] UAW help was important to Carter's early victories and they, in turn, were vitally important in getting Carter's bandwagon under way.

Carter's Eastern Establishment connection through the Trilateral Commission and his ties with the Atlanta Establishment thus played an important part in his success as a presidential candidate. It gave him an edge on the other candidates, an edge that Carter skillfully used. It gave him credibility and acceptability with the media and others who counted in American politics. It was not everything — Carter and his advisory staff and support groups had to struggle at the party level of American politics to win primaries and gain support from local leaders — but his Trilateral connection gave him many of the important advisers and much of the political strategy, campaign financing, and interest-group support which put him on the road to presidential power. It allowed him, as one journalist put it, "to pass muster with the influential Northeast crowd. . . he was thereby credentialed as a centrist and internationalist. . . . "[58] And, as another individual said, this tie "gave him an opportunity to convince the corporate amd media leaders that he was not a rustic yahoo, but a man to be taken seriously."[59] The media establishment did indeed take the Carter candidacy seriously, as will be seen below.

Notes

1. For further case studies of the several ways in which the dominant branch of the American ruling class rules, see the works by Domhoff and Shoup and Minter, cited in footnote 4 of the Introduction.

2. G. William Domhoff, *The Powers That Be: State and Ruling Class in Corporate America* (New York: Random House, 1979), p. 5.

3. Ibid., pp. 84-8.

4. *Atlanta Constitution,* May 11, 1972, p. 26A; Eastern Airlines Annual Report, 1974.

5. *New York Times,* October 15, 1974, pp. 1, 28 and October 16, 1974, pp. 1, 28.

6. *Newsweek,* January 24, 1977, p. 24; Ferdinand Lundberg, *The Rich and the Super-Rich* (New York: Bantam, 1969), pp. 63, 439-440.

7. Laurence H. Shoup and William Minter, *Imperial Brain Trust: The Council on Foreign Relations and United States Foreign Policy* (New York: Monthly Review Press, 1977), p. 94. The Watsons gave one million dollars to the CFR during the 1960s.

8. G. William Domhoff, *The Bohemian Grove and Other Retreats* (New York: Harper and Row, 1974), pp. 216-217, 238-239.

9. Ibid., pp. 118-119, 216-217, *Dun's Review,* December, 1976, p. 94.

10. Kandy Stroud, *How Jimmy Won: The Victory Campaign from Plains to the White House* (New York: Morrow, 1977), p. 201.

11. Shoup and Minter, *Imperial Brain Trust,* pp. 301-302.

12. *Time,* May 31, 1971, pp. 14-20.

13. *San Francisco Sunday Examiner and Chronicle,* December 21, 1976, p. A13.

14. Georgia Department of Archives and History, Jimmy Carter's Appointment Book, entry for November 23, 1971.

15. *Washington Post,* May 8, 1976, p. A5.

16. *San Francisco Sunday Examiner and Chronicle,* December 12, 1976, p. A12.

17. *Newsweek,* June 16, 1975, p. 37.

18. See Appendix for membership lists of the Commission.

19. Council on Foreign Relations, *Annual Report 1976-1977* (New York: 1977), p. 93. For a detailed analysis of the Council, see Shoup and Minter, *Imperial Brain Trust.*

20. George S. Franklin to S. Dan Schwartz, January 10, 1978. A copy of this letter is in the possession of the author.

21. For a more detailed discussion of the origins, nature, personnel, and policies of the Trilateral Commission, see Shoup and Minter, *Imperial Brain Trust,* pp. 254-284.

22. For a detailed account of the Council on Foreign Relations, see Shoup and Minter, *Imperial Brain Trust.*

23. See Appendix 1.

24. *Washington Post,* January 16, 1977, p. A4.

25. Report of Committee for Jimmy Carter to the Federal Election Commission, October 14, 1975, Schedule A, Part 4, page 1; letter Madeleine Jablonski, Office Manager of the Trilateral Commission, to Laurence H. Shoup, November 8, 1977.

26. *Washington Post,* January 16, 1977, p. A4; *Los Angeles Times,* January 24, 1977, p. 13.

27. Jimmy Carter, *Why Not the Best?* (Nashville, Tennessee: Broadman, 1975), p. 140.

28. Ibid., p. 127.

29. Robert Scheer, "Jimmy, We Hardly Know Y'All," *Playboy* (November, 1976), p. 192.

30. *European Community* magazine, March-April 1977, has a picture of Carter sitting with Donovan at a December 1974 Commission meeting.

31. *Los Angeles Times,* January 23, 1977, p. 1.

32. Ibid., January 24, 1977, p. 13.

33. *Newsweek,* June 21, 1976, p. 22.

34. Michel J. Crozier, Samuel P. Huntington, and Joji Watanuki, *The Crisis of Democracy: Report on the Governability of Democracies to the Trilateral Commission* (New York: New York University Press, 1975), p. 96.

35. Ibid., p. 89.

36. Martin Schram, *Running For President: A Journal of the Carter Campaign* (New York: Pocket Books, 1977), p. 6.

37. The Trilateral Commission, *The Trilateral Commission* (New York: March 15, 1973), p. 4.

38. Ibid., p. 7.

39. For details about these plans for a new world order, see Shoup and Minter, *Imperial Brain Trust*, pp. 254-284.

40. *Atlanta Constitution*, April 5, 1976, p. 4A.

41. *Atlanta Constitution*, May 29, 1976, p. 2A.

42. Ibid., July 27, 1975, p. 14A.

43. Max Palevsky to Laurence H. Shoup, January 12 and February 16, 1978; Harold Willens to Laurence H. Shoup, January 11 and February 23, 1978; John Bowles to Laurence H. Shoup, January 8, 1978; Marjorie Benton to Laurence H. Shoup, March 21, 1978; Howard Samuels to Laurence H. Shoup, April 10, 1978.

44. Max Palevsky to Laurence H. Shoup, January 12, 1978.

45. Others who linked Wasserman and Cal Tech to the Trilateral Commission and Eastern Establishment were these members of Cal Tech's Board of Trustees: Trilateral Commissioner William A. Hewitt; Mary L. Scranton, the wife of Commissioner William W. Scranton; Robert S. McNamara, World Bank president and frequent Commission adviser; and Robert O. Anderson, chairman of Atlantic Richfield Company, a director of Chase Manhattan Bank, the Council on Foreign Relations, CBS, and Pan American Airlines. Compiled from Cal Tech's Catalogue, Standard and Poor's Corporate Directors, and *Who's Who in America*.

46. *Atlanta Constitution*, July 27, 1975, p. 14A.

47. John Bowles to Laurence H. Shoup, January 8, 1978.

48. References to Carter's New York supporters were drawn from: *Atlanta Constitution*, November 5, 1975, p. 1A; *New York Times*, March 15, 1976, p. 36; March 29, 1976, p. 23; and May 28, 1976, p. A12; *Business Week*, April 12, 1976, pp. 87-88; *San Francisco Sunday Examiner and Chronicle*, October 31, 1976, Sunday Punch Section, p. 8; and from reports of Committee for Jimmy Carter to the Federal Election Commission.

49. *Atlanta Constitution*, August 16, 1976, p. 2A.

50. Ibid.

51. Ibid.

52. Ibid.

53. *Newsweek*, April 19, 1976, p. 15.

54. *Atlanta Constitution*, May 8, 1976, p. 8A.

55. Leonard Woodcock to Laurence H. Shoup, February 23, 1978.

56. Stroud, *How Jimmy Won*, p. 240.

57. Ibid., pp. 258 and 265; *Atlanta Constitution*, January 15, 1976, p. 14D; and January 18, 1976, p. 16A.

58. *Los Angeles Times*, January 24, 1977, p. 13.

59. *Washington Post*, January 16, 1977, p. 13.

3

Carter and the Media Establishment

During the 1976 campaign it was widely recognized — by the candidates and their key staff members, by political reporters, and by academic observers — that coverage by the mass communications media was "the name of the game," the critically important factor determining the outcome of the race for the presidency. In a nation where the average voter has little contact with parties or politicians, the media of mass communications — newspapers, magazines, radio, and television — are the major intermediaries between the candidate and the electorate. Most voters learn nearly all of what they know about a candidate through these media. This is particularly true of primary campaigns, where the party label is not a factor in the people's choice. No matter how long or hard national candidates may campaign, they cannot make contact with more than a tiny fraction of voters. The news media are their only hope for wide exposure. The owners and managers of the mass communications media are thus an important part of America's political structure, holding great power, especially during the pre-primary and primary periods of the campaign.

The media, especially the elite media, have the power to define the bounds of respectable debate and respectable presidential candidates. As presidential campaign analyst Theodore White put it, the "hereditary press barons. . . can make politicians — and on many occasions, break them."[1]

The interpretation that media leaders put on political events, even which events they consider newsworthy, can thus be decisive. Something which might be ambiguous in reality can be seized upon as the turning point, making one candidate an attractive "winner" and another a humiliated "loser." As CBS newsman Roger Mudd put it on the night of the Iowa caucus: "it's not exactly the precise figures that will be important, it's whether the media and the politicians agree that this man won and this man lost."[2] Thus, even a candidate who lost a primary, yet did better than the media expected, can be labeled the real "winner." This was true of both Eugene McCarthy and George McGovern in the New Hampshire primaries of 1968 and 1972 respectively. Both placed second but won in the eyes of the media.

Given this situation, it is understandable that a man with close ties to the leaders of these major media corporations, with business-oriented middle-of-the-road policy positions, and with an aggressive approach in seeking to influence the media would receive favorable coverage and be taken seriously as a presidential candidate from the start. Interestingly enough, many non-Eastern Establishment reporters did not take Carter's candidacy seriously at first — in fact, some treated it as a joke.[3] Reg Murphy, the editor of the *Atlanta Constitution*, was one example. He wrote a July 1974 column ridiculing the Carter candidacy by saying "the state needed a good belly-laugh, and Carter obliged by announcing he would run for president."[4] Murphy, who was soon replaced as editor (probably because the owners of the *Constitution* were Carter campaign contributors), added that it was "incredible" that Carter was serious about running.[5] As will be shown below, however, *Time* and the *New York Times* reporters and editorial page writers were treating Carter seriously from the beginning of his public candidacy in 1974 and soon the other news media followed. Carter had been screened into the campaign sweepstakes by being defined as a "serious" candidate, while others were screened out.

Hamilton Jordan, Carter's campaign manager, clearly recognized the importance of the media establishment. He wrote in a memorandum to Carter in November 1972 that an "eastern liberal news establishment," specifically the *New York Times* and *Washington Post,*

> has tremendous influence. The views of this small group of opinion-makers in the papers they represent are noted and imitated by other columnists and newspapers throughout the country and world. Their recognition and acceptance of your candidacy as a viable force with some chance of success could establish you as a serious contender worthy of financial support of major party contributors.[6]

He added in another memorandum two years later that the press plays a "very special and powerful role." Its interpretation of results during the first few primaries will "begin to make 'winners' of some and 'losers' of others."[7] Jordan concluded that "hopefully, good press in the early primaries will have solved some of our name-recognition problem and given Jimmy Carter some depth to his new national image."[8]

Jordan had put his finger on Carter's key problem: that the Georgia governor was an unknown, even obscure, figure. In various public opinion polls taken in the fall of 1975 Carter placed so low among Democratic voters that his name was not even listed when the poll results appeared in magazines and newspapers.[9] In the December 1975 Gallup Poll, for example, Carter was reported together with "all others" with 7 percent or less (with Edward M. Kennedy listed) or 4 percent or less (without Kennedy).[10] This put Carter behind Kennedy, Humphrey, Wallace, McGovern, Jackson, Muskie, and Bayh, who were the most popular Democratic presidential possibilities.[11]

As late as the Gallup Poll taken during January 23-26,

1976, Carter was still the first choice of only 4 percent of Democratic voters.[12] It was at this point that his poll ratings took off. He jumped to 12 percent by the end of February (after the New Hampshire primary) — behind only Wallace and Humphrey — and to 26 percent by the second week in March (after the Florida and Massachusetts primaries), only one percentage point behind front-runner Humphrey.[13] Starting from an incredibly low level of recognition and voter support in January 1976, Carter had by early March far surpassed Jackson, Wallace and the other Democratic contenders in the polls and nearly equaled Senator Humphrey's popularity.

By mid-March 1976 Carter was not only far ahead of the active contenders for the Democratic presidential nomination, he also led President Ford by a few percentage points.[14] In the space of only a few months, Jimmy Carter was transformed from a virtual unknown to one of the most popular politicians in the entire nation, on a par with men who had been prominent in national life for decades. This is certainly the most astonishing rise in twentieth century American politics. Carter's sudden prominence in early 1976 was all the more important given the fact that typically about 80 percent of voters make up their minds about whom they will vote for before the general election campaign begins. It is therefore during the pre-primary and primary period that presidents are really made.[15]

Only favorable media coverage of the Carter campaign, attention which led to a positive impression of Jimmy Carter, could have accounted for his rise to almost instant popularity. Such media favoritism was commented on by many people during 1975 and the first months of 1976. Carter himself recognized that he had, on the whole, received a "good press." In early May 1976 he said, "I think the press has treated me well. And I would not be where I am now had the press not accommodated some of my errors. . . . "[16] As early as January 1975 Rex Granum, a Georgia political commentator who later joined Carter's White House staff, noted Carter's favorable press coverage, pointing out that the *New York Times, Washington Post* and *Wall Street Journal* had all had front page stories on Carter's announcement for the presidency and that altogether over 100 newspapers and magazines around the world ran stories on Carter.[17] The tone of these stories was "generally upbeat," treating Carter seriously, and some, like syndicated columnist Gary Wills, "lauded Carter."[18] A few months later the *Atlanta Constitution* reported that Carter "has gotten a good press from the national news media. . . a score of newspapers across the nation have kind things to say about Carter's presidential effort."[19] National news columnists like Joseph Kraft and Tom Wicker both pointed out in mid-January 1976 that Carter was, in Kraft's words, "the media candidate for the Democratic presidential nomination."[20] Wicker added that Carter had received a "good press" and was being "promoted" by the media as the "surprise" of the campaign.[21] Reporter Elizabeth Drew added in a March 1976 report that "the press, on the whole, has been kind to Carter and has played an important part in his buildup."[22] Some of Carter's competitors for the nomination also noticed what Morris Udall called an "incredible flow of press" beginning in the fall of 1975.[23] Thus, *before* Carter had won a single state caucus or primary, many media observers commented on his favorable press coverage. Not one of these leading mass media organizations had yet mentioned Carter's Trilateral connection, despite its importance.

The *New York Times*

The place to begin a detailed analysis of Carter's media buildup is with the *New York Times*, the most important single source of news reporting and analysis in the United States. The influence of the *Times* is massive. Theodore White called it "the major power force in American thinking."[24] The *Times'* role is so central partly because of its news service, but more critically because it is read by virtually all of America's leaders — government officials, academics, business chieftains, and, most importantly for this account, by other opinion makers around the nation — the owners, editors, and publishers of the major news and opinion magazines, book publishers, and national news networks. As White put it, the *New York Times* "is the bulletin board for the editors of the great news magazines, who speed their correspondents to the scene of any story the *Times* unearths; it is the bulletin board of all three television networks, whose evening news assignments, when not forced by events themselves, are shaped by the ideas and reportage in the *Times*."[25] Speaking of journalists, White added that "all of us nurse from" the *Times* which in turn nurses from and is nursed by the upper class world of New York City, heart of the Eastern Establishment.[26] The *Times* lives, according to White, "in the center of a closed loop — it lives in the Manhattan world of opinion makers, and it is impossible to say how much the Manhattan opinion makers influence the *Times*, and how much the *Times* influences the opinion makers."[27]

The *Times'* editors and major journalists were interested at an early date in the changing politico-economic trends in the South and the rise of what were called "New South" politicians. James Reston, long the *Times'* Washington correspondent, showed such an early interest. In his column of October 16, 1974, Reston discussed voter apathy and its cure: the need for "new faces and wider choices" for the 1976 presidential campaign. Reston argued that editors and television network producers should fill the longing of voters for new candidates. Reston held up *Time* magazine as an example of a news outlet that has recognized the problem and covered new personalities "whenever they have had an excuse." Reston closed his column with a mention of some of these "new faces," among them Jimmy Carter, adding that the South "is long overdue at the White House."[28]

Less than two months after Reston's comments came the

Democratic mini-convention at Kansas City. The candidates already openly running for President were there to meet with party activists. R. W. Apple, Jr., the *Times'* presidential campaign correspondent, wrote several articles on this mini-convention. He focused on two candidates — Carter and Jackson. The others, he argued, achieved little in terms of results.[29] Carter was "one of the big winners." Politicians were now taking him "seriously" after Carter "performed impressively" at a dozen state caucuses.[30] Carter also "demonstrated the seriousness of his candidacy by mailing a glossy, full-color magazine describing his career to every delegate a week ago, and he has shaken the hand of every member of many of the state delegations."[31] If shaking hands and sending out a glossy magazine makes a candidate "serious," then nearly anyone with a little time and money can be serious.

Jackson, by contrast, was described as "the super-hawk of the Vietnam era," who had "set up a Pentagon-style logistical system" and was a man trying to disassociate himself from a "Neanderthal" image.[32] Left unmentioned was the fact that Carter too was a Vietnam super-hawk until at least 1971 and a strong Jackson supporter until the fall of 1972 when his own presidential ambitions surfaced.

Strong evidence of the *Times'* pro-Carter bias during the early campaign period comes from a series of editorials on the candidates already contending for the Democratic nomination by the first two months of 1975. These editorials, written by John B. Oakes, a member of the owning Sulzberger family illustrate the *Times'* pro-Carter stance. The editorial on Carter was the most favorable of five which appeared during the December 1974 to February 1975 period. Noting the credibility problem that "progressive" Southern governors have had with other Democrats, the article on Carter stated that this problem was "fast fading." It went on to argue:

> Certainly that problem is not likely to be insurmountable for a Southern candidate with the high personal quality and authentic liberal credentials of Governor Carter. He has given

Georgia an excellent administration, notable for progress in racial matters, bureaucratic reform and freedom from corruption. He is a broadgauged, thoughtful and attractive newcomer to the national scene.[33]

The *Times'* editorial comments on Udall were less favorable than those given Carter, but better than those for other Democratic candidates. He seems to have been the *Times'* second choice. Udall was called "competent, imaginative and effective" as a legislator. The country might respond to him, the *Times* added, but in any event his candidacy will "contribute to public enlightenment."[34] In its comments on Fred Harris and Eugene McCarthy, the *Times* offered nothing in terms of favorable comments about their qualifications and stated that the obstacles to their candidacies were "formidable."[35] On Henry Jackson, the Times said that he "is a strong candidate yet a vulnerable one." He has a long record of policy positions, one "with which adversaries and doubters can find much to quarrel," citing his vigourous support of the Vietnam war long after most Democrats had given up on it.[36] The *Times* ended its editorial on Jackson on a negative note, stressing the "imponderable question" whether Democrats who passionately opposed the war could ever forgive him.[37] While there was truth to the *Times'* statements on Jackson, the very same points — especially strong support of the Vietnam war — were also true in the case of Jimmy Carter, something left unmentioned.

The pro-Carter stance of the *New York Times* continued throughout 1975, when numerous favorable articles on Carter appeared, including a special six-part series by political reporter Christopher Lydon, which ran over the entire year. No other candidate rated a special series on "one man's pursuit" of the presidency. In his first report in January 1975 — accompanied by a large picture of a sincere-looking Carter— Lydon recounted the by now well-known story of the early steps in the Carter campaign, comparing it to the early McGovern campaign. Lydon ended on an upbeat note, saying that Carter's press secretary Jody Powell "believes that thousands of Americans have a vaguely pleasant feeling that there is a fresh face that deserves a second look. In the coming months, Mr. Carter will be doing everything he can to make sure they get it."[38]

Lydon's second article of the series appeared in mid-March 1975. In it he indicated that a bandwagon for Carter was under way, quoting campaign manager Hamilton Jordan's remark that "our only problem is the success we're having . . . the thing is moving fast."[39] Lydon pointed out that Carter's growing popularity was based on personal qualities — the impression that Carter was an honest and sincere individual — and had "precious little to do with 'issues'."[40] Lydon ended this article also in a positive way, quoting a Jordan assistant as saying "we have a candidate who's positioned right to take off. Nobody scares us."[41]

In between Lydon's second and third special reports on the Carter candidacy, he wrote two campaign news reports which stressed the weaknesses of the Jackson and Udall candidacies. The first, with the headline "Democratic Left is Standoffish on Udall's Candidacy," emphasized that the "standoffishness between Mr. Udall and the organized left within the party has become one of the marks of his campaign and clearly part of his fund-raising problem."[42] The second pointed out that Jackson's campaign funds came mostly from "Jewish circles" and that "the labor support he has counted on is still largely immobilized" by AFL-CIO chief George Meany.[43] The bias here is that the problems of other candidates' campaigns were stressed, while the strengths and positive features of the Carter campaign were played up in a special series. The reality was that at the time of this article Udall had raised more campaign funds than Carter.[44] Yet his supposed "fundraising problem" was emphasized whereas the positive side of the Carter campaign was invariably highlighted. In addition, mention of the "standoffishness" of the Democratic left toward Udall was inaccurate, since the reality was that this segment of the party was divided among Udall,

Harris, Carter, and Bayh, with an important segment supporting Udall.

Lydon's third article in his series on the Carter campaign emphasized three themes: Carter as the underdog, his "politics of character," and the wide variety of Democrats who were "impressed" by him.[45] Carter was a "have-not" candidate, according to Lydon, because conservative candidates Jackson and Lloyd Bentsen had much more campaign money in the bank than Carter. Note that Udall was said to have a "problem" with fundraising whereas Carter was given the underdog "have-not" label, a man supposedly bucking the system and, therefore, needing sympathetic support. In any case, with an eighteen-member staff and a daily income of nearly $2000, Carter was hardly a "have-not" candidate in the absolute sense. The real and unmentioned underdog of the campaign was Fred Harris, who was on a much more restricted budget and was without significant media or establishment support. The politics of character had replaced the politics of issues in the Democratic party, argued Lydon, and "an interesting variety of Democrats keep saying they are impressed and a little surprised by Jimmy Carter."[46] Lydon then quoted the Reverend James Wall of the *Christian Century*, scientists at the Argonne Lab near Chicago, and Max Palevsky, Xerox millionaire and a 1972 McGovern backer, as some of those impressed with Carter.[47] Lydon failed to mention that at least some of those who supported Carter at this stage of the campaign, including Palevsky, did so partly as a tactic, because they thought he could knock George Wallace out of the race.[48]

Two additional examples of favoritism towards Carter's candidacy came in July and August of 1975. In late July, *New York Times* editorial board member William V. Shannon rated the chances of the Democratic candidates in an article on the opinion page. In the top group he listed Udall, Bayh, and Carter at odds of eight to one and offered some praise for each man, saying in Carter's case that he "impresses small audiences with his charm."[49] Below these three Shannon ranked Jackson at ten to one because he had too many enemies and "zero charisma."[50] The others he felt were long shots, fifty or a hundred to one, because of various liabilities.[51] What makes this significant is that Carter was ranked in the top group long before he gained significant public acceptance as measured by the polls. Most of the other candidates listed by Shannon had higher poll rankings than Carter as of the summer of 1975. In late May 1975, for example, Carter was ranked twenty-third out of thirty-four possible presidential candidates by Democratic voters and in August 1975 he was listed among "others" with 3 percent or less of the vote, behind Humphrey, Wallace, McGovern, Jackson, Muskie, Bayh, and Shriver.[52]

In August the *Times* ran a news article announcing that Carter had qualified for federal campaign matching grants. The article was run on page eight and accompanied by a large picture of Carter.[53] A month earlier the *Times* had announced that Udall's campaign now qualified for federal matching funds, but this article had no picture and was carried back on page 29.[54] Similarly, when Jackson qualified in April 1975, no picture of him appeared and the small story was on page 21.[55]

Lydon's series on Carter continued in October; this time the theme was Carter's campaign style. Lydon portrayed Carter as an attractive, old style, meet-the-people kind of campaigner in the electronic age. At the same time he managed to get in a dig at Jackson: "If Senator Henry M. Jackson of Washington sometimes seems to view the campaign as a fundraising contest, the Carter campaign can be said to treat politics as a handshaking competition."[56] Handshaking is, of course, one of the rituals of American politics. The candidates get out and supposedly become one with the people by meeting them at factory gates, town meetings, and door to door. The reality was that Carter admitted early that his campaign trips were mainly to get media attention:

"news coverage on every visit has been all I'd want. . . . we use these trips to get heavy local coverage."[57]

By the end of October Carter's buildup in the *New York Times* and other media had already begun to have some effect. While the average voter still knew little or nothing about Carter, sectors of the attentive public — disproportionately made up of the educated, the wealthy, and professionals, the upper levels of society generally and those most active in party politics — were beginning to line up behind Carter in key states. In Iowa, for example, a straw poll was taken among those attending a $50 a plate dinner (the price alone excluded most Democrats). It found Carter ahead and R. W. Apple trumpeted that "Carter appears to hold a solid lead."[58] Carter's coordinator in the state had recruited a diverse steering committee made up of old-line Des Moines courthouse political bosses, an antiwar leader, a retired chief of Woodcock's United Auto Workers, and a conservative former Democratic nominee for governor.[59] In Iowa, as in New Hampshire, Florida, Maine, Oklahoma, and other states, Carter had much more support from local political leaders (machine bosses in some cases) than he would admit.[60]

The drive to create a bandwagon effect for Carter began seriously in November 1975. On November 2 a *Times* article appeared headed: "Carter's Support in South is Broad." It said that "progressive activists of the South" were all behind Carter and his candidacy was "the only game in town" among liberals.[61] In addition Carter's own "calm confidence about the enterprise is beginning to impress doubting well-wishers as well as his rivals for the nomination."[62] The next day another article stated that Carter was "making impressive strides in New England."[63]

Carter's "broad support" in the South was in actuality very narrow until months after the *Times* article. A poll conducted in January 1976 by Darden Research Corporation found that the favorite presidential candidates of the seven southeastern states (the Carolinas, Florida, Georgia, Alabama, Mississippi, and Tennessee) were: Reagan-20 percent; Ford-18 percent; Wallace-12 percent; and Humphrey-3.7 percent.[64] Carter was not even listed since he ranked below Humphrey's 3.7 percent in his own home region! This fact was, of course, not considered newsworthy by the *New York Times,* although it could have been used to create a loser image for Carter since candidates are always expected to do well in their home regions.

The buildup continued in December with the cover story of the *New York Times Magazine* on Sunday, December 14. Written by Patrick Anderson, later a Carter campaign speechwriter, the story stressed Carter's rural roots and personal political history.[65] The magazine's cover was also very folksy, showing a smiling Carter as a barefoot, overall-clad farmer with a sun hat, holding a pitchfork and a bag of peanuts, with a heading entitled "Looking at Jimmy Carter: Peanut Farmer for President." Anderson later said, "It certainly was a very favorable article."[66]

Lydon's fifth report in his series on Carter, accompanied by another picture of the candidate, appeared in late December. It stressed Carter's successes, that he was now "being taken seriously by other Democratic candidates, by party leaders and by the nation's press and broadcast networks." The article also began to focus on what became a central point of *New York Times* reporting during the next few months — that Carter, now a serious contender, would begin to get "close scrutiny" and more criticism.[67] The purpose of raising this point was possibly to deflect the coming criticism of the policy vagueness of candidate Carter. Lydon did this in the final report of his series headed "All the Candidates Fall Short on Defining Issues." Stating that people are wondering what Carter stands for, Lydon argued that this "question applies as well, in varying degrees, to others in the Presidential field" with the exception of perhaps Wallace and Harris.[68]

The *Times* coverage of several other candidates during this period, just before the Iowa caucuses, stands in sharp contrast to the favoritism shown Carter. In the case of Fred Harris, for example, it was stressed that many political leaders in his own state and around the country felt that Harris was too "radical," "far out," and "dangerous" to be elected and govern the country. His candidacy was therefore in "trouble."[69]

In a January 1976 article covering the field, R. W. Apple, Jr., cited Jackson's "drab speaking style" as a main problem, said Shriver was seen as a "lightweight pseudo-Kennedy" and Udall lacked a constituency.[70] Such glib characterizations may or may not conform to the facts in each case, but the point is that Carter was rarely, if ever, characterized in such negative terms, whereas many of his rivals frequently were. While Oklahoma political leaders unfavorable to Harris were quoted by the *Times*, Georgia political leaders who were willing to offer criticism about their ex-governor were not deemed newsworthy enough to appear in print during this critical early period of the campaign.[71] Julian Bond, a prominent black politician in Georgia, was but one ignored critic. Bond opposed Carter because Carter's political record was so conservative. When running for governor, Carter had courted the Wallace vote and said nice things about Lester Maddox. While governor, Carter supported the Vietnam war, even introducing a resolution at the 1972 Governors Conference asking that Vietnam not be made an issue in the 1972 Presidential campaign. A Jackson supporter in 1972, Carter was involved in the "stop McGovern" movement, Bond also pointed out.[72] Carter's close ties with David Rockefeller, the Eastern Establishment, and Trilateral Commission — certainly known to many *New York Times* writers — were also never reported, although the story was certainly important. In fact, the absence of reporting on Carter's connections led one distinguished panel of judges to label "Jimmy Carter and the Trilateral Commission" tᵣ ᵥe the best censored story of 1976, the most important story during that year that the entire American media systematically failed to cover.[73]

On January 19 came Carter's victory in the Iowa precinct caucuses. The next day Apple called it "an impressive victory" and said that Carter's "showing here appeared certain to win him supporters, media attention and financial backing . . . ."[74] Trilateral Commissioner Leonard Woodcock's United Auto Workers backed Carter, playing a major part in his victory over Bayh, who was in second place, a fact that Bayh found "frustrating," since Carter's labor record was unclear to say the least, while Bayh's was solidly pro-labor.[75] The *New York Times* editorialized on Carter in Iowa a few days later, arguing that Carter had shown himself "to be an excellent candidate, attractive, energetic and articulate." Carter, the *Times* went on, "looks like a genuinely national candidate. . . he is taken seriously as a possible President by his political peers. This is a most encouraging development."[76] The *Times* did caution that the Iowa, as well as other early, results might be "greatly overvalued" and that Jackson, Bayh, Udall, Shriver and "others" were also entitled to "careful consideration," but these comments seemed to be mainly an afterthought.

This brief review of the *New York Times* coverage of the Democratic pre-primary and primary campaigns from the fall of 1974 until the end of January 1976 has shown that there were numerous examples of strong pro-Carter bias. Each of these incidents of favoritism might, if taken alone, be dismissed as an isolated case of the reporter's excessive zeal. Taken together, however, the editorials, the special series, favorable news reports, and the close connections of the *Times'* owners and board of directors with other organs of the Eastern Establishment, along with numerous examples of negative portrayals of other candidates, add up to a picture of the subtle merchandizing of a favored candidate.

Time

Time magazine is the most important of the weekly news magazines — the "national newspapers," as they are sometimes called. It has a regular readership of nearly twenty million, more than any other newsmagazine. *Time* has long held a reputation for bias in its reporting of the news and has, for almost as long, been interested in influencing the political process by which a President is chosen. As the late Harvard political scientist V. O. Key said, *Time* is "not bound by notions of objective reporting. Its condensation of the news of the week involves a selectivity dictated by editorial policy, an evaluative tone fixed by the same standard, and often a warped picture of the political world."[77] *Time* first seems to have had an influence in selecting a presidential nominee in 1940 when it was a key element in the Wendell Willkie boom. Theodore White later wrote that *Time* and several other Eastern Establishment magazines "created a man called Wendell Willkie, decided he should be the Republican nominee of that year — and then imposed him on the party. Few naked exercises of press power can compare to their feat. . . . "[78] Henry Luce, a founder, editor, and longtime largest stockholder of *Time, Life,* and *Fortune,* said that he was "influential" in the nomination of both Willkie and, later, Dwight D. Eisenhower.[79]

Time's coverage of Jimmy Carter's campaign for the White House was even more favorable than that of the *New York Times.* It was *Time* which first focused national attention on Carter in 1971 by running a cover of him entitled "Dixie Whistles a Different Tune: Georgia Governor Jimmy Carter." The cover story was entitled "New Day A'Coming in the South" and talked about the "new breed" of racial moderates taking over in the South, featuring Carter as the central figure.[80] Carter's life history was covered in some detail and he was labeled a peanut farmer who looks "eerily like John Kennedy from certain angles."[81] Carter was also put in a presidential context by the report that 1972 presidential hopefuls Muskie, Bayh, Jackson, and Humphrey "have recently called on Carter to discuss the lay of the votes in '72. And Carter and his colleagues in the other Southern states are assembling a caucus to be reckoned with at convention time."[82] Interestingly enough, this cover story appeared nearly five months after Carter's now famous inaugural address as Governor ("I say to you quite frankly that the time for racial discrimination is over"), indicating that this was a carefully planned story and not a response to news events. *Life,* owned by Time, Inc., also featured a "close-up" article on Carter in late January 1971.[83]

Time next featured Carter in December of 1974 when his announcement of his candidacy rated a *Time* story and Udall's and Harris' announcements at about the same time did not. By then Carter had become a friend of fellow Trilateral Commissioner Hedley Donovan, editor-in-chief of *Time*. *Time*'s article was full of positive comments about the candidate. Carter is "noted for his folksy charm," the article stated, and "bears a slight physical resemblance to John F. Kennedy."[84] As "one of the chief political figures to show concern about erasing the remaining gap between black and white in the modern South, Carter as Governor has become the symbol of the moderate shift in Southern politics."[85] Carter's bureaucratic and cost-cutting measures, as well as his "sunshine law," were reviewed favorably and his underdog status in the race was mentioned. *Time* even termed Carter's defeat by Lester Maddox in 1966 as an "impressive showing" by Carter. To win, Carter "will rely on a savvy brand of political toughness underneath his populist, courtly charm," said *Time*.[86] The article ended with Carter's response to a reporter's question about the vice presidency in which he said, "I'm not interested in the vice presidency, but I am very interested in the selection process. I intend to be the one making the selection."[87]

These kind comments on Carter contrast sharply with a

devastating cover story *Time* ran on Senator Henry Jackson's candidacy a few months later. In this article no effort was spared to make Jackson appear unattractive and a loser. Words with negative connotations abound, together with quotes from Jackson's enemies. The article begins at a dinner for Jackson in Los Angeles. Jackson's speech is "flat and dull. He dwells on the energy crisis, pushing out statistics like a bookkeeper."[88] Jackson cannot inspire; the audience offers polite applause but "not the huzzahs of which American political dreams are made."[89] Jackson's announcement for the presidency "could have been the ho-hum event of the year" but with the Democrats so short on convincing leaders it rated much early attention.[90] Jackson is the most prominent Democratic candidate so far, *Time* went on, but will have an uphill fight because, as columnist James A. Wechsler wrote, Jackson "seems to personify a colorless man" who "evokes a surprising amount of hostility from many people."[91] Jackson's views had been so consistent over the years that "some people suspect his mind is closed to new ideas."[92] *Time* said that he was "stridently" in favor of the B-1 bomber and Trident submarine, was a "bitter-end backer" of the Vietnam war, but that "his most dubious effort" was his attempt to tack freer emigration clauses onto U.S.-USSR trade agreements.[93] In his 1972 campaign Jackson showed "traces of demagoguery in his desperate bid for attention."[94] *Time* also linked Jackson with secret illegal campaign contributions.[95] Even Jackson's personal life came under sharp attack. As a long-time Washington bachelor, he lived "in a series of cluttered apartments" and "scarcely took advantage of the glittering social life that was in his reach."[96] Even after Jackson's marriage he "still wears undistinguished suits and black wingtip shoes."[97] Almost needless to say, *Time*'s conclusion was that unnamed "party professionals" believed Jackson could not win and that a "fresh face" was needed to give a "fresh start" to the Democratic party.[98]

Time's next article on Carter in October 1975 stressed that he had "an image elusive enough to qualify as that 'new face' many voters seem to be seeking."[99] *Time* argued that Carter was making "surprising progress" and that wherever he went "his ready smile and unaffected intelligence win friends."[100] *Time* quoted a "professional" at Democratic national headquarters to the effect that Carter was "impressing a lot of people with his style and organization."[101] After a favorable review of his life history and general policy positions, *Time* closed by admitting that Carter "often seems flat and pedantic in front of large crowds," but adding right away that even so he

> effectively conveys a soft-spoken reasonableness and decency in face-to-face talks. . . . So far, he remains well back in the presidential pack. Still, as so many of the candidates keep pointing out, so was George McGovern in a comparable period four years ago.[102]

Time continued its buildup of Carter in December 1975 with an article entitled "Taking Jimmy Seriously." *Time* began with the comment that Carter "has begun to emerge as the fastest of the dark horses racing for the Democratic presidential nomination. Last week the pleasant soft-spoken candidate. . . scored a minor coup."[103] *Time* was referring to Florida's state Democratic convention, where Democratic leaders voted for Carter by a majority of 67 percent. There followed a review of Carter's campaign and an ending stressing that maverick and underdog Carter had made some officials at the Democratic National Committee "nervous" and this for Carter was "a sure sign of progress. . . they are taking him seriously."[104]

What was *Time's* view of other candidates besides Jackson? Wallace was also treated unfavorably — his racism and health problems were referred to — but apparently because Wallace was an unlikely nominee, little attention, even of a negative kind, was paid him.[105] Bayh and Udall were criticized only mildly; while not *Times*'s favorite, they were apparently seen as reasonable alternatives to Carter.[106] Fred Harris was the last remaining candidate that *Time* felt rated strong criticism. In a late December review of Harris's candidacy, *Time* tagged Harris with the "radical" and "loser" images, as another McGovern. Entitling its article "Harris: Radicalism in a Camper," *Time* admitted that Harris was the "best orator" of declared candidates, but since Democrats wanted a winner, they were having "sober second thoughts" about Harris since he "does not look like one."[107] Harris, *Time* argued, was, "if anything, more radical than McGovern. If Harris had his way, the U.S. would be much altered, perhaps beyond recognition."[108]

When *Time* made predictions about Carter's showing in the early primaries, it was careful not to build up expectations too greatly. Discussing Wallace's candidacy in late November 1975, *Time* argued that all Carter had to do to "win" the early March Florida primary was to cut Wallace's margin of victory below that of 1972: "If Carter significantly trims his lead, the Alabamian would be badly hurt."[109] Similarly, in January *Time* stated that "Carter can probably hope to pick up no more than a handful of New Hampshire's seventeen delegates votes."[110] The purpose of keeping expectations low was a dual one — prevent the loser image from developing and conversely to be able to stress the "surprisingly strong" showing of Carter whatever the results were, adding to the bandwagon effect.

When Carter did have success in the Iowa caucuses in January 1976 and some criticism of his policy positions began to be raised, *Time* ran a series of articles defending Carter during February and March. The policies that Carter was most criticized for by various individuals were his support of the Vietnam war at least until late 1972, his support of the death penalty, his opposition to federal aid to New York City, his agreement with anti-union "right to work" laws, and his cozying up to Wallace and Lester Maddox in his

1970 campaign for governor. *Time*'s explanation for why Carter was being criticized was that "any presidential candidate who seems to be breaking ahead of the pack is bound to come under fire."[111] Carter had come under attack because he was "one of the more successful candidates" and "an outsider in the view of the Democratic establishment."[112] Without addressing the substance or validity of the criticism *Time* said that the "liberal" press was "doing a job on Jimmy," attacking him with a vengeance. Reporters were quoted as saying that one Carter critic was a "hit man" out to "do a hatchet job on Jimmy Carter."[113] In early March *Time* continued both to defend and praise Carter with a long cover story. Stating that Carter had been "the surprise and irritant of the politics-as-usual world," *Time* argued that now that he was winning "his opponents' amusement" had "turned to concern and then to hostility. To make up for lost time, they" were "turning more heat on him. So along with the love from his ardent supporters," there was a "wave of hate from some of his opponents."[114] In this and some prior articles on Carter, Andrew Young, one of his major supporters, was quoted favorably on Carter, but Julian Bond and other black critics were not quoted.[115]

Finally, *Time* even attempted to push Carter in its advertising. One writer noted after the campaign that "through 1975, *Time*'s advertising in other magazines [run in *People, Sports Illustrated,* the *Atlantic, Harper's, Forbes, New Times, Smithsonian,* the *National Observer,* and others] for its own campaign coverage looked more like an ad for Jimmy Carter: a half-page picture presented the candidate in a Kennedyesque rocking chair under the caption: 'His basic strategy consists of handshaking and street-cornering his way into familiarity.'"[116]

This brief review of *Time*'s coverage of Carter and other Democratic presidential candidates makes it evident that *Time* favored Carter even more strongly than did the *New York Times*. Since a newsmagazine has more latitude about

what can be defined as news, a greater selectivity can come
into play and thus biases are more clear. This was certainly
the case with the *Time* coverage of Carter.

Other Media

The *Wall Street Journal*, with its national circulation
among businessmen and propertied Americans, is one of the
most influential national newspapers. Speaking from a
generally conservative Republican viewpoint, the *Journal*
found Carter the most attractive of the Democratic candidates, ranking him among the conservative Democrats, in
line with the preferences of the newspaper's audience.[117]
An example of the favorable coverage given Carter by the
Journal is an article by staff reporter Norman C. Miller
which appeared in July 1975. Miller relates Carter's plans
and "dark horse" status, pointing out that, despite this,
"his engaging personality and tireless campaigning are impressing many Democratic politicians around the country.
. . . "[118] Appealing to the *Journal*'s audience of business
managers, Miller says Carter is a fiscal conservative and
that his "boyish shock of brown hair, toothy smile and down-
home style (always Jimmy, never James) disguises a mind
that apparently enjoys grappling with 'zero-base budgeting'
systems. . . and other management methods."[119] Miller
preserves the facade of objectivity about Carter by quoting a
union official — certainly not a favorite occupation of most
Journal readers — who states that Carter is "a posturing
phony."[120] Miller counters this by quoting the head of
Georgia Business and Industrial Association that Carter is
"honest and sincere," a "populist kind of guy."[121] Other
articles stressed Carter's "human appeal" and "surprising
strength" in the early caucuses.[122] Carter's strength was
"surprising" to the *Journal* even in Mississippi where Carter
lost to Wallace by a three to one margin.[123] By contrast the
Journal's articles on other candidates included statements

about Jackson's "can't win" image, Shriver's "clumsy" campaign, and Harris's lack of support. [124] In an editorial in March 1976, the *Wall Street Journal* argued that Carter was the best of the Democratic candidates, for, although a freer spender than Republicans, he was viewed as "the only presidential candidate of his party who is characterized as a foe of Washington's big government" and a man "who sings the praises of the private sector." [125]

The *Los Angeles Times,* the most important newspaper west of the Mississippi, also had articles which were favorable to Carter, helping to produce a positive image for the candidate. The headline of one such article in May 1975 stated: "Georgia's Carter Brings Religion, Idealism to New Hampshire Presidential Primary." The article itself consisted largely of quotes from the candidate's set speech and the comment that Carter's "craggy profile reminds many people of John F. Kennedy. . . . " [126] Another *Times* article in February 1976 featured Carter's hometown of Plains, Georgia, and the candidate's role as a racial moderate in a racist area of the nation. An added feature of this latter article was a stress on Carter's supposedly humble beginnings and the Horatio Alger story of how he worked hard as a boy selling peanuts, investing the proceeds in cotton and later in houses. The writer concludes tnat "the sheer enterprise of the Carter family is one of the things that most forcefully strikes a visitor to Plains." [127]

Newsweek, the second most widely read weekly newsmagazine, also favored Carter in its news reporting. In 1971 and 1975 articles, *Newsweek* stressed the Kennedy-type looks and appeal that Carter had. Carter's gubernatorial inauguration was "Camelot all over again," said *Newsweek*, and he is "something of a ringer for the late President Kennedy." [128] Carter's inaugural speech as governor of Georgia was "dramatic" and "eloquent." [129] In a December

1975 article on Carter's campaign, *Newsweek* quotes one voter as saying that the candidate "looks like Jack Kennedy" and another that "he's a person you take to right away."[130] Carter, *Newsweek* argued, "has succeeded in making Democrats who once dismissed him as a regional non-starter look twice," and he has "the true grit of a campaigner."[131]

In contrast to these positive comments, Jackson was called "grey," a "bland man," and the Democrats' "dullest campaigner."[132] Harris was labeled "unelectable" and Bentsen had "flagged badly" by late 1975.[133] Bayh and Udall were treated favorably, however, indicating that, for *Newsweek* at least, Carter was simply one of three acceptable candidates.[134]

Television in the 1970s is said often to be "more influential and powerful than the government itself."[135] While this no doubt overstates reality, television does have great power in many areas of American life, including politics, because of its influence over people's consciousness and ideology. Television was important in the creation of President Carter. After the election he "acknowledged that television had been his savior."[136] Positive coverage of Carter on television news programs began during the second half of 1975 when very few Americans had even heard of Jimmy Carter. In quantitative terms during the last six months of 1975 network evening news programs (CBS, NBC, and ABC) had as many stories on Carter as on Henry Jackson, and only George Wallace and Hubert Humphrey had more.[137] Of these four most covered Democratic candidates, Carter was the only "new face," the only man who had not been prominent in national public life for at least fifteen years. Qualitatively Carter's coverage by the networks was very good. Carter's appearance on NBC's *Face the Nation* directly resulted in political support in Iowa. After Carter led in the *Des Moines Register and Tribune* Iowa straw poll in the fall of 1975, columnist Joseph Kraft noted that all three networks had "stories favorable to Carter."[138] One of these was a favorable profile of Carter on NBC nightly news on October 31, 1975.[139]

This "profile" was the longest story of the entire newscast and sympathetically reviewed Carter's life history, campaign efforts, and policy views, concluding on the optimistic note that Carter had come a long way from being an unknown. [140] Not all candidates rated a profile by NBC news, and some who did got a negative one. The profile devoted to Fred Harris, for example, concluded on two negative notes, stressing the criticism of Harris by his opponents and that he was given little chance of winning. [141]

Positive stories on Carter continued from fall 1975 on, as indicated by the statement of Chris Brown, Carter's campaign manager in New Hampshire, that Carter's victory in Iowa climaxed a period of helpful media coverage. [142] Once Carter had won in Iowa, he received more positive coverage on network television. His victory was called of great symbolic importance by John Chancellor of NBC. [143] R. W. Apple, Jr., of the *New York Times*, after interviewing Carter supporters in New Hampshire, concluded that Carter, once unknown in the state, "seems to have benefited substantially from television coverage of his victories in caucus states; several backers mentioned seeing such reports." [144]

It was not merely Carter's victories that gave him positive coverage. Reporting was favorable before he won anything and his defeats were minimized. For example, when Wallace defeated Carter by a three to one margin in the Mississippi caucus a week after Iowa, the defeat was deemphasized by the media. CBS reporters, for example, said that Mississippi was not significant; the really important Wallace-Carter contest was Florida in March. [145] The very next story on CBS evening news that night recalled Carter's victory in Iowa and had a film of him campaigning in New Hampshire speaking about his Iowa win. [146]

The contrast between the way in which Carter's victory in New Hampshire and Jackson's victories in Massachusetts and New York were handled by CBS is probably the most instructive example of all. When Carter won New Hampshire

— as the only middle of the road Democrat in a fairly conservative state — with 30 percent of the vote (about 23,000 votes), Walter Cronkite announced: "the first ballots in Campaign '76 have given Jimmy Carter a commanding head start in the race for the Democratic presidential nomination."[147] Roger Mudd added that "Carter's victory was substantial. . . he's now the one with momentum, the one who must be stopped."[148] One week later Jackson won in Massachusetts with 23 percent (about 163,000 votes). Cronkite announced that Jackson's showing "has scrambled the race," and Mudd added that "Jackson's strong finish. . . surprised everyone."[149] Carter's victory was interpreted as "substantial," giving him a "commanding head start" and "momentum." Jackson's victory, which in reality was comparable to Carter's, "scrambled the race," and was only a "strong finish."

Jackson's victory in New York in April was also deemphasized as an unusual coalition, one which "appears peculiar to New York and may not be duplicated anywhere else."[150] NBC said that Jackson had "the appearance of a headline hunter," something of a *non sequitur* in the circumstances.

Carter was also played up by the television networks as an underdog, Horatio Alger hero, the good guy of the melodrama who raised himself to power by his own efforts and those of the people. Roger Mudd even went so far as to say this about Carter and the Iowa caucuses:

> If Carter wins even by one point, that's a substantial accomplisment, because he's done it with hard work, without any real support or alliance or ties into labor or to farmers or to the big-city machines. He's done it outside the political machinery of this country.[151]

Anyone looking at the make-up of Carter's Iowa steering committee — with its leaders of the Des Moines political machine, the ex-president of the UAW, the others — would know that Mudd's comment was an overstatement, although it is true that Carter was not generally the favorite of most party regulars.

A journalist who compared Jackson's treatment by the television networks to Carter's concluded that it was "strikingly different. . . it is difficult to escape the conclusion that the reporters didn't much like Jackson and his politics. . . . "[152] In contrast to this, during February and March "night after night the three television networks carried front-line stories" on Carter.[153] Carter was by then clearly "the newest media star in politics."[154]

CONCLUSION

Given that Carter got a good press, how does such favorable free publicity translate into political support and votes at the polls? Influence over public opinion in the United States and other Western nations has best been described as "trickle down" in nature. Those who own and control the mass media influence both the average voter directly and those opinion leaders, "the attentive public," who follow public affairs closely. These leaders in turn retail to voters perceptions acquired through the media.[155] Thus while the average voter may not read the *New York Times* or the *Wall Street Journal*, influential people in their communities do and spread the word through a variety of means.[156] A recent study has convincingly shown that it is this group, the "attentive public," local opinion leaders, who are usually upper middle class, that is most manipulated by the media.[157]

This "attentive public" — usually politically active, highly educated, and in the top 10 to 20 percent of income earners — learns about a candidate who seems attractive through one of the elite media outlets or via a local newspaper or television station which has picked up a news story or editorial from one of these elite sources or through local coverage of a candidate's visit to the area. Such individuals then become ac-

tivists for the candidate, recruiting other supporters who
then work to elect their man. An example of this process
was the way in which Harry Baxter, Democratic County
Chairman of Burlington, Iowa, became a Carter supporter.
Baxter, a local stockbroker (and thus part of the upper
middle class), saw Carter on NBC's *Meet the Press* in December 1974, was impressed and got in touch with Tim Kraft,
Carter's state coordinator. Baxter and his wife both worked
in many local campaigns and had lists of Democratic activists
in the area. Kraft used the Baxters' lists to build the Carter
organization in that part of Iowa.[158] Their work helped
Carter win the Iowa caucuses in mid-January 1976.

In the process of attracting both this activist support
and votes at the polls, both print and broadcast sources are
important. Various studies indicate that voters in the primary
elections tend to be a well-educated, high-income, civic-
minded minority who usually get most of their information
from print media. In addition newspaper endorsements have
been shown to be probably one of the most underestimated
forces in American politics.[159] In primaries and close general
elections such endorsements can be decisive.[160] Thus the
print media are probably most important during the primary
period, since those who participate in primaries are more
likely to depend on this source for their opinions.

Other studies have shown that television's role in politics,
while often overstated, can nevertheless be very important,
particularly in the area of image building. It is now common-
place that we live in an electronic age in which the images
of the candidates' personalities are becoming increasingly
important in politics. It is clear, as the late V. O. Key said,
that as the mass communications media "mold the public
images of personalities they touch a critical point in the
democratic process."[161] By their portrayal of a candidate
and his personal characteristics — looks, background, habits,
values — media executives and reporters can convey a positive
or negative impression, sometimes subtle, sometimes more

overt. The information supply patterns of the media — especially television — tends to "encourage electoral choices on the basis of personality characteristics of the contenders."[162] Voters whose ideological predispositions are weak are most influenced by such image building. These tendencies were especially evident among Carter voters. There is much evidence that during the primary period Carter was "strongest among those voters without clear views of the issues."[163] As Carter himself put it, "the ones who are casually interested in politics like me. . . . "[164] Carter was successful in appealing to all sections — right, center, left — of the Democratic party, and he could do so because of the multiplicity of favorable images which the media, particularly the broadcast media, helped project.

Finally, although there has been little research on the topic, the mass communications media do appear to be extremely effective in creating opinions on new personalities and issues. To cite but one example, a few months before Fidel Castro came to power only a very small percentage of Americans had even heard of him. A year later the American people knew a great deal about Castro, and had a rather homogeneously negative opinion of him. The mass of Americans had essentially one source for information about Castro, the mass media. This source was effective in creating opinion because the audience had no existing opinions or strong interest in the matter. The case of Jimmy Carter is similar but less obvious and more complex. He was a relatively unknown figure and therefore people did not have opinions about him. He was not in office and had only a scanty public record on national issues. His personality and promises thus could not be easily measured by performance. As a fresh face he was relatively easy to sell. The media establishment cannot sell just anyone, however. The ability of one candidate or another to gather a mass following can and does at times have an effect. If a candidate is, as Carter was, favored by many of the political financiers and the owners of the mass communications media, however, it gives a great advantage in developing such a following. A key function of primaries from the point of view of far-sighted ruling class leaders is to determine which of several acceptable candidates can gain broad support from the American people. A candidate not popular among the voters is, of course, rejected as dysfunctional by ruling class leaders themselves, as a man incapable of leading the American people in directions the ruling class want to go.

It is thus clear that Carter's leap to prominence was not, as has often been argued, solely because of his personal qualities, his abilities as a campaigner, or his campaign strategy. While these factors were sometimes important, other candidates campaigned as hard, had adequate early financing, charm and wit, were good speakers, had the "common touch," and knew that the early primaries and the mass media were the keys to the campaign.[165] What Carter had that his opponents did not was the acceptance and support of elite sectors of the mass communications media. It was their favorable coverage of Carter and his campaign that gave him an edge, propelling him rocket-like to the top of the opinion polls. This helped Carter win key primary election victories, enabling him to rise from an obscure public figure to President-elect in the short space of nine months.

Notes

1. Theodore White, *The Making of the President 1972* (New York: Atheneum, 1973), p. 255.

2. Congressional Quarterly, *Editorial Research Reports,* "Presidential Campaign Coverage," I, April 9, 1976, p. 249.

3. *U.S. News and World Report,* May 17, 1976, p. 16.

4. *The Atlanta Constitution,* July 10, 1974, p. 4A.

5. Ibid.

6. Martin Schram, *Running for President 1976: The Carter Campaign* (New York: Pocket Books, 1977), p. 64.

7. Jules Witcover, *Marathon: The Pursuit of the Presidency 1972-1976* (New York: Viking, 1977), pp. 135-136.

8. Ibid., p. 137.

9. See *United States News and World Report,* September 22, 1975, pp. 53-54; Leslie Wheeler, *Jimmy Who? An Examination of Presidential Candidate Jimmy Carter: The Man, His Career, His Stands on the Issues* (Woodbury, New York: Barron, 1976), p. V; *Los Angeles Times,* October 26, 1975, p. I5.

10. *Los Angeles Times,* December 14, 1975, p.I6.

11. Ibid.

12. Princeton Survey Research Center, Inc., *Gallup Opinion Index #129,* April, 1976, p. 4.

13. Ibid.

14. *New York Times,* March 29, 1976, p. 1; *Gallup Opinion Index #129,* April, 1976, pp. 3-4.

15. Elihu Katz, "Platforms and Windows: Broadcasting's Role in Election Campaigns," *Journalism Quarterly* (Summer, 1971), p. 306.

16. Robert W. Turner, *I'll Never Lie to You: Jimmy Carter in His Own Words* (New York: Ballantine, 1976), p. 10.

17. *Atlanta Constitution,* January 6, 1975, p. 2A.

18. Ibid.

19. *Atlanta Constitution,* April 13, 1975, pp. 1A, 22A.

20. *Atlanta Constitution,* January 15, 1976, p. 4A.

21. *New York Times,* January 20, 1976, p. 36.

22. Elizabeth B. Drew, "Reporter in Washington D.C.," *New Yorker,* May 31, 1976, p. 64.

23. Schram, *Running for President,* p. 19.

24. White, *The Making of the President 1972,* p. 258.

25. Ibid., p. 259.

26. Ibid., vi.

27. Ibid., p. 258.

28. *New York Times,* October 16, 1974, p. 43.

29. *New York Times,* December 9, 1974, p. 45.

30. Ibid.

31. *New York Times,* December 7, 1974, p. 16.

32. *New York Times,* December 9, 1974, p. 45.

33. *New York Times,* December 15, 1974, IV, p. 16.

34. Ibid.

35. *New York Times,* January 21, 1975, p. 32.

36. *New York Times,* February 7, 1975, p. 30.

37. Ibid.

38. *New York Times,* January 5, 1975, IV, p. 3.

39. *New York Times,* March 16, 1975, IV, p. 4.

40. Ibid.

41. Ibid.

42. *New York Times,* March 24, 1975, p. 10.

43. *New York Times,* April 21, 1975, p. 13.

44. *Washington Post,* March 16, 1975, p. A5, Udall had raised $82,000 and Carter $71,000 at this point in the campaign.

45. *New York Times,* July 13, 1975, IV, p. 3.

46. Ibid.

47. Ibid.

48. In a letter to the author, Mr. Palevsky stated that his first interest was to end the Wallace threat. Beyond that he stated, "It was a question of alternatives." It thus seems an overstatement to say that Palevsky was "impressed" with Carter. Max Palevsky to Laurence H. Shoup, January 12, 1978.

49. *New York Times,* July 27, 1975, IV, p. 17.

50. Ibid.

51. Ibid.

52. *U.S. News and World Report,* September 22, 1975, pp. 53-54.

53. *New York Times,* August 15, 1975, p. 8.

54. *New York Times,* July 3, 1975, p. 29.

55. *New York Times,* April 27, 1975, p. 21.

56. *New York Times,* October 26, 1975, IV, p. 2.

57. *Atlanta Constitution,* February 17, 1975, p. 6A.

58. *New York Times,* October 27, 1975, p. 17.

59. Ibid.

60. In Florida, for example, he had the backing of the Dade County (Miami) party chairman as well as the UAW and St. Petersburg chairman. In Oklahoma the governor supported Carter, who had the established local power structure on his side against Harris. Witcover, *Marathon,* p. 217. See also *New York Times,* November 17, 1975, p. 21.

61. *New York Times,* November 2, 1975, p. 53.

62. Ibid.

63. *New York Times,* November 3, 1975, p. 25.

64. *Time,* February 2, 1976, p. 18.

65. *New York Times Magazine,* December 14, 1975, VI, p. 15.

66. Schram, *Running for President,* p. 171.

67. *New York Times,* December 26, 1975, p. 1.

68. *New York Times,* January 11, 1976, IV, p. 4.

69. *New York Times,* December 17, 1975, p. 26; December 27, 1974, p. 1.

70. *New York Times,* January 12, 1976, p. 1.

71. *The Savannah Morning News* (Georgia), for example, printed an editorial on Carter in December or early January 1975 which said that Carter's government reorganization plan did not work: "the maze of bureaucracy in Georgia has, if anything, increased in size, scope, and confusion." See *Atlanta Constitution,* January 2, 1975, p. 4A.

72. *The Nation,* April 17, 1976, pp. 454-455.

73. *San Francisco Bay Guardian,* September 7-15, 1978, p. 4. The nationally eminent judges were selected by Carl Jensen, Associate Professor of Sociology at Sonoma State College, Rohnert Park, California. The panel included a former editor of the *Washington Post,* a former Federal Communications Commissioner, two prominent authors, and two nationally known professors. Jensen sent out over a hundred press releases announcing the findings, but it received no coverage from the major media outlets with the exception of an Associated Press story which was published in just a few small newspapers.

74. *New York Times,* January 20, 1976, p. 1.

75. *New York Times,* January 19, 1976, p. 1.

76. *New York Times,* January 23, 1976, p. 30.

77. V.O. Key, *Public Opinion and American Democracy* (New York: Knopf, 1961), p. 377.

78. White, *The Making of the President 1972,* p. 250.

79. Robert T. Elson, *Time Inc.: The Intimate History of a Publishing Enterprise 1923-1941* (New York: Atheneum, 1968), p. 428.

80. *Time,* May 31, 1971, pp. 14-20.

81. Ibid., pp. 15-16.

82. Ibid., p. 16.

83. *Life,* January 29, 1971, pp. 30-31.

84. *Time,* December 23, 1974, p. 11.

85. Ibid.

86. Ibid., p. 12.

87. Ibid.

88. *Time,* February 17, 1975, p. 11.

89. Ibid.

90. Ibid.

91. Ibid., p. 12.

92. Ibid.

93. Ibid., p. 17.

94. Ibid.

95. Ibid.

96. Ibid., pp. 18-21.

97. Ibid.

98. Ibid.

99. *Time,* October 13, 1975, p. 25.

100. Ibid.

101. Ibid.

102. Ibid., p. 26.

103. *Time,* December 1, 1975, p. 15.

104. Ibid.

105. See, for example, *Time,* November 24, 1975, p. 41.

106. See *Time,* November 3, 1975, pp. 18-20 and August 25, 1975, pp. 16-17.

107. *Time,* December 22, 1975, pp. 24-25.

108. Ibid.

109. *Time,* November 24, 1975, p. 41.

110. *Time,* January 19, 1976, p. 11.

111. *Time,* February 2, 1976, p. 17.

112. *Time,* February 16, 1976, p. 77.

113. Ibid. The attacks on Carter were coming from the smaller circulation newspapers and magazines of the liberal sector of the Democratic party — the *New Republic, Harper's,* and *Village Voice.* An especially sharp attack on Carter by Steven Brill appeared in *Harper's* in March, 1976.

114. *Time,* March 8, 1976, p. 15.

115. Ibid., p. 16; *Time,* February 2, 1976, p. 17.

116. Christopher Lydon, "Jimmy Carter Revealed: He's a Rockefeller Republican," *Atlantic Monthly,* July 1977, p. 51.

117. *Wall Street Journal,* February 19, 1976, p. 1; March 30, 1976, p. 24. This fact is especially interesting since the *New York Times* ranked Carter among the liberal Democrats.

118. *The Wall Street Journal,* July 7, 1975, p. 1.

119. Ibid.

120. Ibid., p. 12.

121. Ibid.

122. *Wall Street Journal,* February 19, 1976, pp. 1, 25.

123. Ibid., p. 1.

124. Ibid., p. 25.

125. *Wall Street Journal,* March 30, 1976, p. 24.

126. *Los Angeles Times,* May 25, 1975, p. I5.

127. *Los Angeles Times,* February 11, 1976, pp. IA2-3.

128. *Newsweek,* January 25, 1971, p. 51.

129. Ibid.; *Newsweek,* February 15, 1971, p. 33.

130. *Newsweek,* December 1, 1975, p. 41.

131. Ibid., pp. 41-42.

132. *Newsweek,* November 3, 1975, p. 17; February 10, 1976, pp. 18-19.

133. *Newsweek,* November 3, 1975, p. 17; December 22, 1975, p. 25.

134. *Newsweek,* December 8, 1975, p. 29; December 29, 1975, pp. 17-18.

135. David Halberstam, "CBS: The Power and the Profits," *Atlantic* (January, 1976), p. 35.

136. Witcover, *Marathon,* p. 14.

137. Compiled from Vanderbilt Television News Archive, *A Guide to the Videotape Collection of the Network Evening News Programs July-December 1975* (Nashville, Tennessee).

138. *Atlanta Constitution,* January 15, 1976, p. 4A.

139. *Los Angeles Times,* November 2, 1975, p. 1A:1.

140. Vanderbilt Television News Archive, *Television News Index and Abstracts, October 1975,* Abstract of NBC Evening News Broadcast (October 31, 1975), p. 2196.

141. Vanderbilt Television News Archive, *Television News Index and Abstracts, December 1975,* Abstract of NBC Evening News Broadcast (Dec. 19, 1975), p. 2250.

142. *New York Times,* February 23, 1976, p. 30.

143. Vanderbilt Television News Archive, *Television News Index and Abstracts, January 1976,* Abstract of NBC Evening News Broadcast (January 20, 1976), p. 132.

144. *New York Times,* February 24, 1976, p. 26.

145. Vanderbilt Television News Archive, *Television News Index and Abstracts, January 1976,* Abstract of CBS Evening News (January 25, 1976), p. 163.

146. Ibid., p. 164.

147. *The New York Times Magazine,* August 29, 1976, VI, p. 51.

148. Ibid.

149. Ibid.

150. Ibid., p. 54.

151. Ibid., p. 56.

152. Ibid.

153. Leslie Wheeler, "Jimmy Who?" p. ix.

154. *New York Times,* January 31, 1976, p. 22.

155. See V.O. Key, Jr., *Public Opinion and American Democracy,* pp. 359-361; Robert D. Putnam, *The Comparative Study of Elites* (Englewood Cliffs, New Jersey: Prentice Hall 1976), pp. 138-139; and John P. Robinson, "Interpersonal Influence in Election Campaigns: Two Step-flow Hypotheses," *Public Opinion Quarterly,* (Fall, 1976).

156. Key, *Public Opinion and American Democracy,* pp. 362, 365-366.

157. Richard Hamilton, *Restraining Myths: Critical Studies of U.S. Social Structure and Politics* (New York: John Wiley & Sons, 1975), pp. 219-239.

158. Kandy Stroud, *How Jimmy Won: The Victory Campaign from Plains to the White House* (New York: Morrow, 1977), 238-239.

159. *Congressional Quarterly,* "Presidential Campaign Coverage," p. 251; "Newsline," *Psychology Today* (September 1974), p. 20; Harold Mendelsohn and Garrett J.O'Keefe, *The People Choose a President: Influences on Voter Decision Making* (New York: Praeger, 1976), pp. 167-168.

160. Two authorities estimate that newspaper endorsements are worth "at least" two percentage points to the Republican Party nationwide, and that Hubert Humphrey might well have won in 1968 with a more even balance of endorsements. See Robert S. Erikson and Norman R. Luttbeg, *American Public Opinion: Its Origins, Content, and Impact* (New York: Wiley, 1973), p. 145.

161. Key, *Public Opinion and American Democracy,* p. 400.

162. Doris A. Graber, "Press and Television as Opinion Resources in Presidential Campaigns," *Public Opinion Quarterly* (Fall, 1976), p. 301.

163. *New York Times,* February 25, 1976, p. 18.

164. Schram, *Running for President,* p. 122.

165. Witcover indicates, for example, that Fred Harris was superior to Carter as a stump speaker and campaigner with the "common touch." Some polls also indicated that Harris' campaign messages were popular ones. But Harris did not get far in his campaign due, at least in part, to the hostility of the media. See Jules Witcover, *Marathon: The Pursuit of the Presidency 1972-1976,* pp. 144-146.

Part II

The Carter Presidency and Beyond

Introduction to Part II

The central point of the first half of this study has been that Jimmy Carter, using a combination of charm, hard work, middle-of-the-road policy positions, and a keen sense of where power lies in America, built his political career by gaining support first from the establishment of his local area, and then from the dominant sector of the national ruling class focused in New York. Traditional Democratic constituencies like labor, intellectuals, minorities, ethnics, and big city machines played a role as time went on; but the key to Carter's victory was the early support given by upper-class groups centered in Atlanta and New York, especially the large financial and media corporations of New York.

The makeup and locus of power in his administration supply strong additional evidence of the validity of this perspective. The individuals Carter chose to fill the central policy-making positions in his administration were overwhelmingly from the Eastern Establishment's key policy-planning organizations: especially the Trilateral Commission and the Council on Foreign Relations, but also the Committee for Economic Development, Brookings Institution and others.

Carter chose mainly from the center and liberal side of the Eastern Establishment, not from its more conservative side (as represented by the Committee on the Present Danger, Business Roundtable, and Business Council). Carter brought into his administration twenty Trilateral Commissioners, at least fifty-four members of the Council of Foreign Relations (at least thirty-one at the State Department and another ten at the National Security Council), and at least five trustees or senior staff members of both the Brookings Institution and Committee for Economic Development. In contrast, his administration does not have even one representative from the 141-member Board of Directors of the hard-line anti-Soviet Committee on the Present Danger despite the fact that two of their leaders, former State Department officials Paul H. Nitze and Dean Rusk, were Carter advisers during the campaign. Table 1 summarizes the connections of leading Carter administration officials to the policy-planning organizations of the Eastern Establishment.[1]

The Carter Cabinet's direct ties with Eastern Establishment big business interests are also substantial. Cyrus Vance and N. Michael Blumenthal served as trustees of the Rockefeller Foundation; Patricia Harris was a Chase Manhattan Bank Director; Harold Brown, Vance and Harris were directors of IBM; Energy Secretary Charles W. Duncan Jr. was President of Coca Cola and lawyers Joseph Califano and Griffin Bell represented that company. Juanita Kreps was a director of J.C. Penney, Eastman Kodak, and R.J. Reynolds Industries and G. William Miller was Chairman of Textron. In addition, only a few members of the Cabinet came from outside the northeast section of the United States. Those members of the Carter cabinet having the narrowest constituencies and most representing the special interests of the party politics level — Agriculture, Labor, Transportation, and Interior — are those least tied to the Eastern Establishment and also the least wealthy cabinet members.[2] These Estab-

Table 1.

High Level Carter Administration Officials and
Policy Planning Organizations (1977-1979)

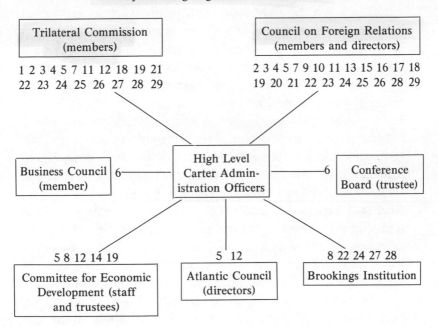

Key:

1. J. Carter, *President*
2. W. Mondale, *Vice President*
3. C. Vance, *Secretary of State*
4. Z. Brzezinski, *Natl. Sceurity Adv.*
5. W. M. Blumenthal, *Sec. of Treas.*
6. W. Miller, *Sec. of Treas.*
7. H. Brown, *Secy. of Defense*
8. C. Schultze, *Chair, Council of Economic Advisors*
9. J. Califano, *Secy HEW*
10. P. R. Harris, *Secy. HUD, HEW*
11. W. Christopher *Dep. Sec. of State*
12. R. N. Cooper, *Undersec. of State*
13. P. Habib, *Under Secy. of State*
14. W. G. Clayton, Jr. *Dep. Secy. of Defence*
15. S. Turner, *CIA Director*
16. D. Aaron, *Dep. to Nat. Sec. Adv.*
17. A. Solomon, *Under Secy of Treas.*
18. P. Warnke, *Arms Control Direct.*
19. A. Young, *Amb. to UN*
20. D. McHenry, *Amb. to UN*
21. E. L. Richardson, *Amb. at Large*
22. H. Owen, *Natl. Security Council*
23. R. Bowie, *Dep. CIA Director*
24. L. N. Cutler, *White House Couns.*
25. H. Donovan, *Spec. Adviser to the President*
26. P. Volcker, *Chair. Fed. Reserve Board*
27. L. W. Benson, *Under Secy. of State*
28. G. C. Smith, *Amb. at Large*
29. J. Sawhill, *Dep. Secy. of Energy*

lishment figures make the important foreign, economic, and domestic policy decisions of the American government today. They set the goals and directions for the government.

It is interesting to note that, while Carter and other Trilateral Commissioners have taken over the American government, several European and Japanese Commissioners have also risen to high positions in their own nations. In France, Commissioner Raymond Barre became Prime Minister and Minister of Economy and Finance in the summer of 1976. In 1977 Count Otto Lambsdorff, also a Trilateral member, became Economics Minister of the German Federal Republic. In Japan, Commissioners Nobuhiko Ushiba and Kiichi Miyazawa recently assumed the posts of Minister of External Economic Affairs and director-general of the Economic Planning Agency respectively, and were cited by *Washington Post* financial writer Hobart Rowen as "key figures" in subsequent economic negotiations with the United States. And in Belgium, Eire, and Norway Trilateral Commissioners have become foreign ministers. Several Commissioners have stated that the goal of the organization is to have a direct influence on government decision-making. Canadian Mitchell Sharp, the deputy chairman of the North American section of the Commission, frankly said, "There's no doubt that the Commission's aim is to affect government."[3] By 1977 this goal had certainly been achieved, most particularly in the United States.

The Atlanta Establishment group in Carter's government, while much ballyhooed in the media, is clearly in a secondary position, although they are substantially represented at the middle levels of power. Carter's political operatives, Jody Powell and Hamilton Jordan, are his main staff members in the White House. They do not handle large-scale policy making, but deal rather with the middle-level nuts-and-bolts jobs connected with building and maintaining a political machine — public and press relations, including the selling of already-decided-upon policies, control of the Democratic Party and its factions, and deciding whom to reward and whom to punish.[4] Griffin Bell, of the King and Spalding law firm and long a close friend of Carter, was selected for the politically sensitive position of attorney general. This cabinet office, with its control over criminal investigations and indictments, is one that presidents — campaign pledges aside — have always tried to control tightly with a close friend or relative.[5]

Another important position filled by a Georgian and Carter political ally is that of Budget Director — first by T. Bertram Lance and, then, beginning in early 1978, by Georgia lawyer James McIntyre. The role of Budget Director includes a seat on the small but powerful Economic Policy Group Steering Committee, which was chaired by Treasury Secretary W. Michael Blumenthal and dominated by Eastern Establishment individuals.

Other high officials of the Carter Administration have both an Eastern Establishment and Atlanta connection. Bell, and Duncan, mentioned above, are two such individuals, as is Deputy Secretary of Defense W. Graham Clayton Jr., who was Chairman of Southern Railroad Company and a CED trustee. Anne Cox Chambers and Jay Solomon, major Carter campaign contributors, were appointed Ambassador to Belgium and head of the General Services Administration respectively.[6]

Some of Carter's media supporters were also brought into government positions to reward past support and to help assure continued favorable coverage. Vance and Brown were, of course, on the boards of the *New York Times* and *Los Angeles Times* respectively. Joining them in the Carter Administration are journalists from the *New York Times* (active CFR member Leslie Gelb, Director of Politico-Military Affairs, Department of State, and William V. Shannon, Ambassador to Ireland); *Time* magazine (Jerrold Schecter, National Security Council press operations); *Los Angeles Times* and the *Atlanta Constitution* (William Drummond and Rex Granum respectively, assistants to Jody Powell); and the *Chicago Sun-Times* (Thomas Ross, Assistant Secretary of Defense for

Public Affairs). In addition, Thomas Reston, the son of James Reston of the *New York Times*, is a State Department spokesman.

The power of the lower level cabinet and government officials is substantially less than those individuals listed in Table I. Policy is made by the Eastern Establishment sector of Carter's government. It is impossible for anyone looking at the evidence to deny that Jimmy Carter's campaign as an "outsider," dedicated to ousting the "insiders," was an outrageous misrepresentation. He has in fact installed a retreaded regime of establishment figures, the same men responsible for the "mess in Washington," which Carter talked so much about. As Ralph Nader put it, Carter's cabinet choices are "conservatives, old-line establishment, traditional inhouse advocates for certain interests and completely main line."[7] As one scholar commented, many would "not have been out of place in a moderate Republican Cabinet."[8] The *average* income of Carter's eleven cabinet officers before taking office was $211,000 a year, when nearly 90 percent of American families earn less than $25,000 a year.[9]

The personnel practices of the Carter Administration as a whole then represent an attempt to serve both the dominant sector of the ruling class, giving it control over "high" policy, and the party politics level of American politics, bringing in at the lower levels of government Carter's political allies and individuals representative of various key constituencies — Democratic party leaders (Robert Strauss), blacks (Andrew Young; his replacement, Donald McHenry; Patricia Roberts Harris), liberals (Sam Brown, head of ACTION, and Joan Claybrook, head of the National Highway Safety Adminis-tration), Eastern "liberal" Republicans (Elliot Richardson among others), and women (Midge Costanza and Juanita Kreps). Organized labor seems to have been excluded entirely. John Dunlop, the AFL-CIO choice for Secretary of Labor, was not appointed. Ray Marshall, the man chosen, was not, however, opposed by the AFL-CIO leadership. These appointments show that the Carter Administration is attempting to build a political machine which can win again in 1980. Appointments are a central part of its strategy.

When the Carter administration entered office in early 1977, it faced serious and long-standing economic and foreign policy problems, difficulties which collectively added up to the worst crisis of the system since the great depression of the 1930s. The sector of the ruling class which put Carter in office — represented by the Trilateral Commission and Council on Foreign Relations — stressed the international aspects of this crisis. From its formation in 1973 the Trilateral Commission issued regular statements pointing out that the current international order was inadequate to handle the problems it faced and that rapid "renovation" of that system was needed. For example the Commission's Executive Committee issued this statement in December 1974:

> The international system is undergoing a drastic transformation through a series of crises. Worldwide inflation reflects, transmits and magnifies the tensions of many societies, while the difficulties produced by the abrupt change in oil prices are accompanied by the entry of major new participants onto the world scene.[10]

A Commission report argued that this was a "critical" turning point in world history and that "the lives and fortunes of large numbers of human beings hang upon the outcome of decisions taken by a small handful of national leaders."[11] Other Commission publications speak of the "serious strains" and "alarming deterioration" in international relations, the resulting "high risk of global anarchy," and threat of "long-term disaster," as well as the possibility that in some industrial nations "the existing social and political system could be endangered."[12] Aspects of this crisis which are particularly worrisome to ruling class leaders include the possible end of United States world hegemony as illustrated by its defeat in Indochina, the rise in relative power of Europe, the Soviet

Union, China and Japan, and the rebelliousness of important parts of the Third World, including the oil-producing nations. These trends have manifested themselves in the dollar devaluations of 1971-72, the quadrupling of oil prices in 1973, the recession of 1974-75 which was the most serious since the 1930s and which affected the entire Western world, as well as the lagging investment and productivity and the inflation and unemployment which have continued since then. An additional aspect of the crisis is the continuing struggle of the left to overthrow capitalism in Europe and the Third World and the unstable political conditions facing many Western nations.

As Commissioner Harold Brown, now Secretary of Defense, put it at a Commission meeting in June 1974, the problem facing the United States was traceable to "a failure of leadership." He added that "trust has been completely eroded in domestic affairs and in moral leadership."[13] A "new synthesis of world view, life style and ethic" was now needed which "will have to come from a new administration. . . and elsewhere."[14] This new leadership

> will have to inspire and then live up to the confidence and trust that has been lacking for a decade. Only such leadership can persuade its people to make sacrifices of individual and group advantages in order to produce the long-term benefits of international economic and political partnership abroad and a just distribution of economic and social benefits at home. Only such a leadership can make possible the adjustments that will be needed in the transition to a national and international situation in which we all shall be living in the world of the year 2000. That world will be one of sharply finite external resources. . . . I should add that such a leadership will be needed not only in North America.[15]

This, then, was Carter's mandate from ruling class leaders — restore trust, "renovate" the domestic and international system in order to preserve intact its basic structure and power relationships. The strategy used to attain these ends, first in foreign policy, then in domestic policy, will now be examined.

The concluding chapter will examine the unfolding future, with special attention given to the personalities and issues likely to dominate the 1980 election.

Notes

1. Drawn from official membership lists and news reports.

2. *Congressional Quarterly Weekly Review*, March 12, 1977, p. 455.

3. *Maclean's*, October 17, 1977, p. 44.

4. Jordan's official title for example, is "Assistant to the President for Political Affairs" and he sits in on policy-making committees in the White House in his words, to "provide whatever political insights are relevant."

5. Carter pledged during the campaign to remove the attorney general from politics. The selection of Bell, who was a part-time fund-raiser and speechwriter for Carter during the campaign, violates this promise. See Jimmy Carter, *A Government as Good as its People* (New York: Simon and Schuster, 1977), p. 48.

6. The Chambers appointment was labeled "a political payoff" by the American Foreign Service Institute. *Newsweek*, November 27, 1977, p. 70. Carter said during the campaign that the practice of "appointing unqualified persons to major diplomatic posts as political payoffs was disgraceful." See Jimmy Carter, *Why Not the Best?* (Nashville, Tennessee: Broadman, 1975), p. 147.

7. *San Francisco Sunday Examiner and Chronicle*, December 12, 1976, p. 1.

8. Gerald Pomper et. al. (ed.), *The Election of 1976: Reports and Interpretations* (New York: D. Mc. Kay, 1977), p. 121.

9. *Harper's*, October, 1977, pp. 37-38.

10. *Trialogue*, Winter 1974-1975, p. 3. This is the Trilateral Commission's own publication.

11. Richard N. Gardner, Saburo Okita, and B.J. Udink, *A Turning Point in North-South Economic Relations*, Triangle Papers 3 (New York: The Trilateral Commission, 1974).

12. *Trialogue*, May-July, 1974, pp. 7-8, and the 1973 and 1978 brochures, *The Trilateral Commission*.

13. *Trialogue*, May-July, 1974, p. 17.

14. Ibid., p. 18.

15. Ibid.

4

Trilateralism in Action:
Carter's Foreign Policy

Judging from Jimmy Carter's presidential campaign image and pledges, together with the 1976 Democratic party platform, the Administration's foreign policy promised to be different from Nixon's and Ford's in both content and tone. Carter and the 1976 Democratic election platform indicated that the lessons of Vietnam had been learned. He promised openness, consultation with traditional allies, and increased idealism. Candidate Carter had pledged to respect the rights of smaller nations, to support broader principles of human rights, to reduce military spending by $5-7 billion, and to cut arms sales abroad significantly. He also promised not to use foreign policy as an escape mechanism to avoid dealing with serious problems at home. A fair evaluation of these promises after more than two years of Carter's actual foreign policy must conclude that most of the pledges have been broken. The real goals of the corporate powers behind the President are such that the majority of these promises must remain a dead letter. Viewed broadly, these goals involve maintaining a dominant world geopolitical position for the United States. To the corporate powers this dominance is the "national interest" of the U.S. Such a position is desired for its own sake, but also for economic and strategic motives, largely due to the needs of American capitalism as presently organized.[1] As Deputy Secretary of State Warren Christopher expressed it: "Nearly ten million American jobs depend upon our exports. Two-thirds of our imports are raw materials that we do not or cannot readily produce. One out of every three dollars of U.S. corporate profits is derived from international activities. These economic issues are crucial to our national security."[2]

These goals have broad support within the American ruling class, although there is sometimes sharp disagreement over which specific policies best serve these ends. Carter has dealt with this conflict over specifics by choosing foreign policy advisers from both of the current main policy tendencies within the Establishment. The leaders of the two main policy views within the Administration are Secretary of State Cyrus Vance and National Security Adviser Zbigniew Brzezinski. That the policy approaches of both these men are within a fairly narrow range is indicated by the fact that before assuming their posts both were closely allied with the Rockefeller family, directors of the CFR and members of the Trilateral Commission.[3] Yet they do have differences, and a review of them is illuminating. Each of these men and their policy approaches competes within the Administration and each has a support group in the outside society. The more combative tendency is represented by Brzezinski and the more measured one by Vance. According to high-level sources interviewed by reporter Elizabeth Drew, Brzezinski's essential reaction to world events "is to see them in terms of the rivalry of the Soviet Union and the United States." These sources say "Brzezinski is frequently eager to take actions that challenge — test — the Soviet Union."[4] Brzezinski sees the Third World as increasingly the key arena of East-West battles, arguing that the United States should "respond forcefully" to Sovet actions there, and link such activities with other issues, such as economic relations and Strategic Arms Limitation Talks (SALT).[5] Thus, Brzezinski is more willing to risk war to keep the USSR from gaining influence in the Third World.

Brzezinski's Soviet policy also includes building up a de facto anti-Soviet alliance with China ("playing the China card") and attempting to undermine Soviet control in his native Poland and other Eastern European nations. The National Security Adviser may be partly motivated by his visceral feelings as a member of Poland's former ruling class, now out of power in his native country. Whatever his motivations may be, Brzezinski's clear desire is to keep the United States the unchallenged number one world power. As Brzezinski revealingly put it in the spring of 1978:

> In the end it gets down to a simple proposition: they would like to become number one, like we did. It's better to become number one from the number two position than be toppled from number one. That's why there is such a serious problem. It's much more destabilizing for our self-esteem, for our role in the world; there is no way of knowing where you will stop once you start going downhill.[6]

While Vance and the Department of State also strongly desire to remain "number one," their emphasis and tactics are somewhat different, resulting in "serious" strains and "in-fighting" within the Administration. Vance feels that Brzezinski is impulsive, instinctually tough, tending to react and go off half-cocked without thinking things through. Vance believes that because of nuclear weapons, a "life or death" issue, the U.S.-Soviet relationship is of "central importance."[7] Therefore, some kind of detente, at least on the issue of nuclear weapons, is crucial and unnecessary abrasions in U.S.-Soviet relations must be avoided. Vance argues that his view should not be confused with uncritical acceptance of Soviet motives; his toughness is "measured," whereas Brzezinski's is "combative."[8] Vance and the State Department also tend more to take into account the local causes and possible local solution of a Third World conflict and counsel against U.S. involvement in a situation simply as a response to Soviet or Cuban actions. These differing approaches, and the fate of Carter's campaign promises, can best be reviewed by focusing on four specific policy areas, each of which will be discussed in turn: (1) increased attention to the Third World; (2) the unity of the Trilateral World; (3) a harder line towards the Soviet Union; and (4) human rights rhetoric.

THE THIRD WORLD

The Carter Administration feels that the Third World — defined as Africa, Latin America and that part of Asia which is neither Westernized nor socialist — has been neglected in American foreign policy in the past and is now of increasing importance for economic and political-strategic reasons. Economically, this part of the globe is the major source of oil and other key raw materials. It is an important market and investment location for large corporations and wealthy individuals from the entire trilateral world.[9] As Anthony Lake, Director of the Department of State's Policy Planning Staff, pointed out in late 1977: "We have a major stake in the health and vitality of the Third World. . . no less than 35 percent of our exports went to developing countries, while almost half of our imports came from them."[10] Western Europe and Japan depend upon the Third World for economic needs even more than the United States. Politically and strategically, areas of the Third World sit astride key sea and air routes connecting world trade and transportation — places like Panama, Suez, the Cape of Good Hope, Gibraltar, and Singapore. Their weight is also important in international forums like the United Nations. Therefore, as Carter has said, "we need their friendship and cooperation."[11] Recognizing that such friendship and cooperation could not be had without at least the appearance of changes in the

Nixon-Ford-Kissinger foreign policy, the Carter Administration, led by trilateralists, has moved to attempt to mold the character of the "profound transformation" now taking place in Latin America, Asia, and Africa.

The growing importance of the Third World in American foreign policy makes it an excellent place to begin a comparison of Carter's rhetoric with reality.

CARTER'S MIDDLE EAST POLICY

Since its oil is absolutely crucial to the stability of the U.S. and world economy, the Middle East is a central focus of Carter Administration foreign policy. Several leading officials, including Secretary of State Vance, have indicated that the area is considered so important that the United States will, if need be, go to war to preserve unrestricted access to Mideast oil for the U.S. and its Western European and Japanese allies. For example, in early 1979, Secretary of Defense Harold Brown said, "protection of the oil flow from the Middle East is clearly a part of our vital interest. In protection of those vital interests we will take any action that is appropriate, including military force."[12] This strong stand was partly the result of the loss of U.S. influence in Iran following the overthrow of the Shah by a popular upheaval inspired by nationalism, a religious revival and desire for an end to corruption and terror. The Iranian revolution was in large part directed against the United States, which the Iranian people correctly blamed for the misrule of the Shah.

The Shah's regime was installed by a 1953 coup orchestrated by the American CIA, and U.S. policy since then had been total support for the brutal dictatorship. The anti-American tone of the new government should therefore not be surprising. Ironically, in light of subsequent events, it was Carter's human rights statements in early 1977 which helped provide the catalyst for a slight easing of the Shah's repression of his opposition. That opposition was, at the same time, encouraged by Carter's proclaiming the centrality of human rights to American foreign policy and a group of prominent Iranians formed a "Committee for the Defense of Human Rights and Liberty" which soon became the focal point of demands for fundamental change. The slight easing of repression allowed the massive disenchantment with the Shah's regime to surface, express itself and grow, and once in the open, even the severe repression that the Shah unleashed during 1978 — when thousands of unarmed demonstrators were shot down on the streets by heavily armed soldiers — was inadequate to stop the revolutionary surge.

By late 1977 the Carter Administration had dropped its human rights concerns in Iran, and Carter toasted the Shah on December 31, 1977 in Tehran by saying "Iran under the great leadership of the Shah is an island of stability in one of the more troubled areas of the world. This is a great tribute to you, your majesty, and to your leadership and to the respect, admiration and love which your people give to you."[13] Throughout 1978, the Administration expressed its support for the Shah and his regime again and again, and the sole object of American policy seemed to be to find ways to help the dictator survive. In early September of 1978, just after hundreds of Iranians had been shot by the Shah's American-equipped soldiers, Carter took time out from his Camp David summit meetings with Egypt's President Sadat and Israeli Prime Minister Begin to telephone a message of good wishes and support to the Iranian ruler. The Administration shipped fuel to Iran to help the military cope with the oil workers' strike. Brzezinski was also in constant touch with the Shah and his closest advisers during the crisis, offering advice and moral support.[14] Once it was clear the Shah himself was doomed, the U.S. embraced Prime Minister Shapour Bahktiar, appointed by the dictator and essentially his surrogate, and helped ease the Shah out of the country, hoping this would coopt the revolution. Bahktiar was, of course, also overthrown, and U.S. influence in Iran dropped sharply. These actions help illustrate that Carter's human rights stand was mere rhetoric and his catalytic role in the Iranian revolution was, as one academic expert put it: "both inadvertent and innocent."[15]

The aftermath of the Iranian revolution saw leading ruling class thinkers like Kissinger and Brzezinski talking and worrying about an "arc of crisis" along the shores of the Indian Ocean stretching from India to the Horn of Africa. With Iran no longer considered an "island of stability," U.S. geopolitical strategists feared that the Soviets might fill the vacuum left by Iran's withdrawal from its former role of regional policeman for U.S. and Western interests in the Persian Gulf area. These events in Iran form the backdrop for Carter's Mideast actions of spring 1979.

Since at least 1975, American policy has attempted to split the Arab world in order to build a strong and stable pro-U.S. bloc in the area composed of Israel, Egypt, Iran, Saudi Arabia, Morocco, Kuwait, Sudan, and Jordan. During Carter's presidential campaign and first year in office, he promised a change in these past policies, including a change in the step-by-step diplomacy toward a separate peace between Egypt and Israel. He and his top advisers correctly claimed that the only way to a viable and stable Middle East peace involved a comprehensive settlement, including recognition of Palestinian rights and negotiation with their representatives. Inevitably, the Palestinian Liberation Organization (PLO) would have to be a part of any lasting settlement. The Administration also made clear that it supported a return to the Geneva Conference, where all conflicts could be settled at once, and the Soviet Union could be a participant and help enforce any agreement which could be reached. This approach was discarded after Sadat's trip to Jerusalem in late 1977, and a separate peace decided

upon. The key decisions on this change in American strategy
were decided in secrecy behind closed doors, disregarding
professions of post-Watergate candor and the need for public
debate.

What emerged as the new U.S. policy in early 1978
was warmed-over Kissinger: deny the Soviets any role in the
peace process; ignore the PLO (Brzezinski summed up U.S.
policy as "bye-bye PLO"); and take no sanctions against
Israel to force negotiations on any but Egypt's Sinai front.
The Kissinger-Nixon policy of a regional bloc was thus
resurrected, and various means, ranging from arms sales and
foreign aid to an Egypt-Israeli peace treaty have been used
to try to solidify this bloc. In the area of arms sales and
military aid, for example, during 1978 the Administration
sold U.S. combat jets to Egypt and Saudi Arabia for the
first time despite outcries from the Israeli lobby. Military
aid to Morocco was increased by over 50 percent, giving
King Hassan important aid in his fight against the POLI-
SARIO guerrillas in the colonized western Sahara.

In fiscal year 1978 just three Middle East nations — Iran,
Israel, and Saudi Arabia — acquired nearly three-quarters
of all U.S. arms shipments to the Third World as a whole.
This policy of creating a bloc of client states tied to the U.S.
has serious internal contradictions including the possibility of
revolutionary upheavals overthrowing one or more of the area's
reactionary regimes, as has already happened in Iran. The
most serious contradictions, however, are the conflicts between
Palestinian and Israeli nationalism and the Arab-Israeli
conflict over Israel's expansionism. These conflicts disrupted
the flow of oil to the West and Japan in 1973 and made it
easier for the Organization of Petroleum Exporting Countries
(OPEC) simultaneously to raise prices greatly, disrupting
the world economy. Continued conflict could again endanger
world economic stability. To prevent this danger President
Carter has personally involved himself in the peace negotiations begun by Egypt's President Sadat with his journey to

Jerusalem in November 1977. Sadat has, since 1974 at least, pursued what could be labeled an "American strategy," aimed at achieving a separate peace with Israel by closely allying his regime with the United States and attempting to use any leverage gained to force concessions upon Israel. The reception given Kissinger and Nixon in Egypt and the laudatory statements showered on Jimmy Carter by Sadat must be seen in this light. After succeeding in getting Carter to play the role of middle man — a role Carter was not too reluctant to take, since it was believed that the renewed danger of large scale war was the likely alternative — the preliminary Camp David Agreement was signed in September 1978, and a final peace treaty was initialed in Washington in March 1979.

This "peace," worked out in marathon bargaining session by Carter, Sadat, Begin, and their aides, has the ultimate aim of providing the stable base for a power bloc which Washington hopes will dominate the region from Afghanistan to Algeria and south to Yemen and into Africa. The peace is in effect an alliance bringing together the two most powerful states in the area — Egypt, with its great manpower, and Israel, militarily the most advanced in the area — and the United States, which is now in a much better position to project its military power into the region. It can now be expected that Egypt in particular will use its armed forces to police the Middle East and east and central Africa in the interests and at the behest of the United States. For example, Sadat promised after meeting with Secretary of Defense Harold Brown that Egypt will meet "any external threat against the Arab states in the Gulf."[16] The details of the peace illustrate this aim. Egypt politically and economically recognizes Israel — agrees to trade, diplomatic relations and use of the Suez Canal, and in effect, renounces its previous alliance with the other Arab states. In exchange, Egypt obtains peace, the return of valuable land in the Sinai and the promise of military and economic aid from the United States. The Carter Administration hopes to obtain the stability it wants in this strategic area and appears ready to back the treaty with military force if need be. In the long run force may be necessary, because the accord is seriously flawed. First and foremost, the Palestinian demand for national self-determination and the related issue of the disposition of the West Bank of the Jordan remain unresolved. These are left to future talks which will take place with an Israel which has a peace with its main Arab enemy already in hand and is intransigent about a Palestinian state or even negotiating with the Palestine Liberation Organization (PLO) which is recognized by most of the world as the legitimate representative of the Palestinian people.

Israel's spurious "autonomy" plan for the Palestinians in the occupied West Bank is colonial in nature; all real economic and political power would remain in Israel's hands and it would retain its occupying military forces there for the foreseeable future. In the aftermath of the peace treaty, the Begin government is pushing ahead with additional settlements on the West Bank, and declares unequivocally that it will never allow a Palestinian state to arise on the West Bank. [17] Thus, it is likely that these talks will eventually break down without resolving the West Bank-Palestinian problem. Second, the peace treaty leaves the questions of the Israeli-occupied Golan Heights and East Jerusalem also unresolved. Finally, the more conservative Arab nations, most noticeably Saudi Arabia, are joining the more militant ones in an economic and diplomatic boycott of Egypt. While the Saudis can be relied upon not to try to push Egypt to the wall and thus encourage revolution there, Carter and his advisers did not expect the Saudis to react even that strongly. The action of the Saudis — taken apparently because of fears that Palestinian radicals could turn against the Saudi monarchy and cause serious destabilization within Saudi Arabia where many exiled Palestinians work — puts pressure on Carter to try to squeeze concessions in the next round of talks from an intransigent Begin government.

Carter is not able to push the Israelis too far, however, be-cause of the "Israel Lobby" within the United States, and because American geopolitical strategy in the Middle East relies on an Israel which is militarily strong and allied with Washington. Because of these weaknesses, the Middle East "peace" signed in March 1979 is unlikely to be lasting. The human and national rights of the Palestinians as well as Syria's national rights are totally ignored by this much bally-hooed "peace."

United Nations Ambassador Andrew Young discovered these realities the hard way when he attempted to begin a dialogue with the PLO in August 1979. Young was spied upon by either Israeli or American intelligence when he secretly met with the PLO's U.N. Ambassador and was ousted from the Carter Administration after not telling the full story when questioned by other members of the Depart-ment of State. Young's demise—due to a Middle East policy he labeled "foolish"—led to a reassessment of past Middle East policy positions by many leaders of black America, erosion of black support for Israel (which has close relations with South Africa), and perceptible movement towards recognition of the PLO. As Mayor Richard G. Hatcher of Gary, Indiana, summed up: "it is now time for us to take another look at the whole question of Israel and Middle East policy, oil and South Africa."[18]

Oil, power and geopolitical calculations count for much more than human or national rights in Jimmy Carter's foreign policy. Further illustration of the fact is the recent U.S. intervention in Yemen's civil war. In March 1979, at the same time Carter was trying to finalize the Egypt-Israel peace, he rushed an emergency package of several hundred military and civilian advisers and about $400 million in U.S. arms to tiny North Yemen, population roughly seven million, whose conservative military rulers are fighting local insur-gents backed by Soviet-supported Marxist South Yemen. The reason for U.S. intervention in this Vietnam-type conflict is to prevent all of Yemen, strategically located at the southern tip of the Arabian peninsula, from uniting under a radical government, something which could threaten the existence of the Saudi Arabian monarchy. The Saudi rulers are worried about the situation — not only because of Yemen's strategic position, but also because about two million North Yemenis have left their own poverty-stricken country to work at menial jobs in Saudi Arabia, and following a revolution at home, they could represent a radical force within their host country. The Saudis are thus heavily subsidizing their North Yemen client government. The $400 million in U.S. arms represents a vast sum in North Yemen; on a per-capita basis, it works out to nearly $60 dollars in weapons for every man, woman and child in a nation which has only an $80 dollar per capita yearly income. These facts, together with the military aspects of the Egypt-Israeli-U.S. treaty, illustrate the dangerously interventionist post-Iran Middle East strategy of the Carter Administration. In the Persian Gulf, at least, the post-Vietnam military policy no longer applies. After wise restraint in Iran, it appears that the mood in Washington is now far more assertive, and the U.S. will be increasingly likely to deploy U.S. combat troops directly in key areas where local allies cannot meet the test. The groundwork for such intervention is being laid by a stepped-up naval presence in the Indian Ocean. In this respect, American policy-makers have learned nothing from the Vietnam war and Iranian revolution. The main danger to the conservative regimes in the Middle East is not external aggression but the internal rot characteristic of unjust regimes. More U.S. arms and Marines or an American fleet in the Indian Ocean will not deal with the mass revolutionary trends in the region. The Saudis and other conservative regimes are being offered the same prescription that helped to oust the Shah. By abandoning the attempt at a comprehensive, all-sided peace in the Middle East in favor of a short-range pact between Egypt and Israel, Carter has helped make continued conflict, turmoil and tragedy inevitable.

The Middle East is thus certainly not in for peace now. Continued class and national struggle, against local ruling classes and especially between Israeli and Palestinian nationalism, is more likely, although Egypt appears to be at least temporarily out of the geopolitical military equation, reducing the chances of full-scale war. But it is also not impossible that Egypt could rapidly again become an enemy of Israel. Several top Egyptian officials have already declared that in certain circumstances Egypt could militarily support the PLO and Syria. There is little chance of peace in the Middle East until the fundamental conflicts have been resolved. In particular, the Palestinians will have to be considered seriously and with justice. Such consideration is difficult in Israel and the U.S., because of the emotion arising from centuries of persecution against Jews and because current U.S. geopolitical interests in the Middle East dictate support for Israel. The feelings of most Palestinians about the Egypt-Israel agreements were expressed by Yasser Arafat, leader of the PLO, when he said that all it offered was a "new slavery, for an unlimited period of time," and by another PLO official who declared: "It's true there can be no war without Egypt, but there can be no peace without the PLO."[19]

AFRICA

The Carter Administration has shown an interest in Africa unmatched by any of its predecessors. This new interest is mainly due to the rapid pace of events on a continent whose southern cone is characterized by poverty, inequality, and racist repression as severe as anywhere else in today's world. This situation has generated a revolutionary response which appears to be heading for victory in Zimbabwe (Rhodesia) and Namibia (Southwest Africa) with South Africa itself (called Azania by the native blacks) the next target for revolution. Since Africa as a whole and particularly the southern cone are an important source of raw materials, markets, and profits through investment for all the Trilateral nations, the Carter Administration has attempted to manage the developing crisis and has "issued more pronouncements, deliberated more hours, logged more official miles and held more high level consultations on African issues — including the first state visit to the continent — than that of any other administration."[20]

Secretary of State Cyrus Vance summed up Africa's importance in a major policy address in June 1978. Mentioning copper, manganese, cobalt, and potash among other raw materials, Vance stated that:

> Africa supplies us with between a quarter and one-half of our imports of these and many other raw materials, including 40 percent of our petroleum imports. Similarly, our exports to Africa are increasing rapidly—Africa provided a market last year for well over $1 billion worth of U.S. agricultural produce.[21]

Anthony Lake, the State Department's Policy Planning Director, pointed out the importance of African nations in another context. They play "a central role in the multilateral negotiations on such issues as commodities."[22] Africa is also strategically located on the routes between the Middle East and its oil and the U.S. and Western Europe. U.S. investments in the three white-ruled nations of the southern cone now reach $5 billion and western Europe's investments are even greater. Thus the Carter Administration has ample incentive to try to assure that the radical and revolutionary forces in these nations do not gain power.

The guiding goal of Carter's African policy is a "Kenya-Zaire solution." The objective is to implant relatively tame pro-Western and pro-capitalist local blacks to replace the increasingly endangered white regimes of the southern cone. The major tactical maneuverings are best understood in this context. These tactics have included the strong stand against growing Soviet-Cuban involvement on the continent, the propping up of Mobutu's corrupt regime in Zaire, the attempt to impose a Western solution in Zimbabwe and Namibia, and verbal warnings to the South African government without substantial action. Such tactics include, in shifting proportions, older nationalistic perspectives with Trilateral ideas. The hard-line view sees African conflicts in cold war, communist versus anticommunist terms; the Trilateral outlook stresses the softer, more positive language of "community" and tries to influence natural processes which occur in the Third World in cooperation with western European powers and local pro-Western African regimes.

The Brzezinski-Vance division within the Carter Administration shows up more in African policy than in the Middle East. Brzezinski's tendency has been to respond to Soviet-Cuban actions by backing the opposing side whatever its nature, or withholding U.S. cooperation in another area of interest to the USSR. Vance and the Department of State have given more consideration to the local causes and possible local solutions to a conflict, rather than treating every event as part of the East-West duel. That the Brzezinski-Vance division reflects a wider split within the ruling class is indicated by the 1978 report of Winston Lord, President of the Council on Foreign Relations. Lord reported that within the CFR, there was "a sharp divergence" on Africa "between those preoccupied with the need to counteract Soviet-Cuban actions, which they saw as having global ramifications, and those who gave priority to alignment with black aspirations as not only morally imperative but also the wiser course in geopolitical terms."[23] It should always be kept in mind that the neocolonial goals are the same for both tendencies and only the tactics to best achieve such goals differ. Developing events affect the rise and fall of these two main tactical outlooks within the administration.

During the relatively calm period of 1977 the Vance perspective, with U.N. Ambassador Andrew Young as one of its

main advocates on Africa, held the high ground. This changed
early in 1978. The Cubans and Soviets, while continuing their
role in defending Angola's government acted on a request from
the new Ethiopian military government to aid in fending off
attacks from internal foes aided by Somalia. The Brzezinski
tendency towards a harder, cold war line began to manifest
itself and dominated American policy for several months
during early 1978. From roughly February to late June there
were many hard-line statements made and some actions taken
by the Carter Administration.

The new approach was reflected in Carter's Wake Forest
University speech in mid-March. In what the *New York Times*
termed a "strongly worded speech," Carter warned that the
Soviet growth in military power and "ominous inclination"
to use this power to intervene in Africa could jeopardize
cooperation with the United States.[24] Calling the Cubans in
Africa "proxy forces" and "mercenaries," Carter added that
U.S. cooperation with the USSR in economic, social,
and scientific fields could be cut back due to such activities.
Even more serious is the still fragmentary evidence that
Brzezinski wanted to "punish" the Angolan government and
the Cubans there by supporting the opposition guerrillas, a
group called UNITA. Despite a May 4 Carter statement
that "we have no intention to intercede in any war in Angola,"
a few days later CIA chief Stansfield Turner, along with
Brzezinski's chief deputy David Aaron, asked Senator Dick
Clark (D. Iowa) if he would agree to a plan to give UNITA
rebels military equipment through a third party. Clark, who
had co-authored the 1975 Clark-Tunney amendment for-
bidding any kind of U.S. intervention in Angola without
congressional authorization, refused, as did enough other
senators to prevent this apparent trial balloon from ever
fully surfacing. Senator Patrick Moynihan (D.-New York)
had indicated that other senators were contacted; he
stated in late May that "for about a month now, this
administration has been talking to senators about sending

aid to Savimbi," the leader of UNITA.[25] Indirect evidence also indicated that $10 million in overt aid for UNITA was being collected among "a consortium of nations," including South Africa, Saudia Arabia, Iran, France, and Morocco, and quite possibly under the secret direction of the United States.[26] Senator Clark summed up the evidence by concluding that "it is increasingly clear that President Carter has made the decision to reinvolve the United States in the Angola civil war."[27]

That same month, May 1978, only days after the meeting between Turner, Aaron, and Senator Clark, Zairian rebels seized the mineral-rich province of Shaba. Portrayed as an "invasion" from Angola by the Carter Administration, other Western governments, and most of the Western press, the rebel action was in fact a classic example of popular rebellion aimed at toppling a government widely known for its repression, corruption, and general venality. One conservative Western journalist called the Mobutu government "quite possibly the most corrupt and incompetent regime in all Africa."[28] President Julius Nyerere of Tanzania said it was "universally recognized" to be "corrupt" and "a bunch of murderers."[29]

To save this regime, where Western economic interests are very extensive (U.S. corporate investments alone exceed $2 billion and French and Belgian investments are probably even higher), Western intervention was mounted for the *Zaire* second time in just two years. United States forces were placed *(and China)* on alert, but only French and Belgian paratroopers were actually ferried into Shaba by the U.S. Air Force to fight the rebels. At the same time President Carter sent fuel supplies and released $17.5 million in military assistance to Zaire along with communications and other equipment.[30] These actions temporarily defeated the insurgency, but the administration then decided that Cuba, the USSR, and Angola were behind the "invasion" of Shaba by its own people. As in Vietnam, a civil war was portrayed as foreign aggression

Zaire IMF relief, too

by communists, and the Carter Administration acted just like former ones in backing a despotic, corrupt, and unpopular regime against a revolutionary movement. Carter said Angola and Cuba "must bear heavy responsibility for the deadly attack" on Zaire.[31] This accusation could not be substantiated, however, and Congress, many sectors of the press, and even some figures in the State Department itself remained skeptical about Carter's accusations.[32]

Despite this skepticism, Carter continued his rhetorical attacks on the Soviets and Cubans in Africa and strongly supported Western intervention in Zaire. At a NATO parley on May 30, 1978, Carter stated that "I welcome the efforts of individual NATO allies to work for peace in Africa, and to support nations and peoples in need, most recently in Zaire."[33] Then in a final attack on Soviet and Cuban troops and military activities in Africa, Carter indicated again that they were responsible for the rebellion in Zaire, stating in his Annapolis speech on June 7 that:

> We are deeply concerned about the threat to regional peace and to the autonomy of countries within which these foreign Cuban and Soviet troops seem permanently to be stationed. That is why I have spoken out on this subject today, and that is why I and the American people will support African efforts to *contain such intrusions as we have done recently in Zaire.* [emphasis added][34]

The final sentence of Carter's statement referred to a Western-organized and supplied "Pan-African" military security force apparently first proposed in National Security Council meetings in Washington. Discussions on the strike force among NATO allies and some conservative African states were also going on in Paris and Brussels.

Such statements and plans were apparently too much for many African states to stand, however, for the very next day Julius Nyerere, one of Africa's most respected and important leaders, launched an angry and impassioned counterattack on the "hysterical voices" dominating the Carter Adminis-

tration's foreign policy.[35] Nyerere's major address was directed
to all foreign envoys accredited to Tanzania, assuring that
his views would be rapidly communicated to the United States
and Western Europe. Nyerere began by pointing out that
Cuban and Soviet forces were significantly involved in only
two nations, Angola and Ethiopia, and in both cases were
there only at the request of the "legitimate and recognized"
governments of those nations. They were there "for reasons
which are well-known and completely understandable to all
reasonable people."[36] Western objections to Soviet and Cuban
activities were thus unjustified, Nyerere went on, and talk
by the Western powers of establishing a "Pan-African" Security
Force "is the height of arrogance."[37] "Those who have put
forward this idea, and those who seek to initiate such a
force," he added, "are not interested in the freedom of Africa.
They are interested in the domination of Africa."[38] Nyerere
termed this domination "neo-colonialist" and claimed it was
more dangerous to Africa than Soviet and Cuban activities
since "the West still considers Africa to be within its sphere
of influence and acts accordingly."[39]

Since Nyerere's view was supported by Nigeria, politically
and economically the most important state in black Africa,
the Brzezinski perspective was defeated in Washington. The
Carter Administration, after a policy review, dropped its
hard-line stance, substituting the more subtle, low-key approach of Vance and Young.[40] To do otherwise would threaten
to undo Western efforts to achieve peaceful solutions in
Zimbabwe and Namibia, since these efforts require the cooperation of nations like Nigeria and Tanzania. The new
approach was announced in a major Africa policy speech
made by the Secretary of State on June 20, 1978. Vance
reiterated what had been U.S. policy prior to early 1978;
African problems should be seen and dealt with in their
own context and not "simply as an arena for East-West
competition."[41] U.S. policy "will not... mirror Soviet and
Cuban activities in Africa, because such a course would not

be effective in the long run. . . our best course is to help resolve the problems which create the excuse for external intervention. . . "[42]

The policy shift proposed a new direction in regard to Angola. A "more normal" U.S. relationship with that country was proposed, dropping the threat of renewed covert action against the Neto government, "in order to improve the prospects for reconciliation between Angola and Zaire, as well as for achieving a peaceful settlement in Namibia."[43] This new policy resulted in negotiations between Neto and Mobutu towards normalizing relations and ending the support of guerrilla warfare in one another's nations.

Vance and the administration also developed, in partnership with the British government, a proposal for solving the problem of white-minority rule in Rhodesia. The plan has several elements, but at its core is the idea of restoring a British administration and holding free elections with outside supervision. The American role has, step by step, become more and more central to achieving a negotiated peace which would keep out both the Cubans and Soviets, as well as the more radical of the black nationalists, headed by Robert Mugabe and the Zimbabwe African National Union (ZANU). Since Mugabe's group has been doing most of the fighting which threatens to bring down the Smith regime, however, it has become very difficult to exclude ZANU entirely. The Carter Administration has therefore attempted to pressure the Ian Smith-Abel Muzorewa government into an "all parties conference" and government as a device to keep ZANU and its less radical guerrilla allies, ZAPU, headed by Joshua Nkomo, from taking absolute control in Zimbabwe. The problem, as always, has been the refusal of the colonialist Smith-Muzorewa government to give up its hold on power except under the direst of pressure. As of this writing in the summer of 1979, the chances for an overall agreement appear to be dim, although the situation is fluid and could change quickly.

One source of change could be U.S. policy. Support

within the U.S. political elite for the Vance approach is fairly thin. Influential Republicans like Kissinger, Reagan, Ford, and Connally, as well as many conservative Democrats, have argued that Smith's "internal settlement," bringing compliant local black leaders like Abel Muzorewa into his government, and holding elections for a black majority government with whites retaining a veto power — should be given a chance. Brzezinski also appears to favor this option.[44] A shift within the Carter Administration back to Brzezinski's harder line could result in the lifting of economic sanctions and covert or overt forms of U.S. intervention to prop up Smith and his black allies and divide and exclude the nationalist guerrillas.[45] Guerrilla warfare, after all, was responsible for Smith's yielding a partial share of power to the black majority. A change in U.S. policy to support Smith's "internal settlement" against ZANU and ZAPU could create a serious rift between the Carter Administration and independent Africa, however, so it will be taken only very reluctantly. A powerful motive for U.S. policy in southern Africa generally has been the desire to build close, cooperative relationships with independent Africa, because of its control over vital raw materials.

Finally, the United States, along with four of its Trilateral partners — Britain, France, West Germany, and Canada — has attempted to impose a settlement between South Africa, which controls as a colony the territory of Namibia or Southwest Africa, and the black nationalist guerrilla organization known as SWAPO (South-West Africa People's Organization) which has been contesting South African control. By the summer of 1978, negotiations seemed close to achieving a solution on the basis of free and fair elections in the territory under United Nations supervision, followed by a South African military withdrawal. But South Africa unilaterally announced in late September its intention to proceed with its own elections in Namibia without outside or SWAPO participation, effectively sabotaging the Western plan. South Africa then held a rigged election in December

1978, angering many African states which are ever more forcefully demanding U.S. economic sanctions against Pretoria.[46] Such sanctions, especially on oil, would hurt South Africa badly, but since they would also hurt Western economic interests which have large investments and trade relationships with South Africa, this demand has been met with U.S. vetoes in 1974 and 1977. While such vetoes put Washington and its allies in an awkward position and have an adverse effect on relations with black African states, the West has been unwilling so far to harm its own multinational corporations. This problem will manifest itself even more strongly as the mass of South African blacks escalate their struggle against the racist white regime in Pretoria. The possibility that Cubans and the Soviets may become more deeply involved will grow, as will the danger of a U.S.-USSR confrontation over the future of this mineral-rich area of the world. Many have commented on the explosive potential of conflict in the area. Brzezinski observed in the spring of 1978, for example, that "what makes the South African conflict so dangerous is that it is racial, North-South, nationalistic and ideological — all four rolled into one."[47] Immanuel Wallerstein, a former president of the African Studies Association in the United States, stated late in 1977 that South Africa will be a Vietnam "ten times worse" because it is both politically and economically so important. It will probably cause a major world and domestic crisis.[48]

Aside from ineffective rhetoric, the Carter Administration has so far developed no real policy for dealing with this major emerging problem. Such a policy would have to address the reality that American and Western economic aid to the South African government via private investment, loans, and trade is in fact a major support for the racist apartheid regime. A new policy would require an end to all such support. But there is no sign that any American government intends to do this soon, especially given the fact that an arms embargo supposedly put into effect in 1963-64 has been totally lacking in enforcement.

Shipments of arms to South Africa have continued both covertly and overtly. Secret illegal arms shipments through dummy companies and third countries were made in 1977 and 1978 by Space Research Corporation of North Troy, Vermont, a company with close Pentagon connections. The exposure of the activities of this corporation by the British Broadcasting Corporation resulted in a belated impanelment of a Federal grand jury to look into Space Research's activities, but at last report, the jury is meeting only once every three weeks, indicating the low priority the Carter Administration attaches to enforcement of the embargo.[49] Even more overtly, the administration has allowed American corporations to supply military equipment by, as one Colt Industries employee put it, "looking the other way," when presented with fraudulent export declarations.[50] The government has also classified certain types of counter-insurgency equipment — such as helicopters, radar sets and transport planes — as "non-combat" and issued export permits.[51] A similar policy of covert aid has been followed in the case of the United Nations' arms embargo against the Rhodesian regime of Ian Smith and Abel Muzorewa. A 1979 report to the U.N. Sanctions Committee has charged that since 1976 the Smith-Muzorewa regime has successfully purchased Bell helicopters, Cessna-Reims reconnaissance aircraft and other military equipment from the United States for use in raids on neighboring African countries and counter-insurgency warfare.[52]

Finally, the Carter Administration has continued a long-standing policy of nuclear cooperation with South Africa,[53] even as evidence mounts that the apartheid regime is developing nuclear weapons and may even have already secretly produced an atomic bomb. The rationale for this policy — which even resulted in a joint U.S.-British-French Security Council veto of an African sponsored U.N. resolution which would have banned any nuclear cooperation with South Africa — was explained by Andrew Young on October 30, 1977 when he ruled out an American ban on the shipment of nuclear fuels to South Africa because, as the *New York Times* reported, "such a prohibition might encourage South Africa to step up development of its own capacity to produce atomic weapons."[54] Due to sentiment in Congress and the international community, however, the Carter Administration did make an unsuccessful attempt in late 1977 and early 1978 to pressure South Africa to sign the 1968 treaty to halt the spread of nuclear weapons and allow international inspection of its atomic facilities.[55] The South Africans' refusal to sign and the growing nuclear capabilities of that government — which possesses 20 percent of the world's raw uranium reserves, whose scientists have been trained by the U.S., whose first atomic reactor was supplied by the U.S. in 1965, and much of whose nuclear equipment comes from leading U.S. corporations — is certainly a frightening indication of their intentions.[56] The Carter Administration's failure to end nuclear cooperation with South Africa is additional evidence of its desire to take no actions that might actually undermine the racist regime. The enforcement of the arms embargo is so feeble that even one Commerce Department official remarked that "when people realize what a joke it is, it is really going to hurt our image."[57]

ECONOMIC POLICY IN THE THIRD WORLD

The two main manifestations of current U.S. economic policy toward the Third World have been in the policies and practices of the International Monetary Fund (IMF) and in the recent "North-South dialogue" in Paris and Geneva. The Trilateralists have short-and long-range plans for the IMF, which is a banking and monetary stabilization institution still controlled by the United States and other Western powers. In the short run, the IMF will increasingly be used — as it has been for several years now — to force indebted nations to impose austerity programs on their people. The situation of indebtedness developed because the economic crisis of the 1970s has hurt the Third World nations most of all, forcing many of them to seek new loans on top of almost $180 billion they already owed by the mid-1970s. As poor credit risks, they had to approach the IMF as a main source of loans. The Fund agreed to extend credit, but only under certain conditions. These normally included policies aimed at cutting domestic consumption, devaluation of a nation's currency, placing Fund employees in positions of economic power in the nation's government, curbs on wage increases, and higher taxes. Such measures often result in severe hardships for the working class in the country in question, sometimes accompanied by riots, strikes, and protests.[58] So far, twenty-one nations, mostly Third World, are subject to such IMF intervention, which is aimed at preventing default and assuring that not only will the Western banks and governments continue to have their $180 billion in loans repaid with interest, but that defaults will be prevented from spreading and threatening the entire credit structure of Western capitalism. The long-range Trilateral plan is to turn the IMF into a world central bank for national central banks. This change would allow for even more "central guidance" of the world economy by the U.S. and other Western powers than is now possible. Commissioners Richard N. Cooper, now Undersecretary of State for Economic Affairs, Karl Kaiser, and Masatake Kosaka wrote in a 1977 Commission report that:

> It is desirable that the International Monetary Fund increasingly evolve into a central bank for national central banks. It already performs this function as a source of financial support, although it is not yet a true lender of last resort due to limitations on its resources.[59]

In the long run, the Commission thus wants to give the IMF power to create or restrict the creation of money, so far called "Special Drawing Rights" (SDR) or "Bancor" which would eventually replace gold and the dollar as the world monetary unit. As Cooper, Kaiser, and Kosaka put it: "If SDR's become the principal reserve asset, the IMF will play a central role as a creator of international reserves."[60] Needless to say, this would give the IMF tremendous power in the world economy. This power basically represents a projection of Trilateral, expecially U.S. (which still holds a veto over IMF actions) power, under the convenient auspices of an international institution.

The "North-South" dialogue held in Paris and Geneva in 1977 had the aim of reaching agreement on a Third World plan for a "Common Fund" to stabilize the prices of eighteen key commodity exports. The Third World has had the problem in the past of greatly fluctuating prices for its exports, resulting in boom and bust cycles in development. Such a fund has been a key part of the Third World's demand for a "New International Economic Order" put forth in the United Nations and other forums since 1974. The Third World's goal seems to be to impose a rise in real prices of the raw materials they export in order to get resources which could, with new technologies, finance a new stage of industrialization in their countries. This, in turn, if Trilateral markets were opened up, could open the way for a high level of exports to the Trilateral world. In the short run at least, the success of such a Third World program would further shift control of commodity trade from consumers to producers, increasing costs of raw materials imports and therefore increasing domestic inflation. It is therefore opposed by the chief Trilateral powers, led by the United States. As C. Fred Bergsten, an active CFR member, co-author of a Trilateral Commission Report, and now Assistant Secretary of the Treasury for International Affairs, expressed it, "The U.S.'s primary purpose in pursuing international commodity agreements is to reduce the risk of inflationary pressure at home."[61] Since the Third World's "Common Fund" approach does not stabilize commodity prices at a low level, but rather has the opposite effect, the Carter Administration opposed this approach and caused the failure of both meetings.

The United States and other Trilateral nations have so far only been willing to offer minor concessions aimed mainly at splitting the Third World nations. So far at least this has not been successful. At the same time, the core Trilateral states — U.S., Japan, West Germany, and the United Kingdom — have maintained unity and a hard line, although other Trilateral states, especially the Netherlands and Scandinavian countries, have been willing to accept Third World proposals. As this issue deals with fundamentals of the world economy, structure of power, and domestic health for many nations, early and easy resolution of the conflict does not appear likely.

THE PANAMA CANAL TREATY

While few concessions have been forthcoming on fundamental international economic issues, the Carter Administration has tried to win the confidence of the Third World by eliminating the more obvious vestiges of outright colonialism, as in the case of the Panama Canal. The State Department called this a "litmus test" of U.S.-Third World relations.

While ambiguous in some respects, the Canal treaty, negotiated under several presidents and passed by the Senate in the spring of 1978, can best be described as an attempt to preserve the substance of American imperial power while giving up its annexationist form. American ownership of the Canal will be given up by the year 2000 but the right to intervene militarily after 1999 to preserve the "neutrality" and sustained operation of the canal was written into the treaty. Thus blatant imperialism — holding the territory of another nation — was replaced by its more modern neo-colonialist form, political/economic influence backed by the threat of force. Both the Carter Administration and its supporters and the Omar Torrijos regime in Panama agreed that this was the real nature of the treaty. Two former Trilateral Commissioners, Secretary of Defense Harold Brown and treaty co-negotiator Sol Linowitz, made such statements during the debate over the treaty.

Brown was asked by Senator Richard Stone (D-Florida) if the United States could militarily intervene to deal with an internal situation in Panama that the U.S. believed might threaten the neutral operation of the canal. Brown replied that U.S. officials would have "the right to take whatever action we considered necessary."[62] Linowitz also made a similar statement during the debate over the treaty, pointing out that the U.S. would decide if and when the Canal's "neutrality" was jeopardized and would then "be in the position to take such steps as might be deemed necessary."[63]

For this reason among others, the Torrijos regime in Panama was reluctant to sign the treaty, but because of its need for the increased revenues the new treaty would bring, combined with the bleak alternative of guerrilla warfare to overthrow U.S. rule, Torrijos gave in and signed. At the signing ceremony he indicated his misgivings, stating that it was not pleasant to accept an arrangement "that places us under the protective umbrella of the Pentagon."[64] Significantly, he added, "this pact could, if not administered judiciously by future generations, become an instrument of permanent intervention."[65] It is, therefore, evident that this arrangement has the overall aim of maintaining U.S. geo-political dominance of the Caribbean, while making the absolute minimum of concessions to Panamanian nationalism.

THE TRILATERAL WORLD

A main focus of the Carter Administration's foreign policy is its stress on the need for unity of the "Trilateral World" (Western Europe, North America, and Japan). Carter's address to the Trilateral Commission in June 1978 illustrates the importance he attaches to this approach:

> The President greeted his former brethren in the East Room with praise so generous that it was mildly embarrassing to some. "I was dumfounded by some of the things he said," said a Trilateral executive. "I would love to get permission to quote him in our fundraising. . . ." Carter told the 200 movers and shakers from America, Europe, and Japan that, if the Trilateral Commission had been in business after World War I, the world might have canceled World War II.[66]

In a 1976 speech, written by Brzezinski, Carter outlined his basic foreign policy as follows: "The time has come for us to seek a partnership between North America, Western Europe, and Japan."[67] Trilateral thinkers, like Brzezinski, stress that the nations of these three areas are linked by a multitude of ties. In the economic realm alone the relationships are intense enough to create massive interdependence, with trade in the hundreds of billions of dollars annually and investments in each other's nations at a similar level. Having capitalist market and property systems in common is an additional economic link. These three areas also have common socio-political values, such as parliamentary democracy, as well as long-standing military allegiances like NATO and the U.S.-Japanese defense treaty. These connections are reinforced by joint memberships in a multitude of public and private organizations like the Organization for Economic Cooperation and Development, and, of course, the Trilateral Commission itself. The Trilateralists stress that these nations thus make up a natural bloc which should be strengthened in order to deal with the current world crisis. In essence this may result in bringing Japan into NATO organizations and extending their joint activities into the economic realm. The result would be not mere cooperation — which has, after all, existed between these nations for over thirty years — but increasingly coordinated domestic and foreign policies in the political, economic, and military realms.

This bloc of nations — collectively making up roughly two-thirds of the world's economic power and military strength — can, in the view of Trilateral thinkers, maintain an over-whelming geopolitical preponderance against any threat if unity is maintained. The problem is that the world political/economic crisis, combined with domestic class struggle within these nations, makes it difficult to maintain this unity. Thus intra-Trilateral conflict could destroy the basis for a renewal of American and Western world hegemony.

The key problem is the threat of protectionism caused by nationalistic elements — workers trying to keep jobs and economic security and domestically oriented businesses. As Trilateralist and Secretary of the Treasury W. Michael Blumenthal put it at a recent Trilateral Commission meeting:

> There is increasing pressure for providing additional security to workers and consumers against change that arises from rapid movements in the trade field. The net result has been that, over the years, protectionism has manifested itself in the intensification of a variety of trends and measures which existed in earlier times but not nearly to the extent to which we find them today . . .68

The Trilateral strategy for dealing with these dangers has several parts. First, the Commission itself tries to develop class solidarity more intensively among the ruling classes of these main capitalist powers. If this can continue to be done, then the main directions of both domestic and foreign policy can be more easily designed and implemented. Toward this aim the Commission has carried on its work of meetings and joint Trilateral policy statements. These Commission activities — in the words of Commissioner Gerard C. Smith — aim to

> seek a private consensus on the specific problems examined
> in the Trilateral analysis. Consensus-seeking must be a central
> element in the Trilateral process . . . the commission will seek
> to educate attentive audiences in the three regions, so that
> public opinion in Japan, North America, and Europe will
> come to reflect the private consensus.[69]

Second, at the Commission's urging, the political leaders of all three regions have been holding yearly meetings since 1975. At these meetings the focus has been on interlocking world and Trilateral economic problems — protectionism, inflation, unemployment, energy, balance of payments deficits, North-South relations, etc. — and what to do about them. A pattern has developed which reveals the difficulties involved. Every meeting reaches a generalized consensus about the broad direction of their domestic and foreign economic policies but then each nation has difficulty implementing its promises when its leaders return home. Part of the problem is that these nations are natural competitors in world markets and each wants the others to pay the price — in inflation and unemployment — by having an open door for imports.

At the Bonn Summit in July 1978, for example, President Carter promised to cut energy imports and improve the American balance of payments in order to cut inflation and stabilize the dollar. That this was more easily promised than carried out is illustrated by the weakened energy bill reported out of Congress, a continued high level of oil imports, and the continued inflation and fluctuation of the dollar, now combined with recession.

To cite an additional example, at the May 1977 London Summit the final declaration urged Japan and Germany, nations with a strongly positive balance-of-payments position, to "ensure continued adequate expansion of domestic demand within prudent limits."[70] The final three words obviously gave the two nations the freedom to stimulate demand very little if they chose, as they did, since they feared a renewal of domestic inflation. The summit meetings do, however, tend to prevent an increase in the trend towards protectionism and economic nationalism and open the possibility that the economic crisis can be kept within bounds.

The Trilateralists call the overall policy position for dealing with all these interlocking issues "piecemeal functionalism." The basic concept of piecemeal functionalism is that conflicts can be solved more easily "if the issues can be kept separate."[71] For example, instead of comprehensive negotiations with the Third World on a new international economic order, the problem can be divided into all of its component parts and be discussed by smaller groups limited to the nations directly involved. The effect would be to split the Third World's "Group of 77" on specific issues, allowing the unified Trilateral World to achieve its goals more easily. The United States is at the center of the entire process, since the U.S. is the only nation dealing at the same time with the Soviet Union and strategic arms, energy and the Middle East conflict, Africa, North-South issues, and unifying the Trilateral world. The Carter Administration has, however, made a practice of consulting with and involving its allies in certain issues, Africa especially, but also the neutron bomb and economic questions.

Finally, connected to piecemeal functionalism is the belief that the desire for national autonomy is an obstacle to the achievement of joint solutions to world problems. Therefore solutions should be "pragmatic" and technocratic and thus beyond the purview of popular discussion and decision. There is much talk among the Trilateralists about "interdependence" and the related need for a decline in national sovereignty. Brzezinski has argued for years that the very concept of the "national interest" is now outdated and must give way to a merging of foreign and domestic policies both within and among nation states beginning with the Trilateral bloc. As Brzezinski stated

The concept of national interest — based on geographical factors, traditional animosities or friendships, economics and security considerations — implies a degree of autonomy and specificity that was possible only as long as nations were sufficiently separated in time and space.[72]

The Trilateral goal, reflected in the policies of the Carter Administration, is a "community" or bloc of the advanced capitalist nations, led, naturally enough, by the United States, thereby greatly magnifying its and the Trilateral nations' power. Trilateralism is therefore combined in practice with the more traditional concern with the U.S. national interest. In many ways it is simply another way to pursue that interest, broadening the definition of "national interest" to include Trilateral allies.

U.S.-USSR RELATIONS

The election of Jimmy Carter marked the beginning of a new period of U.S.-Soviet relations. If the era from roughly 1945-46 until 1963 and the test ban treaty could be called one of "cold war" and from 1963 until the mid-1970s one of "detente," then the rise of the Trilateralists to power marks the beginning of a third period. This new era is best characterized as a mixture of the first two periods — both confrontation and cooperation are simultaneously being pursued. This said, it should be immediately added that so far at least, the tendency toward conflict and a return to a Cold War mentality and mode of behavior has been stronger overall than a cooperative stance. To some extent, the greater tendency toward Cold War is a structural one, growing directly out of the Trilateral stress on relations with Western Europe, Japan, and the Third World. Emphasis on building up a stronger Western bloc and on improving relations with the Third World inevitably must downgrade relations with the Soviet Union.

There is, however, another important factor at work. Recent foreign-policy writings of the Trilateral Commission and other ruling class organizations have emphasized the relative increase in Soviet military power during the past fifteen years. They argue that in spite of detente the Soviets have

> made a steady, sustained effort to improve their relative position in the military balance—in the fields of strategic nuclear weapons, world-wide conventional mobility and regional theater strength in Europe.[73]

This Trilateral Commission policy paper adds that this attempt "to improve their relative position has been crowned with considerable success."[74] Ruling class leaders have generally interpreted this Soviet drive to build up military power in the traditional Cold War terms — a desire for world domination, to be achieved step by step through political, military, and economic activities.[75] The fact that the USSR has, as compared to the U.S., a much more negative geopolitical position — it faces powerful hostile nations like China and the NATO group on two of its borders — is conveniently ignored in this perspective. A very large percentage of Soviet military spending, for example, is China-border related. A more realistic assessment of Soviet power and aims might include these basic facts, as well as recent failures of Soviet policy in areas like the Middle East and Japan, and conclude that world domination by the USSR is extremely unlikely for the foreseeable future. A large sector of the American ruling class has, however, taken to heart Henry Kissinger's 1976 statement that "the problem of our age is how to manage the emergence of the Soviet Union as a superpower."[76] Anti-Soviet groups like the Committe on the Present Danger can be expected to take a tough stance, but the more "moderate" ruling class organizations like the Council on Foreign Relations are also becoming more hard line. Recent discussions at the Council on the Soviet Union, reported CFR President

Winston Lord, "seemed to reflect the toughening of attitude in the nation as a whole."[77]

The overall hardening of the American position on U.S.-Soviet relations during the Carter regime can be illustrated in each policy area, beginning with military policy and the question of arms control. Other issues, such as economic relations with the Soviets, U.S. policy toward Eastern Europe, China, and Turkey, and Carter's emphasis on human rights will also be discussed.

As this is being written about half way through Carter's third year in office, the complex negotiations for a strategic arms limitations treaty (SALT II) are now complete. Such a treaty represents to Secretary of State Vance the bare minimum in U.S.-Soviet relations necessary to prevent a massive destabilization in the dangerous area of nuclear weapons. The importance of such a treaty is probably being oversold, however. The preliminary information so far available on the new treaty indicates that numerous aspects of the nuclear arms race are excluded from the agreement. Weapons systems which are included will be allowed to grow substantially in numbers and quality.[78] The treaty is more accurately seen as a means of institutionalizing a continuation of the arms race and maintaining rough parity, rather than a means of reducing or really controlling the threat to the world's people posed by nuclear weapons. In the words of one expert, the new agreement places "limits on obsolete, redundant, or ineffective weapons, while giving free rein to the weaponry that decisively escalates the arms race."[79] Thus, the cruise missile and Trident submarine, both frightening weapons, with first strike capability, are exempted from the agreement. As Daniel Ellsberg expressed it, SALT is "essentially a hoax, a cover, a distraction for increases in the arms race."[80] Despite these facts, and the fact that according to relatively independent studies the United States "could devastate the Soviet Union even *after* a massive, surprise Russian attack aimed at destroying American nuclear forces,"[81] approximately one-third of the Senate of the United States opposes a SALT II treaty. The presence of this hard-line group in the Senate, representing mainly the South and West, strengthens the Brzezinski wing within the Carter Administration. This group wants to pursue overwhelming superiority vis-a-vis the U.S.S.R.; and continued expansion of military spending during the Carter Administration indicates that this group has won precedence against any dissenters.

In other military policy areas the administration has itself more clearly taken a hard line. The U.S. has strengthened its forces in Europe; and the NATO governments, at the prompting of the United States, have decided to raise defense budgets (and thus force levels) by 3 percent per year (above inflation levels) for the next five years.[82] Carter has increased U.S. military spending by a similar amount, clearly breaking a campaign promise to reduce defense spending by $5-7 billion annually.[83] Civil defense efforts within the United States are being revived after over ten years dormancy. President Carter submitted the new plans to Congress in June 1978, overriding objections of both Brown and chief disarmament negotiator Paul Warnke, both of whom felt civil defense exercises were largely futile in case of nuclear warfare and, in fact, could make such warfare more likely.[84] In this context, the government moves for a re-imposition of the military draft are especially ominous. While it is the leaders of the military establishment and congressional hawks on the House and Senate Armed Services Committees who are pushing step by step reintroduction of the draft, Carter and many congressional liberals are supporting the move, trying to modify it, if at all, in the direction of "national service" for both sexes. The first step, already passed by one congressional committee, is mandatory Selective Service registration for all eighteen-year-old American males.[85]

Lying behind the drive for a new draft is the desire to both psychologically prepare the nation and its people for a more interventionist foreign policy, especially in the Third

World, and have the cheap manpower available to carry out such a foreign policy. The all-volunteer army is seen as inadequate on several counts. It is more expensive, less skilled, smaller and most importantly, since blacks and other minorities are disproportionally represented in the volunteer force, it may prove unreliable if called upon to put down uprisings at home or in the Third World. The push for a new draft is being led by that part of the ruling establishment which wants overwhelming military superiority vis-a-vis the Soviet Union, and increased capability to police the world in their interests. President Carter's request for an increased budget for the Selective Service System again shows that he is a supporter of this imperial aim.[86] The new emphasis on the revival of the draft is additional evidence that the rulers of America are in the process of redefining the "national interest" in an aggressive way, building up the supposed danger that the Soviets will invade Western Europe and the imagined threat to the United States posed by liberation movements in the Third World. If left unchecked by the American people, this aggressive tendency is likely to lead to American military intervention abroad in the not too distant future.

Development of complex and terrible new weapons systems — the Trident submarine, cruise and MX missiles, and neutron bomb — is also proceeding. In the case of the neutron bomb, there had been some indications that its production was to be dropped, but on October 18, 1978, Carter ordered that the necessary components for the bomb be produced. These new weapons are an additional symbol of the renewal of the U.S. elite's goal of global strategic dominance, if not the overwhelming supremacy the right wing of this ruling class desires. Such weapons give them the feeling of being able to face down the Soviet Union in a crisis.

Finally, the policy of high arms sales, partly for economic and partly for strategic reasons, has continued, even increased, under the Carter Administration despite a campaign promise to reduce such sales.[87] An arms embargo against Turkey, instituted during the invasion of Cyprus (where American-supplied arms were used illegally), was lifted following "an intense, two-month lobbying effort by the White House and the State and Defense Departments."[88] Carter had said this was the "most important foreign policy issue facing Congress."[89] The reason such an effort was made was, in Carter's words, to move "toward strengthening the vital south flank of NATO."[90]

While NATO and U.S. allied nations on the southern flank of the USSR are being strengthened militarily, the Carter Administration at the same time is moving toward closer relations with other nations on the Soviet border — China and the Eastern European nations. It is naturally Brzezinski who has been anxious to play the "China card," subtly playing the Chinese and Soviets against each other, helping to create conflict which will mainly benefit the United States. This policy is not new, however, but has been going on since the first Nixon Administration.

The intensity of the American-Chinese relationship has greatly increased under Carter, however, with diplomatic recognition, expanded trade and other economic relationships, educational and cultural exchanges, and state visits by high officials from both sides. This closer relationship was foreshadowed by a Trilateral Commission policy paper written during 1977 and published in 1978. The authors of this report consulted with no less than ten current Carter Administration officials in the course of its preparation. The report states that "the present degree of Sino-Soviet hostility. . . tends to benefit the West; and the West should help ensure that the present situation continues to be worthwhile for China. In particular, it is clearly in the interest of the West to grant China favorable conditions in economic relations."[91] Additional signs that the U.S. ruling class was ready to ally itself informally with China came during the summer of 1978, when two former Trilateral Commissioners within the

Administration, Secretary of Defense Harold Brown and Assistant Secretary of State for East Asian Affairs Richard Holbrooke made speeches clearly indicating that China's political and military stance against the Soviets improved the U.S. position in Northeast Asia and arguing that American ties with China should be strengthened as a way of containing the Russians.[92] The economic advantages to both sides developing out of China's desire to become a modernized world power were an additional reason for the establishment of diplomatic relations. The vast China market is the "biggest new market" to appear in many years, and business executives are ecstatic about the prospects, using words like "phenomenal," and "without limits," to describe the possibilities.

Both the Carter Administration and Japan's rulers want to integrate China economically, politically and militarily into the Trilateral world as a junior partner, then, for both economic and geopolitical (anti-Soviet) reasons. Japan, for example, recently signed a gigantic trade agreement with China, and several top U.S. corporations have also made large-scale economic deals. If implemented, these pacts will create a U.S.-Japan-China bloc, a defacto alliance dominating the entire Pacific Basin. Mexico's rulers also seem anxious to join, and other states allied with the U.S. will no doubt fall into line. The anti-Soviet aspects of the alliance make it risky, however, as illustrated by China's decision to attack Soviet-allied Vietnam after the latter's invasion of Chinese-allied Kampuchea (Cambodia). The Chinese leaders had apparently decided to play their "American card," to try to force the United States to choose between them and detente (and a SALT agreement) with the Soviet Union, and show the right wing in America that they are a reliable anti-Soviet ally. The Carter Administration is walking a tightrope in trying to have both detente with Moscow and a de facto alliance with Peking. Chinese leaders have proved to be clever political operators, and their attack on Vietnam, coming right after Vice Premier Deng Xiaoping's state visit to the U.S.,

made it appear that Carter and his advisers encouraged the
aggression against a Soviet ally. The mild criticism of the
invasion by American leaders only served to underscore U.S.
collaboration with the invasion, especially compared to the
sharp denounciations of Soviet military involvement in Africa,
for example. The U.S. use of "hegemony," the Chinese code
word for containment of the Russians, in two recent Sino-
U.S. official documents — the agreement to establishment
of diplomatic relations, and the "joint press communique"
during Deng's visit — also indicated the current tilt of the
American government. It is therefore clear that at the same
time that the U.S. is attempting to play China off against
the USSR, China is trying to make sure the U.S. and
USSR are at each other's throats. These maneuvers certainly create dangerous political currents in international
affairs, increasing the chances of great-power conflict and
possible war.

Another theme in the Carter Administration's foreign
policy towards the USSR — the desire to improve relations
with the Eastern European nations as a way to weaken Soviet
influence over them — was also stressed in an early 1978
Trilateral Commission policy paper. The report argues that
control over Eastern Europe "tends to pose increasing problems for the Soviet leaders — both of an economic and of
an ideological kind."[93] Eastern Europe's economic ties with
the West are now great; the human rights principles of the
Helsinki Accords have stimulated dissident groups there;
and both together constitute "an unprecedented challenge
to Communist authority."[94] Brzezinski, a native of Poland,
clearly wants to take advantage of this situation to try to
roll back Soviet power in Eastern Europe, an area, he says,
which is in "a condition of rigidity, which fractures when all
of a sudden that rigidity is challenged by dynamic processes."[95] So far, at least, this policy has not gone beyond
state visits — Carter to Poland and Mondale to Yugoslavia
— and verbal statements about the need for independence,

human rights, and, as Carter put it, "genuine self-determination."[96]

Economic diplomacy is another area where U.S.-Soviet relations are on the downslide. Economic relations with the USSR are now definitely seen as a tool to encourage some modes of behavior and discourage others. Presidential Directive #18, issued in August 1977, outlined this tactic, arguing that the United States must take advantage of its economic and technological superiority "to counterbalance adverse Soviet influence in key areas of the world and promote human rights and national independence."[97] If the Soviets do not respond as desired, the "United States and its allies will eventually have no choice but to begin to close the door of economic detente."[98] Such a closing of the economic door depends upon gaining cooperation from the other Trilateral nations, as well as strengthening executive branch control over East-West trade. Such tightening of trade and linkage of economic relations with other issues began in July 1978 when President Carter canceled the sale of a U.S. computer system for the Soviets' official news agency, Tass, and brought proposed sales of oil drilling equipment to a halt at least for the time being.[99]

A final area where U.S.-Soviet relations are becoming more strained is on the level of rhetorical attacks, including the important question of human rights in both the United States and the Soviet Union. Such attacks have sharply escalated since Carter took office, especially during 1978. The strongest speech to date, marking a low point in U.S.-Soviet relations, came in early June 1978, when President Carter devoted the major part of his commencement address at the Naval Academy to a harsh critique of the Soviet Union.[100] The critique focused on military and human rights issues and argued that the Soviets are continuing an "aggressive struggle" for political advantage and are guilty of a military buildup "excessive far beyond any legitimate requirements." As for human rights, Carter said that "the abuse of basic human rights in their own country — has earned them the condemnation of people everywhere who love freedom."[101]

Marshall D. Shulman, the Department of State's top adviser on the Soviet Union, has himself pointed out often that such confrontation talk is more likely to increase political repression in the USSR than ease it. As Shulman put it, "frontal pressure directed against the system, demanding of it steps that go beyond any reasonable scale of feasibility in the near future, can and does have counterproductive effects."[102] Thus an external demand for chage is not necessarily the best means for changing the internal policies of the Soviet Union. On the contrary, it may increase the siege mentality and strengthen the conservative forces causing such repression in the first place.[103] Not surprisingly, about a month after Carter's speech, the USSR put Jewish dissidents Anatoly Shcharansky and Alexander Ginzburg on trial despite warnings from Washington that this would "do severe damage to relations."[104] The previous long delay in trying the two men suggests that a less strident approach in Washington would have been of more help to them.

These facts suggest that the real goals of the human rights campaign and hard-line anti-Soviet rhetoric are other than to influence the USSR, especially considering the fact that quiet diplomacy is always an alternative to public speeches on such sensitive issues. This leads to the final general topic of the chapter — the actual aims of Carter's "human rights" campaign.

THE HUMAN RIGHTS CAMPAIGN

The unifying, overarching theme of the Carter Administration's foreign policy is the "human rights" campaign. It was designed to give credibility and a new image to a foreign policy badly weakened at home and abroad by the Vietnam debacle. More specifically, the campaign has three interrelated aims. First, it

exactly

seeks to build a domestic consensus to support a foreign policy with interventionist and confrontationist tendencies at a time when this kind of a foreign policy had become partially discredited. Consensus is possible because the issue of human rights has wide appeal across the political spectrum. As one administration official explained to a reporter: "It appealed to Henry Jackson and others on the right in the sense that it applied to the Soviet Union and its treatment of Jews, and it appealed to the liberals in terms of Korea and Chile."[105]

exactly

Second, since the campaign's real thrust is aimed primarily at the Soviet Union, it has a strong tendency towards anticommunism and a renewal of the ideological Cold War. In this case the human rights campaign has been selectively aimed only at the USSR and some of its allies and not against all communist governments (China, for example, has been exempt from "human rights" attacks). The ultimate aim here is to try to weaken the unity and strength of the Soviet bloc by encouraging dissidents both within the USSR and in their Eastern European client states. Conversely, since the Soviet Union can be relied upon to respond to attacks with a heavy-handed approach to domestic dissidents, this approach helps build unity in the West.   *yes*

Finally, adding a moralist dimension to American foreign policy helps provide an image of benevolence, integrity, and justice deeply needed in reconstructing U.S. hegemony in the post-Vietnam era. It helps to legitimate American involvement and interference in political struggles around the world. In short, the human rights campaign allows the United States to leave behind the defensive position it was in after Vietnam and begin to take the offensive again.   *yes*

Only these geopolitical and pragmatic aims can explain the gross inconsistencies in the application of the policy. Even a brief review of the policy's application will provide clear illustrations. The best place to begin such an analysis is with Carter's own definition of "human rights." On his inaugural day Carter issued a "message to people of other nations," saying that U.S. foreign policy will be based on the need to guarantee "the basic right of every human to be free of poverty, hunger, disease, and political repression."[106] Carter himself thus correctly defines the term "human rights" broadly to include the right to adequate levels of nutrition and health as well as civil and political rights.

Despite this useful definition, the Carter Administration has spent most of its verbal effort criticizing violations of civil and political rights within the Soviet Union, while ignoring the grossest violations of the spectrum of human rights in U.S. client states. The only actions taken have been cuts in aid or trade with Ethiopia and a few other small, internationally powerless nations and cutbacks in economic relations with the USSR. Trade, recognition, and aid have continued to U.S. totalitarian client states guilty of torture, mass murder, political repression and gross economic exploitation resulting in malnutrition, dire poverty, disease, early death, unemployment and illiteracy. Examples of such nations include Morocco, Peru, Brazil, Zaire, Chile, the Philippines, Indonesia, Thailand, Guatemala, El Salvador, Argentina, South Korea, Taiwan, and others. While volumes could be written documenting the human rights violations of these regimes, some idea of the magnitude can be grasped by considering that in Latin America — an area long under U.S. hegemony — oppressive military dictatorships rule in a large number of states. Torture and murder by government officials are common in Chile, Argentina, Guatemala and Brazil. In Argentina alone, Amnesty International estimates that fifteen thousand people have disappeared and eight to ten thousand are subject to the horrors of torture in the junta's jails.[107] America's harsh words have been aimed at nations like the Soviet Union where U.S. influence to affect internal events is minimal. Meanwhile, nothing is done to change conditions in areas under U.S. influence. Trilateral Commission member Richard C. Holbrooke, now Assistant Secretary of State for East Asian and Pacific Affairs, has summed up the reasons for this stance. Holbrooke spoke of the need for continuing aid to the Marcos dictatorship in the Philippines. Although pointing out continued human rights violations in that country, Holbrooke argued:

> Given the importance of our bilateral political, security, and economic relations, we believe we will have more influence with the Philippine Government with regard to the human rights situation if we continue our assistance, rather than if we reduce or terminate our programs.[108]

The logical conclusion is that stability is much preferred to progress on human rights in nations like the Philippines, Zaire, Brazil, and others, while destabilization and an overthrow of Soviet power is the goal in the Soviet Union and Eastern Europe.

Not only has the Carter Administration done little or nothing to improve human rights in client states, many of the Administration's policies have actually worsened human rights conditions in these nations. A recent Institute for Policy Studies report. *Supplying Repression: U.S. Support for Authoritarian Regimes Abroad,* found that tens of billions of dollars worth of U.S. arms were sold to ten governments considered the worst violators of human rights in the world. The continued U.S. policy of large weapons shipments to dictatorships like Morocco, for example, strengthens the armed forces there and makes it much more difficult for needed change to take place. Equally destructive of human rights is the use of the International Monetary Fund to force governments to cut various forms of welfare spending in order to repay Western banks. In several instances, such actions have resulted in widespread protests and government repression. The example of Peru in May 1978 was reported in *Matchbox*, the Amnesty International newspaper:

> Constitutional guarantees were suspended and a state of emergency decreed in Peru on May 20 in response to widespread disturbances. The unrest followed austerity measures which doubled public transportation fares and raised basic food prices by an estimated 80 percent. The measures were introduced after government negotiators met a team from the

International Monetary Fund in Lima to discuss credits to ameliorate Peru's severe financial crisis. Opposition spokesmen have protested that the conditions imposed by international financial bodies would seriously jeopardize the elections, scheduled for June 18, and would lead directly to violations of human rights. During the course of the initial, nationwide disturbances and a general strike on May 22 and 23, at least 38 people were killed by security forces. Over 3,000 persons, mostly trade unionists, were detained.[109]

This is an example of a worldwide trend. The IMF has carried out similar measures in over twenty nations. Since the U.S. government has a veto power over IMF policies, it certainly must take a large share of the responsibility for these actions and their results.[110] This is a disturbing picture which indicates that, despite its moral pose, the Carter Administration is continuing to maintain the United States as a leading violator of human rights.

Finally, the Administration's record on human rights at home is at least worth mentioning. Has Carter done much of anything to lessen the continuing poverty and unemployment and the hunger, crime, prison sentences, and disease that go with those evils? Has a domestic "human rights" campaign been launched to liberate the "hundreds, perhaps thousands" of U.S. political prisoners which U.N. Ambassador Andrew Young spoke of? The lack of decisive human rights action on the home front again indicates the hypocrisy of a human rights crusade abroad.

CONCLUSION: A MOVE TOWARD A NEW COLD WAR?

Based on the preceding analysis, the Carter foreign policy can be summed up with several interrelated propositions. First, it can be said that this foreign policy does have a coherence and internal logic. It is not, as some observers have argued, in any real sense a random or haphazard policy. Second, the overall aim is to reconstruct American hegemony in all its former power, using a policy of closer alliances to form a trilateral bloc now including China, to help deal with the threat posed by the power of the USSR and by revolutions and nationalism in the Third World. Overall, the Carter Administration's policy toward the Third World can best be described as a sophisticated form of neo-colonialism, aimed at eliminating or disguising the more overt forms of political colonialism whenever possible, but retaining various forms and degrees of informal political and economic control. Third, the cement for a more closely allied trilateral bloc is not merely more summit meetings and attempts to build stronger economic ties, but is also composed of an emphasis on the external threat to the West posed by the Soviet Union. Unity among capitalist states who compete in the world market is difficult to achieve except when there is a strong outside threat, and the USSR is the obvious candidate for bogey man.[111] Fourth, the crisis mentality created by stressing the danger of the Soviets is also useful in dealing with the domestic economic crisis within the United States. People are more willing to accept cuts in living standards and acquiesce in the suppression of dissidents if there is a perception of strong external threat. An ambitious foreign policy thus aids in solving domestic problems. While the trend is not yet conclusive, it is increasingly evident to those closely watching the actions of leaders of the American ruling class. A Trilateral Commission book, entitled *The Crisis of Democracy*, stressed the problem of "an excess of democracy" and "decline of government authority" within the United States.[112] A renewal of the Cold War increasingly appears to be a goal of the Commission and the dominant sector of the ruling class which it represents as a way of dealing with the crisis they face at home and abroad. International tensions strengthen anti-democratic elements both in the U.S. and the USSR, resulting in the potentially dangerous situation of continuous rounds of actions and counteractions, each one further strengthening hard-line elements. Fifth, policy makers should learn

[margin notes: Schurmann 1973; yes; good prediction]

from the failures of U.S. policy over the past twenty years, but clearly they have not. Vietnam showed the ultimate bankruptcy of military interventionism strategy in the Third World. Iran has now illustrated that the policy of arming client states to make them regional policemen for imperial interests is also inadequate to deal with our revolutionary times. The failure of U.S. policy in Iran has raised the demand for a return to interventionism instead of a realistic change of U.S. goals. Sixth, Carter's campaign promises, on idealism and human rights, on arms sales abroad, on serious reductions in military spending, and in regard to respect for the rights of small states, clearly were false. Geopolitical and geoeconomic equations, based on the systemic needs of the American's current capitalist political economy, take precedence over campaign promises. Those promises are useful mainly to get elected, but they do not govern policy decisions once the candidate is in office.

Finally, given the continuation of the grandiose foreign policy goals of the past thirty-five years, certain other past policies — such as executive secrecy, high military spending, covert CIA actions, some repression of dissidents at home, intervention in foreign crises, tough anticommunist speeches and so on — tend to be necessary to achieve these ends. Thus, there is a need for fundamental change in the goals of American foreign policy, and therefore in the socio-economic system and structure of power that have defined past goals. To this domestic area we now turn our attention.

Notes

1. For elaboration of this general point, see Laurence H. Shoup and William Minter, *Imperial Brain Trust: The Council on Foreign Relations and United States Foreign Policy* (New York: Monthly Review, 1977), and the literature cited there.

2. Warren Christopher, "Agenda of International Economic Issues," The U.S. Department of State Current Policy No. 25, June, 1978, p. 1.

3. Vance was Chairman and a trustee of the Rockefeller Foundation and Vice Chairman of the Council on Foreign Relations (Chaired by David Rockefeller); Brzezinski is a close friend of David Rockefeller, and was the Director of the Trilateral Commission.

4. *The New Yorker*, May 1, 1978, p. 98.

5. Ibid., pp. 117-118.

6. Ibid., p. 111.

7. Ibid., p. 118.

8. Ibid., p. 129.

9. For frank statements of this view, see articles by C. Fred Bergsten and Zbigniew Brzezinski in *Foreign Policy* Summer, 1973 and Summer, 1976 respectively. Bergsten, long active in the CFR and a co-author of a Trilateral Commission report, is now Assistant Secretary of the Treasury for International Affairs.

10. Anthony Lake, "The United States and the Third World: Economic Issues," November 5, 1977 speech, The U.S. Department of State, Bureau of Public Affairs, 1977, p. 2.

11. *New York Times*, May 23, 1977, pp. 1, 12.

12. *New York Times,* Februrary 26, 1979, p. A12.

13. *Dollars and Sense,* February, 1979, p. 12.

14. *Newsweek*, January 29, 1979, p. 44.

15. *Foreign Policy*, Spring, 1979, p. 12.

16. *Seven Days*, March 30, 1979, p. 30; see also *N. Y. Times*, March 8, 1979, p. A15.

17. *San Francisco Sunday Examiner and Chronicle*, March 25, 1979, p. 17A; *Guardian*, April 4, 1979, p. 15.

18. *New York Times,* August 20, 1979, p. 1,A6.

19. *Guardian*, September 27, 1978, p. 18.

20. *Africa News*, April 10, 1978, p. 2.

21. Cyrus Vance, "The United States and Africa," June 20, 1978 speech, The U.S. Department of State Publication 8950 Africa Series 59.

22. *Africa News*, March 10, 1978, pp. 3-4.

23. Council on Foreign Relations, *Annual Report 1977-1978* (New York: CFR, 1978), p. 12.

24. *New York Times*, March 18, 1978, p. 1.

25. *Africa News*, May 29, 1978, p. 2.

26. Ibid., pp. 2, 11.

27. Ibid., p. 2. See also I.F. Stone's article in the July 20, 1978 *New York Review of Books*.

28. Gwynne Dyer in the Hearst press's *San Francisco Sunday Examiner and Chronicle World*, June 11, 1978.

29. *Africa News*, June 19, 1978, p. 9.

30. *Africa News*, May 22, 1978, p. 11; *San Francisco Sunday Examiner and Chronicle*, September 17, 1978, p. 18A.

31. *Newsweek*, June 5, 1978, p. 48.

32. For example, see *San Francisco Chronicle*, June 15, 1978, p. 22.

33. *Vital Speeches of the Day*, June 22, 1978, p. 522.

34. Ibid., p. 516.

35. *San Francisco Sunday Examiner and Chronicle World*, June 18, 1978, p. 18.

36. *Africa News*, June 19, 1978, p. 6.

37. Ibid., p. 7.

38. Ibid.

39. Ibid., pp. 6, 10.

40. See *Newsweek*, June 12, 1978, pp. 26-37 for background, and *Newsweek*, July 3, 1978 for the change in African policy.

41. Cyrus Vance, "The United States and Africa," June 20, 1978 speech, The U.S. Department of State Publication 8950, Africa Series 59, p. 2.

42. Ibid., p. 3.

43. Ibid., p. 11.

44. *Africa News*, January 19, 1979, pp. 6-7.

45. See the analysis of the evolving situation presented weekly by *Africa News*, P.O. Box 3851, Durham, N.C. 27702.

46. *Africa News*, October 23, 1978, p. 2.

47. *The New Yorker*, May 1, 1978, p. 110.

48. See Wallerstein's article in *The Nation*, November 12, 1977, pp. 489-492.

49. *The Nation*, July 28-August 4, 1979, p. 76.

50. Ibid., p. 75.

51. Ibid.

52. *Africa News*, August 17, 1979, p. 11.

53. John J. Berger, *Nuclear Power: The Unviable Option* (Palo Alto, Calif.: Ramparts Press, 1976), p. 221.

54. *New York Times*, October 31, 1977, p. 1; *New York Times*, November 1, 1977, p. 1.

55. *New York Times*, December 20, 1977, p. 10.

56. *New York Times*, October 31, 1977, pp. 1, 13; *Guardian*, July 18, 1979, p. 13.

57. *Africa News*, April 10, 1978, p. 5.

58. Examples include food riots in Egypt, strikes and riots in Peru, and protests in Portugal, three nations which have recently had IMF austerity plans imposed upon them.

59. Richard N. Cooper, Karl Kaiser and Masataka Kosaka, *Towards a Renovated International System*, Triangle Papers 14 (New York: The Trilateral Commission, 1977), p. 49.

60. Ibid.

61. *In These Times*, September 28-October 4, 1977, p. 8.

62. *Foreign Policy*, Spring, 1978, p. 75.

63. Ibid., p. 77.

64. Ibid., p. 71.

65. Ibid., p. 75.

66. *Washington Post*, June 19, 1978.

67. Jimmy Carter, *A Government as Good as its People* (New York: Simon and Schuster, 1977), p. 116.

68. *Trialogue*, Summer, 1978, p. 11.

69. *Atlantic Community Quarterly*, Fall, 1974, p. 350.

70. *New York Times*, May 9, 1977, pp. 1, 12.

71. Cooper, Kaiser and Kosaka, *Towards a Renovated International System,* p. 32.

72. Zbigniew Brzezinski, *Between Two Ages: America's Role in the Technetronic Era* (New York: Viking, 1970), p. 4.

73. Jeremy R. Azrael, Richard Lowenthal and Tohru Nakagawa, *An Overview of East-West Relations*, Triangle Papers 15 (New York: The Trilateral Commission, 1978), p. 37.

74. Ibid.

75. Ibid., pp. 38-40. See also The Committee on the Present Danger's policy statement "Common Sense and the Common Danger," November, 1976.

76. See *New York Times*, December 24, 1975, pp. 1, 7.

77. Council on Foreign Relations, *Annual Report* 1977-1978, p. 11.

78. *Inquiry*, July 24, 1978, pp. 16-19.

79. *The Progressive*, December, 1978, p. 9.

80. *In These Times*, March 1-7, 1978, p. 2.

81. Study done by the Congressional Budget Office, reported in the *San Francisco Sunday Examiner and Chronicle,* July 2, 1978, p. A2.

82. *San Francisco Sunday Examiner and Chronicle World,* July 9, 1978, p. 30.

83. *New York Times*, June 18, 1976, p. A12.

84. *San Francisco Sunday Examiner and Chronicle World,* June 25, 1978, p. 7.

85. *Inquiry*, April 16, 1979, pp. 17-18; *Guardian*, June 6, 1979, p. 9.

86. *Inquiry*, April 16, 1979, p. 19.

87. See *The Nation*, September 24, 1977, pp. 268-273.

88. *Congressional Quarterly Weekly Review*, August 5, 1978, p. 2041.

89. *San Francisco Sunday Examiner and Chronicle World*, August 6, 1978, p. 23.

90. Ibid.

91. Azrael, Lowenthal and Nakagawa, *An Overivew of East-West Relations,* p. vii.

92. *Trialogue,* Summer, 1978, p. 5.

93. Azrael, Lowenthal and Nakagawa, *An Overview of East-West Relations,* p. 24.

94. Ibid., p. 25.

95. *Trilogue,* Fall, 1977, p. 12.

96. In Carter's Naval Academy speech, reprinted in *Vital Speeches of the Day,* June 15, 1978, p. 515.

97. *Foreign Policy,* Fall, 1978, p. 65.

98. Ibid., p. 69.

99. *San Francisco Sunday Examiner and Chronicle,* July 30, 1978, pp. A16-18.

100. It was the African aspects of this tough speech which President Nyerere responded so sharply to.

101. *Vital Speeches of the Day,* June 15, 1978, pp. 515, 516.

102. *New York Times,* April 16, 1978, IV, p. 4.

103. *New York Times,* April 2, 1978, IV, p. 6.

104. Ibid.

105. *Congressional Quarterly Weekly Review,* August 5, 1978, p. 2047.

106. *Atlantic Community Quarterly,* Spring, 1977, p. 5; Vance made similar statements in his April 30, 1977 speech at the University of Georgia.

107. Estimates made by Amnesty International in their publication *Matchbox,* Spring, 1978, pp. 9-12.

108. Richard Holbrooke, "U.S. Economic and Social Programs in East Asia," *The U.S. Department of State Bulletin,* April 4, 1977, pp. 325-326.

109. *Matchbox,* Summer, 1978, p. 4.

110. Several Congressmen have recognized the implications of this policy. Representative Thomas Harkin (D. Iowa) for example, pointed out that IMF policies cause "violations of human rights." See *In These Times,* April 20, 1977, p. 14.

111. It is interesting to note in this connection that Brzezinski wrote a few years ago (*Foreign Policy,* Winter, 1974-75, pp. 63-66), that until recently the U.S.S.R. played the role of "unifier" of the Western system by posing a threat. Since the threat was becoming less credible, the result was a "crisis" for the West.

112. Michel J. Crozier, Samuel P. Huntington, and Joji Watanuki, *The Crisis of Democracy: Report on the Governability of Democracies to the Trilateral Commission* (New York, 1975, pp. 113 and 106 respectively.

5

Serving the Powers That Be: Carter's Domestic Policy

Carter's domestic policy, like his rise to power and his foreign policy, has its origins in the response of powerful upper class business groups to the economic crisis of the 1970s. If it is clear that the Carter Administration's foreign policy is traditionally Democratic in the sense of being both ambitious and interventionist and therefore requiring high military spending, it can be said that its domestic policy is much closer to a traditional Republican one, with some new elements as well. While both major parties have long agreed on the necessity of promoting domestic prosperity by using public policy to promote the profitability of business, Democrats have, especially since 1933, also stressed innovation in welfare programs and an even-handed policy toward the organized working class in order to maintain domestic harmony and the legitimacy of the system in the eyes of the majority of the American people. With the Carter Administration, this liberal Democratic welfare tradition is rapidly dying. In this sense, the advent of the Carter Administration marks something very new, the end of an era of expansion of the welfare state by succeeding Democratic administrations and subsequent acceptance of these measures by Republicans.

The complete picture of the coming new era in the history of the American political economy is as yet unclear. What is evident, however, is that the Carter Administration is moving the nation toward <u>a more fully developed form of the American corporate state,</u> which involves decreasing the economic and political power of the average American in order to give more to the corporations. The overall goal is <u>to restrict labor's share of the national income</u> in order to increase corporate profits. The rulers of America expect that greatly increased wealth in corporate hands will result in increased investment and a rejuvenation of the American and world capitalist economy. In the long run what is apparently hoped for is structural change in the economy amounting to <u>a new industrial revolution</u>, which will result in a period of future prosperity. Put another way, we are witnessing the initial stages of an attempt to lay the groundwork for <u>a new stage of capital accumulation</u> and economic growth. The last time changes this basic were made was between the Depression and World War II. The level of class struggle coming during the 1980s may well be as sharp as during that period.

To deal with the present crisis and lay the basis for the future the Carter Administration is attempting to increase corporate profits by following an economic policy which can be characterized as a blend of <u>laissez-faire deregulation</u> (in areas that directly affect corporate profits), traditional <u>Keynesianism</u>, and the Nixonian policy of <u>"zapping labor."</u> The specifics of the program can best be described under two headings: first, a tightening of executive and ruling class control over the federal government's budget and spending policies in order to curtail all non-military spending; and second, disciplining the American working class and at the same time helping big business increase its profits. Carter hopes that success in these two areas will give him the required political support to achieve re-election and will allow big business the economic wherewithal to overcome the stagnation and recession tendencies of American capitalism in the late 1970s.

Before turning to these two topics, we must discuss a key source of domestic policy — the Business Roundtable. If the Council on Foreign Relations and the Trilateral Commission run the Carter Administration's foreign policy, it may be said that another big business group, the Business Roundtable, wields the most influence over his domestic policy. The Roundtable is a private lobbying organization of about two hundred chief executive officers of major American corporations. Founded in 1972, it rapidly recruited the leaders of the giants of capitalism, including the three largest auto companies, seven of the largest oil companies, the three largest banks, and the major steel producers, mining corporations, retailing organizations, and utilities. Its 1978 chairman was Thomas A. Murphy, Chairman of General Motors, and its vice chairmen were the chief executive officers of General Electric, Exxon, and Goodyear. Its policy committee included men like David Rockefeller of Chase Manhattan Bank, Walter B. Wriston of Citibank, John de Butts of ATT, Irving S. Shapiro of DuPont, and Frank T. Cary of IBM.

The Roundtable's leadership is heavily interlocked with other big business groups. In 1977 the number of interlocks between the Roundtable's forty-five member policy committee and members of the Business Council was thirty-three, with the Council on Foreign Relations eighteen, the Committee for Economic Development thirteen, the Conference Board eight (1976 list), and the Trilateral Commission three. Even though only three leaders of the Roundtable were at the same time members of the Trilateral Commission, those three were key individuals: David Rockefeller; Carter friend and early supporter J. Paul Austin, chairman of Coca-Cola; and David Packard of Hewlett-Packard (see appendices for complete lists of the members of each of these organizations). The extremely high level of overlap between the Business Roundtable and the Business Council suggests that the two organizations act in close concert, with the Roundtable acting as the lobbying arm of both. This connection extends to common leaders — in 1977 the Chairman of the Roundtable was a vice chairman of the Business Council and two other Roundtable co-chairmen were a Council vice chairman and a member of its executive committee. In 1976 Edmund W. Littlefield, then chairman of the Business Council confirmed who does the lobbying with his comment that "we leave the advocacy to the Business Roundtable."[1]

The Roundtable's great strength is based on the active participation of its two hundred or so chief executives who meet to discuss domestic developments and plan strategy, then lobby the government to carry out their will. The Roundtable brings its chief executives to Washington to pressure the Congress and White House personally. It uses its influence over the media to spur propaganda blitzs about the virtues of "free enterprise," a "growing capital shortage," and "excessive government regulation." Its domestic clout has made the business community, in *Fortune*'s words, by far "the most effective special-interest lobby in the country."[2] *Business Week* added that the Roundtable has eclipsed older lobbies and is now business's "most powerful lobby in Washington."[3] The *Los Angeles Times* credited the Roundtable with "enormous power," pointing out in 1975 that the organization, only a few years old, "has veteran 'we've seen everything' Washington lobbyists standing up and taking notice."[4]

From the beginning the Carter Administration courted Roundtable leaders. Irving S. Shapiro, chairman of the Roundtable when Carter took office, was part of the group with which Carter consulted before making key cabinet appointments.[5] S. Stephen Selig III, White House liaison with business, told the *New York Times* in early 1978 that the administration continues to clear with Roundtable leaders "many" of its proposed appointees to high Federal office. This was true, for example, of the appointment of G. William

Miller, an active member of the Business Council and co-chairman of the Conference Board, to head the Federal Reserve Board.[6] The *New York Times* reports that Carter himself meets "regularly" with Roundtable and other big business leaders, calling them "Carter's Corporate Brain Trust." The President, as Shapiro puts it ". . . is accessible. He talks. We have no trouble getting ourselves heard."[7] These facts led one Carter watcher to remark that ". . . no President in living memory has courted big business as ardently as James Earl Carter."[8] The *New York Times* added that "in fact, big business has the ear of Jimmy Carter, Democrat, to a greater degree than was true of Richard M. Nixon and Gerald R. Ford, Republicans."[9] An excellent example of Carter's deferential attitude toward big business and his willingness to serve corporate leaders is his December 1977 speech before the Business Council. The Council's meeting was held at the posh Mayflower Hotel, with John de Butts, Chairman of American Telephone and Telegraph, presiding. Carter began his talk by stressing his friendship with the chief executives: "John de Butts and many of you have been very close friends of mine since I've been in the White House as President, and I've relied upon many of you already to give me advice. . . "[10] During his speech Carter related how, as a small businessman in Plains "you were the leaders in our nation that I looked to and admired," and how "I am honored to be invited to come" to speak to and learn from the "top business executives of our nation," humbly adding that "I've got a lot to learn, and I'm learning rapidly. I've had some good teachers."[11] The President then said: "I'd like to answer a question or two, if you'd let me" and "thank you very much for what you've contributed to our country. I hope that I can perform my job in such a way that will make you proud."[12] Even worse than such a deferential posture was Carter's willingness to turn governmental policy over to the leaders of the big corporations. In closing, the President said that if the businessmen find anything "that unnecessarily encroaches on your own effectiveness, I hope you'll let either my Cabinet officers or me know, and I'll do the best I can to correct it. . . if you will let me have those recommendations, I'll do the best I can to comply with your request."[13] Jimmy Carter, a man who always wants to do his best, has certainly complied with the requests of the lords corporate. The result of this closeness between the Carter Administration and big business has been domestic policies precisely in line with corporate wishes.

ZAPPING SOCIAL WELFARE SPENDING: GOVERNMENT REFORM, CARTER STYLE

The Carter program of improving business profits to deal with the economic crisis of the late 1970s, combined with the growing objections of a majority of Americans to high taxation, means that overall government spending must be reduced. Two characteristics of the federal government pose impediments to such necessary retrenchment — the party politics level of American politics, especially in the Congress, and the "clientist" nature of policy formulation in the federal bureaucracy. In Congress the party politics level of American politics is very close in practice to what could be called "the special interest process." This is the process by which narrowly defined, specific interests get favors of all kinds from the federal largesse, ranging from contracts to tax breaks, grants, and so on. The process has a momentum of its own in the sense that each member of Congress has his or her own pet water project or tax exemption or military contract for a local industry and trades votes with other members of Congress to assure his project becomes part of the budget. Since re-election often depends on getting such favors for local special interests, members of Congress fight hard for their pet projects. This process has resulted in both vast corruption and honest employment for many Americans. It is also very expensive.

Since the New Deal, public policy in the federal bureaucracy has been fashioned in what is often a "clientist" manner. This term means that powerful, private special interest groups in effect took over the section of the federal bureaucracy which directly concerned them. Thus the Department of Agriculture was dominated by organizations of wealthy farmers like the American Farm Bureau Federation, the Department of State by organizations like the Council on Foreign Relations, the Interior Department by various private forestry, mining, and other interests, and so on. After a time these government bureaucracies began to lobby for more for these private interests than for either big corporations or the American people as a whole, with the private interests successfully and expensively advancing their own interests. This process was acceptable while the American economy was rapidly expanding, but when stagnation and high inflation appeared in the 1970s, the existing system increasingly could not afford it.

Carter's response to this budget or fiscal crisis has been twofold. First, since Carter was put in office by the dominant sector of the ruling class and serves their general interests as a class, he has often opposed the party politics/special interest policy in Congress. Many have remarked how Carter hates to bargain and make deals with Congress to achieve his program. The President, as House majority leader James Wright (D.-Tex.) put it, "has an instinctive aversion to patronage," and hates "to indulge in quid pro quo."[14] Another Congressman complained that Carter "deals with issues on a vertical plane. He won't say to you, 'I need your vote on the Mideast arms sale and therefore I will give you the dam you want in your district.'"[15] The reason for this is less from any moral scruples than from the desire to break up the log-rolling special interest policies of the Congress and thereby hold down spending. In other words, wheeling and dealing is expensive and should be reserved for what Carter defines as the really crucial issues — not national health insurance, labor law reform or aid to the cities, but rather foreign policy questions like the Panama Canal treaty or the repeal of the arms embargo against Turkey and domestic policy issues like natural gas deregulation. Many remarked how intense the White House lobbying effort was for these three policy questions, but no such effort took place on programs which would serve the social needs of the American people.[16] This view is reinforced by an analysis of Carter's vetoes as President. He has been quite willing to take on vested special interests like specific military lobbies, the complex of interests which want numerous dams and water projects in the West, as well as other "pork-barrel" congressional bills. In the fall of 1978, for example, Carter vetoed a $10.2 billion public works bill for water and energy development, a move which outraged the Democratic leadership in the House. A "well-organized" lobbying effort, together with a large number of Republican votes, helped Carter stop the efforts of Democratic leaders in the House to override his veto.[17] In the summer of 1978 Carter even vetoed a $37 billion weapons appropriations bill — the first such veto in more than 125 years — because it had in it $2 billion for an unnecessary nuclear carrier. The original bill represented a victory for the navy and the nuclear sea-power lobby, but was overturned by the President. The money Carter saved by vetoing the carrier went into other military spending, illustrating again that militarism is one area where spending cuts are not permitted.[18]

In both his vetoes of special interests and his general policy on pork barrel spending, Carter's actions were correct but for the wrong reasons. Serving the special interests in the Congress and federal bureaucracy is expensive and lines the pockets of those wealthy and powerful enough to influence those branches of government. But the reason for Carter's policy was to give the President, and thus the ruling class level of American politics, more control over public spending. Such control will be used to serve the specific interests of the ruling class as a whole — instead of a special interest sector of that class — rather than promote the general welfare of the American people. In other words, while it is necessary and proper to control the special interests, what must be substituted is programs and government by the people and for the people. This, however, is precisely what the Carter Administration is unwilling to do.

Second, Carter has dealt with clientism in the federal government through several kinds of government "reorganization," civil service reform, eliminating or minimizing government regulation in several areas and strengthening the Office of Management and Budget and certain cabinet positions. Carter called Civil Service reform the "centerpiece of government reorganization during my term in office."[19] The "reform" bill passed by Congress made it easier for managers to fire and transfer federal employees, while allowing federal workers to join unions, but not to strike or bargain collectively on pay and fringe benefits.[20] This program, plus Carter's lid of 5.5 percent on pay raises for federal workers and partial freeze on federal hiring lays the basis for enforced productivity increases, called "speedup" in factories.[21]

Carter's reorganization also included moving towards "free market competition" in several areas formerly under government regulation. This was true in the case of the Civil Aeronautics Board, where route and fare restrictions were dropped, and natural gas, which was deregulated after an intense and complex fight among Carter, businessmen on both sides of the issue, consumers, and the Congress. This is in response to cries on the part of businessmen like David Rockefeller of "excessive government regulation" of business.[22] What such an approach ignores is the always inflationary consequences of deregulation of sectors of the economy with monopoly characteristics. Due to deregulation, for example, higher prices for natural gas are now inevitable, costing the American consumer billions in higher bills.

Carter has also, in effect, created a domestic economic council with a centralized policy-making role similar to the

National Security Council for foreign policy. The head of the Office of Management and Budget, the Treasury Secretary, the Vice President, and the Chairman of the Council of Economic Advisers are the key individuals on this council. These stronger sectors of the bureaucracy, with power to look at the big picture and make overall national economic policy, can thus sharply decrease the "clientism" more characteristic of other departments, such as Agriculture, Interior, Labor, HEW, Commerce, and so on. The result promises to be the ability to cut spending more severely than ever before and at the same time give more centralized power over the "welfare state" to the President and his top advisers. By extension, this weakens the party politics/special interest process in the federal government and, conversely, strengthens the control of the ruling class. The purpose of these policies is to give the capitalist class control over the welfare state to deal with the economic crisis.

One additional example, Carter's proposed "welfare reform" plan, provides another clear illustration of the aims and effects of government reform Carter-style. The origin of this plan is what corporate leaders perceive as overly "generous" welfare payments and unemployments benefits which discourage workers from accepting low paying employment in the private sector. Since employers want to find it easy to hire workers on profitable terms (i.e. at low wages), they oppose adequate welfare payments and want, in *Fortune*'s words, to "put a moratorium on social programs designed to redistribute income."[23] Carter's original plan, introduced in the summer of 1977, attempted both to do this and cut administrative overhead (i.e. lay off some of the social workers who run the welfare bureaucracy) along with a series of "reforms." These included merging the main programs into one, setting nation-wide minimum benefits, and instituting stringent work requirements on childless individuals, two parent families, and single parents with children over fourteen. This final provision would require a cutoff of benefits in the event that *any* job was refused. This reform program pleased few and angered many. The conservatives in Congress disliked the $18 billion price tag above what the federal government had been spending. Welfare rights groups were angry about the low benefit levels and the work requirement without any choice of jobs. Therefore the program failed to pass during the 95th Congress. The Carter Administration reintroduced a revised, more conservative version into the 96th Congress in 1979. Benefit levels will be reduced even further, since the cost to the federal government will be reduced substantially. The stringent "workfare" provision will be retained, requiring everyone on welfare except mothers with children under six to register with state employment offices and seek work.[24] Public employee unions and others have pointed out that experimental programs carried out in several states by the Department of Health, Education, and Welfare have demonstrated that work requirements for welfare recipients are unnecessary when adequately paid employment is available.[25] The problem is, of course, that decent jobs are scarce and especially difficult for disadvantaged groups to get. The effect of the workfare aspects of the program would be negative not only from the point of view of the welfare recipient, who must take *any* job, no matter how low paying or unsatisfying, but it also would result in layoffs of public employees presently receiving adequate, if low, pay and their replacement by a group of superexploited welfare recipients. This has the effect, ominous from the point of view of the American working class, of downgrading part of the work force, thus lowering the bargaining power of the entire class. The working class lives by selling its power to labor and the attempt to pull down a sector of this class has threatening implications. The success of this plan may indeed allow big business to cut their labor costs substantially and drive down the living standards of the majority of the American people.

THE CARTER ADMINISTRATION AND
THE CORPORATE CLASS WAR

Due to the economic crisis as well as additional factors already mentioned, the 1970s saw the American ruling class on the attack in labor relations on a scale not seen since the great Depression. Once a perspective of the right wing of this class, anti-unionism has spread to sectors once considered "liberal" in such matters. As *Business Week* put it, the cooperative spirit between business and labor is fading "because of stiffening employer opposition in Congress and at the bargaining table."[26] This is part of a larger picture, a political and ideological offensive against the working class as a whole, both organized and unorganized.[27] The obvious aim is to save on wages, pensions, and fringe benefits, as well as government social welfare by weakening the bargaining power of workers. That such policies are now accepted by mainstream business is indicated by the presence of the leaders of Texas Instruments as important members of the Trilateral Commission, Business Council, Conference Board and Committee for Economic Development.[28] Texas Instruments is a notorious anti-union corporation paying near minimum wage levels. The *Wall Street Journal* found that it would immediately discharge any worker even suspected of being pro-union. Also indicative is the fact that R. Heath Larry, the leader of the Council on a Union-Free Environment — an organization founded in 1977 to advise business on techniques of defeating union organizing drives — is also a leader of the Council on Foreign Relations, Conference Board, and Committee for Economic Development.[29] In 1978 Larry was also the president of the right-wing National Association of Manufacturers and a director of the Morgan Guaranty bank. The recent anti-union actions of corporations known for their liberalism, like the *Washington Post,* the *New York Times*, and the *St. Louis Post-Dispatch*, make the case conclusive. The *Post* broke a strike and one of the unions at its plants, now runs a partly non-union shop, and is in the process of attacking the paper's remaining labor organizations. The *New York Times* tried to cut the number of press operator jobs, but was only partly successful, due to an extended and unified strike action by its employees during the summer of 1978. In St. Louis about two thousand workers at the *Post-Dispatch* walked out in November 1978 over publisher demands to reduce press operator jobs.[30]

Even conservative union leaders like AFL-CIO president George Meany have begun to recognize that corporate executives, as Meany put it, "have joined with the right-wing anti-labor forces" in "class warfare" against unions, minorities, and the working class generally.[31] Douglas A. Fraser, president of the United Auto workers, stated even more strongly when resigning from the blue ribbon advisory committee, the Labor-Management Group, in July 1978: *(he dropped this line)*

however)

I believe leaders of the business community, with few exceptions, have chosen to wage a one-sided class war today in this
country — a war against working people, the unemployed, the
poor, the minorities, the very young and the very old, even
many in the middle class of our society. The leaders of industry, commerce and finance in the U.S. have broken and
discarded the fragile, unwritten contract previously existing
during a past period of growth and progress . . . I am convinced there has been a shift on the part of the business
community toward a confrontation . . . now, business groups
are tightening their control over American society.[32]

Part of the "tightening control" of business which Fraser points out is manifested in the political arena where the policies of Congress and the Carter Administration have more and more blatantly favored big business over the average American. In current circumstances, government actions which hurt labor normally help business. Both topics will therefore be discussed in this section.

The first serious confrontation between the organized working class and the Carter Administration came in April

1977 when hundreds of thousands of textile workers briefly walked off their jobs to protest the Carter trade policies. The demonstration, organized by the Amalgamated Clothing and Textile Workers Union and International Ladies Garment Workers Union, was the largest one against government policies since the 1970 antiwar actions and was probably the largest labor demonstration ever against the U.S. government. The unions want the administration to restrict foreign imports, whose far cheaper labor costs enable them consistently to undersell American-made products. Such imports have cost American workers at least 100,000 jobs a year since the 1960s.[33] Employment in the clothing industry has fallen 30 percent in only nine years for example.[34] The Carter Administration, guided by the Trilateral Commission-CFR perspective favoring "free trade," opposes import quotas, significant tariffs or other restrictions, warning that these could cause retaliatory trade wars that would not only damage American exports, but have unforseen political and economic consequences worldwide.

Carter's refusal to agree to import quotas to protect the jobs of American workers prompted a bitter response from Lane Kirkland, secretary-treasurer of the AFL-CIO and probable successor to George Meany as president. Kirkland pointed out that the decision-making process

> reminds us again that in national and world affairs, whether the winds blow left or right, cold war or detente, Republican or Democrat, big business adapts and comes to winning terms. When the Republicans are in, business wins because it owns the party. When the Democrats are in, business wins because it exacts the price of "business confidence." That price usually includes the sacrifice of the main elements of the Democratic platform and of labor's program. . . ."[35]

The ties of Kirkland and Meany to the Eastern Establishment are close, however — Kirkland is a member of the Trilateral Commission and a director of the CFR and Meany is a director of the Atlantic Council — making it unlikely that their oratory is anything more than that. Still, it shows that even conservative labor leaders must now strike a more militant pose and that labor's close cooperation with the corporate ruling class and its governmental arm is becoming increasingly difficult.

Despite this conflict between the Carter Administration and the organized working class during 1977, it was not until 1978 that Carter's honeymoon with labor was definitely over. Carter's response to events during that year showed decisively whose side he was on. The coal strike was the first great worker-capitalist battle during the Carter Administration and came early in 1978. The coal owners, organized in the Bituminous Coal Operators Association (BCOA) took a hard-line stance when the United Mine Workers (UMW) contract expired. The owners demanded "give backs," a roll back of gains in past miners' contracts, such as free health care, decent pensions, and safety provisions. Due to the trend toward concentration in the American economy, the coal owners are now predominantly large multinational corporations, like Kennecott Copper, Gulf Oil, Utah International, Continental Oil, U.S. Steel and others. The leaders of these corporations are, in turn, connected with the influential ruling class organizations that have been previously discussed. To cite just a few examples, the chairman of Kennecott is on the policy committee of the Business Roundtable, the chairman of Utah International was, before its recent merger with General Electric, on the Business Council's executive committee, the chairman of Gulf Oil is a trustee of the Conference Board, and two directors of Continental Oil are members of the Trilateral Commission.

The crisis point came in early March 1978, when coal supplies were getting dangerously low and the miners had rejected by a 2-1 margin a contract negotiated by their union president. That this rejected contract was unfair was admitted even by the business daily, the *Wall Street Journal*, which remarked in an editorial on March 7, "if we were a coal

miner we'd have voted against the proposed contract too"
since any wage gains would have been eaten up by increased
medical costs and taxes.[36] The *Journal*'s editors, not usually
sympathetic to the problems of workers, added that "the
miners have a point. But nobody seems to listen to them."[37]

This contract rejection put the strikers in a strong position;
they had now sacrificed for months to reach the point where
they had some real leverage. Carter than partly destroyed
this leverage by issuing an injunction under the 1948 Taft-
Hartley Act ordering the miners back to work for an 80-day
"cooling off" period. At the same time he declared a "bargaining impasse," meaning that the corporations could legally
be released from the obligation to engage in industry-wide
bargaining, a crucial condition of the workers' unity and
leverage against the owners. Divide-and-conquer tactics could
then by imposed through settlements on a company-by-company
or regional basis. Acceptance of this by the miners would have
effectively broken the strike and severely weakened the union,
since after eighty days the summer months of low demand
would have begun, giving the miners no bargaining power to
deal with the hard-line operators.

Carter also moved to reopen non-union mines with federal
marshals assisted by state police. He could have seized the
mines and reopened them after signing a federal contract
with the miners. The miners would have welcomed such a
policy since it would have offered them a chance to gain
some of their demands under federal auspices. Since this was
not done, however, the miners in the main refused to return
under these semi-slave conditions, risking bankruptcy of the
union and jail terms for union officers. Since the miners
would not return to work, both the corporations and the
Carter Administration feared chaos, and were more forthcoming, resulting in a settlement a short time later. The
armed might of the state had been put on the side of strike-
breaking and union-busting by a Democratic president attempting to coerce the workers into accepting a "give-back"
contract.

LABOR: THE LEGISLATIVE FRONT

During the first two years of the Carter Administration, organized labor had its most important legislative agenda in more than a decade. After eight years of vetoes by Republicans in the White House, the organized working class, with a Democratic Congress and President, hoped to achieve a breakthrough on the legislative front with the 95th Congress. Among the laws labor wanted were a higher minimum wage to help the most poorly paid workers, a consumer protection agency, reasonably full employment guaranteed by the federal government (the Humphrey-Hawkins bill), and, as the capstone, labor law reform.

This last bill aimed essentially at protecting workers' rights to organize, but did little to aid workers already in unions. It was a modest measure meant simply to guarantee enforcement of labor legislation already on the books since the Wagner National Labor Relations Act passed more than forty years ago. Business resistance and such delaying tactics as appeals through the courts have prevented millions of workers from gaining their union rights. This partly explains why union membership as a percentage of the total work force has been declining since 1947. By 1976 only 20.1 percent of the work force was unionized and today's figure is no doubt lower yet.[38] When the 95th Congress recessed in October 1978, labor had lost on every issue with the exception of a compromise minimum wage act and a Humphrey-Hawkins bill totally gutted of its essential features. As the *Congressional Quarterly* stated, the Humphrey-Hawkins bill was diluted to the point where "it was little more than a symbolic statement about Congress' desire to limit unemployment and inflation."[39]

How did these failures come about — despite a nearly $1 million lobbying campaign (the best financed and most sophisticated ever undertaken by the AFL-CIO), and support from the entire spectrum of liberal, women's, and environmental organizations? First of all, it should be pointed out that the AFL-CIO leadership was afraid to mobilize their own rank and file membership in demonstrations and direct action. Such activities could have put pressure on reluctant members of Congress and the Carter Administration, just as civil rights marches and agitation forced the Kennedy and Johnson administrations to push through measures ending formal segregation and assuring voting rights. Conservative, timid labor leadership, tied in with leading capitalist organizations like the CFR, Atlantic Council, and Trilateral Commission, is obviously not conducive to victory in broader struggles with the ruling class.

Second, the world's biggest corporations and their lobbying organizations — the Business Roundtable, U.S. Chamber of Commerce, and National Association of Manufacturers to cite just three — were united and extremely active in opposing labor's program. Business lobbying on the consumer protection agency bill, for example, was so intense that House Speaker Thomas O'Neill exclaimed before the vote that "I have never seen such extensive lobbying."[40] A Business Roundtable representative said, "I've never seen such an intense and unified front by business in all my years here," adding that "it's the first time small and big business have gotten together on something like this."[41]

Finally, if business lobbying was effective, the efforts of the Carter Administration on behalf of labor's program were entirely the opposite. In the final analysis, this was the key factor in the failure of labor's program. Why were Carter and his administration so ineffective in getting a Democratic Congress to pass a mild reformist program? The careful student must conclude that, on these issues and several other ones like an adequate urban policy to aid the poor in the cities, the Carter Administration was not interested in seeing Congress pass such legislation and did not make a serious effort in its behalf.

While there has been a great deal of talk in the establishment press about Carter's inability to deal with Congress, news reports have neglected to point out that during his first two years in office, Carter lobbied hard for and achieved everything he wanted on issues he seriously cared about. For example, on the natural gas deregulation bill in the fall of 1978 many were initially opposed, but Carter won thanks to "the most extensive administration lobbying on a piece of domestic legislation since Carter took office."[42] Some in the Congress mentioned the White House's hard-nosed pressure tactics, something Carter supposedly eschewed. Representative Clarence J. Brown (R.-Ohio), for example, said the White House used "threats, promises, and warnings" to gain votes.[43] On the attempt to override Carter's public works veto, *Congressional Quarterly Weekly Review* spoke of how Carter "blitzed the House with well-organized lobbying."[44] On foreign policy issues the administration won an uphill fight on the Panama Canal Treaty after successfully applying "intense pressure" on Congress and won on ending the Turkey arms embargo after "an intensive two-month lobbying effort."[45]

In contrast to these successes, Carter's efforts on labor-sponsored bills were lax to put it mildly. On the consumer protection bill, one lobbyist remarked that "I don't know of a single vote he changed."[46] On the urban program, which also failed to pass Congress during 1978, it was noted that

> news reports in recent months describe Carter as never personally supporting some of the larger spending items in the urban package. He reportedly was worried about their inflationary impact and the new bureaucracies the program would require. . . . With Carter and his chief economic advisers focusing increasing attention on reducing the budget deficit, some congressional observers have concluded that the administration really did not have its heart in the fiscal aid bill.[47]

One congressional supporter of the bill later described the administration's lobbying efforts in its behalf as "a bunch of second tier Treasury people rap-tap-tapping on everybody's door."[48] Since aid to the nation's decaying cities is in effect aid to the working class, the poor, and minorities which are inordinately concentrated there, Carter's disinterest is another example of ignoring the needs of these working people.

Carter's actions on labor's legislative capstone, labor law reform, reinforces this conclusion. Before the bill was even presented to Congress Carter demanded that labor strike some key sections and compromise on the minimum wage bill. This resulted in labor's painful abandonment of the attempt to repeal Section 14(b) of the Taft-Hartley Act, the so-called "right-to-work" clause permitting states to prohibit union shops, as well as agreeing to a $2.65 an hour minimum wage — a rate which allows a full-time worker to live only at the poverty level — instead of the $3.00 an hour wage the unions wanted.[49] As *Congressional Quarterly* put it: "Only after months of negotiations did labor succeed in gaining administration support for a major labor law revision proposal intended to facilitate union organizing."[50]

Once the law reform was before the Congress, the Administration said it favored the measure, but did practically nothing to help it when a filibuster threatened to block even a vote on the issue. *Congressional Quarterly* remarked that "the White House lobbying office has not been particularly active" in support of the bill, and quoted a White House spokesman denying "suggestions by some opponents that Carter was lukewarm to the measure."[51] After defeat of the measure — cloture (to cut off the filibuster) failed by only two votes — labor's representatives joined business in concluding that Carter was not interested in such a bill passing.[52] An analysis of the senators on each side is also indicative. Nearly all northern, midwestern, and western Democrats voted for ending the filibuster against the reform law as did northern state Republicans. The defeat came because thirteen southern Democrats and twenty-three Republican senators from the west, midwest, and south voted against cloture. Just two additional votes from these two groups would have broken the filibuster. It stretches credibility to believe that had Carter really wanted to he could not get even two additional votes out of thirteen from his own party and region. Both senators from his home state of Georgia voted no, as did two Republican senators, John C. Danforth (Mo.) and William V. Roth (Del.), who are also members of the Trilateral Commission.[53] Carter's actions and lack of action make it plain that when sides have to be chosen, it is not the business community that Democratic politicians can afford to turn against.

HELPING BUSINESS: THE CARTER ADMINISTRATION'S ECONOMIC POLICIES

Obviously the anti-labor actions mentioned in preceding pages have a pro-business effect. But this is also true of Carter's energy and tax programs, as well as the economic policies he instituted in the fall of 1978, such as his anti-inflation plan and the connected dollar support, social welfare and budget cutting programs. An analysis follows.

CARTER'S TAX PROGRAM

During the Carter Administration's first two years in office, mass dissatisfaction with an unfair system of taxation swept the United States. This dissatisfaction was manifested in a number of ways, not the least being Carter's own election, since he campaigned partly on a tax reform platform, stating strongly during the 1976 campaign that the tax system was so unjust that it was "a disgrace to the human race."[54] The "tax revolt" had three aspects. People wanted tax reform to eliminate unfair structures at the federal, state, and local levels; tax cuts; and a curb on what was seen as waste in government spending. The causes of this tax revolt were deeply rooted in the American political economy — high rates of unemployment, inflation, and stationary or declining real wages — in short the stagnation and crisis of the 1970s. As people had a more and more difficult time making ends meet, taxes, always a source of grumbling, became the prime target for change.

The Carter Administration responded to these pressures by emphasizing the second and third aspects of the tax revolt — how much was being paid and government efficiency — rather than the tax reform which would shift the burden to those who could afford to pay. Carter's tax program, presented to Congress in early 1978, contained only minor reforms, designed to make his tax proposals more popular, along with some cuts and some proposals which would make the system even more unjust by giving tax breaks to the big corporations. The "reforms," which Carter did not lobby for hard enough to get past a Congress dominated by special interests, included a reduction in allowances for business meals and entertainment, the so-called three-martini lunch, and other tax loopholes. To aid big business, Carter proposed that the corporate tax rate be cut from 48 percent to 44 percent, although the effective rate, due to numerous loopholes, would remain much lower. One of these loopholes, the 10 percent investment tax credit, was broadened in Carter's plan to include construction of new plants, something which, if passed, would accelerate the flight of businesses overseas and to the non-union low-wage South from eastern and midwestern cities, increasing unemployment and urban decay in those two areas. Tax reductions of almost $25 billion were proposed: $17.8 billion to individuals and $6.2 billion to business.[55]

Carter had "aid" from the Business Roundtable in formulating his tax proposals, a fact which no doubt helps explain why reform in the areas of capital gains taxes and loopholes for the wealthy and large corporations were entirely left out of his tax package.[56] In his December 1977 speech to the Business Council, Carter told the businessmen that "we evolved the tax proposal in a way that I think you would have had you been in office" and that he had consulted with "many of you" personally or through his Cabinet officers.[57] On a deeper level, however, the logic of Carter's entire economic approach dictated that taxes for business had to be cut, not increased to make the rich pay their fair share. For at about the same time that the tax proposals were being given Congress, key members of the administration were publicly concerned about "business confidence" and the rate of business investment. In the Annual Report of the President's Council of Economic Advisers and in a May 1978 speech by Treasury secretary Blumenthal, the need for an increase in the "profitability of American enterprise" was cited and thus the need to cut business taxes.[58]

In this and many other areas, such as labor relations, favoritism toward big business and those with capital to invest is objectively necessary as long as the present economic system exists. Unless a new system — based on an alternative method of development such as an American version of the socialist model of public instead of private accumulation, investment, and ownership — is being proposed and implemented, government has to be solicitous of the needs of the private individuals and corporations with capital to invest. This is the engine of development, employment, production, and thus individual and collective survival. Even with massive government assistance in the form of tax breaks and subsidies, capitalists will not invest unless they believe they can make a profit. In fact, top American corporations are, according to *Business Week*, "sitting atop a record $80 billion pile of cash" which has not been invested because management doesn't trust the future of the American economy.[59]

Taking their cue from the administration's own top economic spokesmen, Congress took Carter's conservative program and turned it into a reactionary one, giving large tax breaks to the rich and business. The tax system that Carter called a "disgrace to the human race" became a bigger disgrace when the President signed the new tax bill into law in the fall of 1978. Called by one congressman "a Republican bill with a Democratic label," the new law gave over 85 percent of the tax cut for individuals to the minority of the population making over $15,000 a year.[60] Not one of Carter's mild "reforms" passed, but the entire pro-business tax program did and then some. The corporate tax rate was reduced, the investment tax credit expanded, and corporate and individual capital gains taxes were cut drastically with over 90 percent going to that 1 percent of the population with annual incomes of $50,000 or more.[61] The effective rate of taxation on American corporations is now down to only about 13 percent.[62]

Filling the gap in federal revenue created by tax cuts for corporations and the rich is the recent large rise in social security taxes passed by the 95th Congress. As an exclusive levy on wages, the social security tax is even more regressive than the sales tax. It is deducted directly from only the first $20,000 of an individual's income, so that those with higher incomes pay a smaller percentage than those with lower ones. Certain forms of income, from investment and capital gains for example, are not taxed at all. The money from these social security taxes is put into a unified budget and is used for general needs such as military spending as well as for old age pensions. That these retirement "benefits" are inadequate is indicated by the fact that the Congress, presidents, military officers, and corporate executives are provided for in separate and generous retirement and medical care systems which provide real benefits. Most Americans, however, must rely on an inadequate social security system.

The net result of Carter's tax proposals and congressional action is an *increase* in the total tax bill for the average American making less that $20,000 a year and a *decrease* for the rich and big corporations.[63] Wealth and income are being redistributed upward instead of down to those who are increasingly squeezed by the failures of the economic and political system. What started out in the 1976 presidential campaign as a drive to reform an outrageous tax system to make it more just had degenerated by the end of 1978 into an orgy of tax cutting for the wealthy which is likely to create serious economic and political problems in the 1980s.

ENERGIZING CORPORATE POWER: CARTER'S ENERGY PROGRAM

While having some conservation and increased production aspects — such as tax credits for installation of energy-saving devices and materials in the home and industry, oil import quotas, increased coal use, a slight increase in developmental funding for solar energy, higher summer and lower winter thermostat settings in public buildings, increased aid to mass transit systems, and a massive, federally financed crash development of synthetic fuels — which make it superficially attractive to the American people, Carter's energy plan is an additional example of a program which actually helps big business. The real essence of the Carter program is conservation and new production through much higher energy prices.[64] The massive profits from these higher prices will mostly go directly or indirectly, to the same private corporations which have largely (with help from other giant corporations like the auto, rubber and allied businesses) created the energy problem in the first place.

Carter's program has no vision and offers no long-range solutions. Even in the short run, it is, in the words of environmentalist Barry Commoner, only "a plan for manipulating supply," not cutting demand significantly, let alone moving toward a crisis-free future based on safe, renewable energy sources.[65] Not surprisingly, Carter's plan essentially corresponds to the recommendations of the Trilateral Commission. The Commission's magazine *Trialogue* stated in the summer of 1978 that higher prices were "the only way to encourage new production and moderate the growth of energy demand."[66] The Commission therefore recommended the deregulation of natural gas and the elimination of price controls on crude oil.[67] Both of these proposals were implemented during Carter's first two and a-half years in office. The Commission's argument, adopted by the Carter Administration, about this being the "only way" to increase production and limit demand, is inaccurate. It ignores the need to develop new energy sources like solar, wind, geothermal and biomass (gas from agricultural and other waste matter) and ration existing oil supplies through the market. The market is unfair and inefficient since it only rations the middle and lower sectors of society, while allowing those with enough money to have all they want.

Carter's energy program is instructive for what it leaves out as much as for what it includes. A brief look at its massive shortcomings indicates why it is inadequate to solve the problem. The Carter plan concentrates on the final stages of consumption — burning gasoline in a car, using natural gas to heat a home or run industry — and hopes that putting a higher price tag on these things will significantly reduce consumption and increase production. Thus much higher natural gas and gasoline prices are coming because of price deregulation on both. This move toward the "free" market as a "solution" to the problem will not work. It is too little, too late. America's overall economic policies over the last fifty years have been based, in large part, on putting the welfare of the automobile and related industries like oil, steel, rubber, and highway construction above almost everything else. By 1977, such policies had made auto and oil corporations the top four (and seven of the top ten) industrial corporations in the United States. This has helped provide enough economic stimulation to maintain American capitalism on a fairly even keel, but has had serious negative consequences. This policy, besides the enormous waste of scarce resources involved, has created a pattern of dependency on autos which cannot be reversed merely with higher gasoline prices. The pattern includes large scale suburbanization, federally funded highway construction, destruction of urban mass transit systems, massive public subsidies to the oil corporations, and allowing the decline of the railroads. Significantly reducing the use of the automobile requires a credible alternative — mass transit as well as a change in many of the consumption and living patterns created during the period of cheap and abundant oil supplies. Creative, even visionary ideas are needed to redesign society and change existing energy consumption patterns, but these are exactly what is missing from Carter's energy program because they threaten the investment and profit priorities of the giant corporations. Such ideas suggest planning, public ownership and control of scarce resources, and alternative forms of transportation. In other words, basic change in a wasteful, unplanned capitalistic system is required to deal with the energy crisis which is upon us, and a long-range solution requires political action.

What Carter's decontrol plan means in practice is massive price gouging by the oil monopolies and shortages which are contrived to force out the smaller independent oil retail dealers and force the public to accept much higher prices. The gasoline shortage of the spring and summer of 1979 is an instructive example. The Federal Trade Commission (FTC) and the House of Representatives Subcommittee on Investigations found in May 1979 that irrespective of OPEC and the Iranian revolution, there was no crude oil shortage and the scarcity of gasoline was created when refineries suddenly cut back on production despite sufficient supplies of crude oil. Domestic U.S. oil producers held down production in anticipation of future higher prices due to decontrol.[68]

To make his plan more acceptable politically, Carter has proposed a token "windfall profits" tax. The much-ballyhooed tax is an all-too-typical example of the President's ringing rhetoric matched with lax performance. The White House's own figures showed that the extra profits from

Carter's oil deregulation would present the oil companies with an additional $14.5 billion in 1982 alone, while the windfall profits tax, if implemented at all, would require the industry to pay only $1.7 billion more in federal taxes than it would otherwise owe for that year. Over the next six years the administration's figures show that the oil industry would reap $57 billion in profits, while paying out only $7 billion extra in taxes under Carter's windfall profits tax scheme.[69] The truth is that the oil corporations, as recent profit figures have shown, have been receiving windfall profits for some years now, and Carter's decontrol plans will give them additional wealth on a massive scale — wealth taken mainly from American working people. Instead of public investment in and control over decentralized and renewable energy sources, such as methane gas from biomass, solar, wind, geothermal, and photovoltaic cells, Carter has increased the power and already huge profits of the oil monopoly more than any President in the last fifty years.

Carter himself, and several members of his Cabinet are known to be strong supporters of nuclear power. Even after the near disaster at the Three Mile Island nuclear power plant in the spring of 1979, the President argued that "nuclear power must play an important role in the United States. . . ."[70] — despite the obvious long-term health dangers posed by lethal radioactive byproducts of reactors and bombs. Nuclear waste — such as plutonium — can kill or cause genetic damage unless it is successfully contained. The risks extend half a million years into the future, yet nuclear plants have been constructed without a solution to the problem of disposing of waste or safely containing it. Common sense tells us that we cannot predict what the world will be like in a hundred or a thousand years — let alone a half million years. The risk to humanity — born and unborn — posed by nuclear weapons and nuclear power is very intense, yet the Carter Administration still views both as viable options for the future.

INFLATION AND CARTER'S NEW ECONOMIC POLICY

During 1977 and 1978, as the American and world capitalist economy gradually recovered from the 1974-75 recession, inflation again began to increase. This increase was frightening to corporate and government leaders since they feared that long-term high inflation levels would cause severe economic instability and undermine the American people's confidence in the entire political economy. As *Business Week* warned in spring 1978, high inflation was a threat "to the basic structure of American society."[71] It was inevitable, then, that such political and economic pressures would assure that the Carter Administration would make inflation fighting its number one economic priority. In the spring of 1978 Carter began jawboning — verbally suggesting that unions and corporations hold down wages and prices — to try to limit inflation.

Inflation is endemic to advanced capitalism, since it is deeply rooted in the social, political, and economic fabric of the consumption-oriented advanced Western capitalist nations. Its three main causes are: 1) monopoly pricing — price competition is nonexistent in large sectors of the economy, including such basics as oil, steel, automobiles, and finance; 2) the ability of organized labor to achieve wage increases to keep up with price rises; and 3) Keynesian deficit government spending, including extremely high military spending, both to preserve the system and to regulate the ups and downs of the capitalist business cycle. To control inflation one has to attack the most basic of these three causes. Which one is attacked is a key decision with important political and economic consequences.

Carter made his decision as inflation heated up in early 1978. Labor was to pay the price to stop inflation. Monopoly pricing, actually the main structural cause of inflation, since wage hikes are largely a response to price rises, was largely ignored. Carter's initial moves on the inflation front, taken in the spring and summer of 1978, reflected this pro-corporation bias. Actions to discipline the federal work force came first. Carter limited pay hikes to 5.5 percent. The President's hard-line position on pay increases and other benefits for postal workers during 1978 is also indicative of the trend in ruling class and government thinking.

That trend became even more clear in May 1978 when administration leaders spoke at a Business Council meeting. Vice President Mondale told the assembled businessmen that the Administration has "no higher priority than controlling inflation."[72] Treasury secretary W. Michael Blumenthal added that the federal budget should be moved "toward balance," foreshadowing the even stronger line on budget deficits later taken by the administration.[73] Federal Reserve chairman G. William Miller echoed business leaders pronouncements at the meeting by later stating that what was needed was a long-term shift in resources from the public to the private business sector along with balanced budgets.[74]

Anti-labor, pro-business policies by the Carter administration increased during the second half of 1978. During the early summer of 1978 there was a struggle within the government and the textile workers union over the level of cotton dust allowed in textile factories. Administration hard-liners, led by Charles Schultze, chairman of the Council of Economic Advisers, wanted lax regulations as an anti-inflation aid so that "unnecessary or uneconomic costs" are not imposed on American industry.[75] The Occupational Safety and Health Administration had to compromise and allow higher levels of cotton dust in factories than the Amalgamated Clothing and Textile Workers Union regarded as safe. Since the Labor Department itself estimates that 150,000 of the 800,000 cotton mill workers in the U.S. today are already suffering from the killing "brown lung" disease caused by breathing cotton dust, Lacy Dawkins of the Brown Lung Association was not far off the mark when he bitterly commented that workers will "pay with their lives for Carter's war on inflation."[76]

These actions during the summer of 1978 were merely preliminary, however, to the much stronger measures taken in the fall of 1978 and winter of 1978-79. The Carter Administration's anti-inflation program outlined in October, November, and December 1978 amounted to an open declaration of war on the American working class, especially blue collar workers, minorities, and the poor.

Carter's long-awaited comprehensive "voluntary" anti-inflation program was announced in late October 1978. Focusing on wage and price hikes, it had these features:

on wages — annual increases in wage and fringe benefits should be held to 7 percent or less. Workers making under $4.00 an hour are exempted along with those who can demonstrate productivity increases. The proposal also includes a complex "real wage insurance" scheme for tax rebates if inflation is over 7 percent in coming years, something which must be passed by Congress.

on prices — business should limit price rises to 0.5 percent below the average rises of 1976 and 1977. Price hikes cannot exceed 9.5 percent in any case. Exemptions exist in farm prices, interest rates, and in case raw materials prices rise too fast. Business profits should not exceed the average of the best two of the last three years.

on government spending — the federal government will reduce its budget deficit by cutting social welfare programs, slashing federal hiring, limiting federal pay hikes to well below the current rate of inflation, and other measures like deregulation of some areas of the economy (mentioned above). Enforcement of this "voluntary" program lies with the administration's Council on Wage and Price Stability, which will monitor the plan and use federal contracts, import powers, and other means to punish those who violate the program.

Evaluation of the program must begin with the fact that wages are much more strictly controlled than prices or profits. Business has a vested interest in restricting wage hikes and, with the power of the government on the side of business, it increases the difficulties of workers in trying merely to keep up with inflation, let alone begin to alter a grossly unfair distribution of income and wealth in America. Since unionized workers sign multi-year contracts and have to wait until the existing contract expires to gain increases, while business can raise prices at will, it is evident that the inflationary spiral is not caused by wage hikes. There is an obvious double standard involved in restricting wage hikes to 7 percent. To cite a few examples, in early 1977 Congress voted themselves a nearly 30 percent raise (to almost $60,000 a year) and after Carter's guidelines were announced politicians in Ohio, Illinois, and Chicago voted themselves salary increases ranging from 30 to 60 percent. Baseball star Pete Rose negotiated a 200 percent pay increase (to $800,000 a year). In addition, the tax program which Carter signed just before announcing his anti-inflation program gave large windfalls to the rich. These facts make it plain that neither politicians nor the wealthy, powerful, and famous accept Carter's 7 percent guideline. They expect their own salaries, capital gains, tax breaks, and dividends to soar high above the inflation rate and they have the power to make sure they do. The 7 percent wage guideline is for everyone else, especially the powerless. Needless to say, nothing has been done by the Carter administration about *these* excessive pay hikes, but much is being done, as we shall see, to limit workers whose average income is below $20,000 to 7 percent or below.

If a double standard exists on wage rises, almost no standard at all exists in the area of price hikes. Several important sectors of the economy — food, fuel and interest rates, for example — are entirely excluded from the program. The enforcement mechanism is totally absent in this most crucial of areas. To begin with, the very structure of the program — allowing price hikes of up to 9.5 percent and allowing numerous exemptions — favors business. In addition, businesses, especially large ones, have numerous ways to escape these or any price guidelines. For example, the price on an item could remain the same and the quality or amount contained in that item (a bar of soap, box of cookies, sheet of steel, etc.) could be allowed to deteriorate, increasing profits. Similar techniques abound. One practiced recently by U.S. Steel is to raise prices on popular items and maintain the same price on those which are not selling anyway, giving a low "average" price hike which is then widely publicized. Another tactic is to eliminate lower-priced lines entirely, forcing consumers to buy a higher priced model whose price has "only" gone up a few percentage points. Since, under the present system, the government must rely on business to supply all the statistics needed to determine compliance, there is additionally the possibility of manipulation of statistics. All this illustrates that it is impossible — as shown by the experience of price "controls" during the Nixon administration — really to control monopoly prices without large-scale government intervention in the affairs of private corporations and a serious national emergency like that faced in the World War II years.

The lack of serious enforcement mechanisms in the price area strongly suggests that the primary purpose of the Carter program, as it was under Nixon, is to "zap" labor and redistribute income to big business in order to spur investment. The government's strong efforts to control wages reinforces this conclusion. One example is the 1978 intervention of Barry Bosworth, a former Brookings Institution economist and a leader of Carter's Council on Wage and Price Stability, in the strike of the Western Pulp and Paper Workers. The workers demanded a 10 percent per year pay hike over a three-year contract and improved pensions. They pointed out that such a raise will only keep them even with the current inflation rate. Bosworth has called this an "outsized and alarming" demand and told the companies — giants like Boise Cascade, Crown Zellerbach, and Georgia Pacific —

that the government could not approve such a hike and that they should refuse to grant it. Thus encouraged by the Carter administration, the companies have imported scabs from all over the nation to attempt to break the strike and the union.[77] An additional example exists in the case of negotiations for a new contract in the trucking industry, where the old one expired in March 1979. The Council on Wage and Price Stability recommended to the Interstate Commerce Commission (ICC) that it should disallow future increases in the trucking freight rate. The ICC has, in turn, warned truck owners that they must "hang tough" at the bargaining table, and Bosworth informed them that the government planned to intervene in the wage negotiations if necessary. This put the Teamsters Union on the spot; its corrupt and undemocratic leadership relies on large wage and benefits settlements to stay in power against several rank and file movements. The trucking union, due to its key role in the entire American economy, however, was able to get a 10 percent a year wage and fringe benefit hike after a short strike. The Carter government is still threatening to undermine the union by deregulation of the entire trucking industry, encouraging more non-union, owner-operated trucking.[78] Similar government actions siding with employers can be expected in the coming months as numerous contracts in other industries expire. This is the answer to the question of whom the Carter Administration wants to pay for inflation. It is obviously the working class. As one labor spokesman put it, "the government and the corporations are accomplices in trying to hold down wages."[79]

The second part of Carter's new economic policy was announced only a week after his anti-inflation message. It consisted of a full percentage point rise in the Federal Reserve Board's discount rate — the fee it charges its member banks to borrow money — to 9.5 percent, a record high. In the summer of 1979 the rate was raised even higher. The last time the rate was raised a full point was at the depth of the depression in 1933, giving an indication of how serious the economic crisis of the 1970s has become. The Fed also required banks to hold higher reserves, further tightening credit. The administration also promised to sell more gold and take other actions to support the value of the dollar, which had been rapidly falling on the international market. Such a fall in the dollar increases inflation by raising the costs of imports and enhances the likelihood of further oil price hikes by the Organization of Petroleum Exporting Countries. Carter's actions pleased David Rockefeller, Wall Street, and business generally and they responded by investing in the stock market and buying dollars. The dollar gained and the stock market rose dramatically, erupting with a 35.34 advance in the Dow Jones Index on November 2, 1978, the biggest one-day advance in history.[80] This temporarily ended the "capital strike" by investors, who had doubted Carter's anti-inflation program would work and so were putting money in other currencies, nations, and investments rather than the dollar and stock market. The boom was not sustained, however, and subsided after a short time.

Carter's new high-interest policy helped cause a recession during 1979 and a worsening unemployment rate. In the days and weeks following Carter's action, a recession had been predicted by many economists, union leaders, some corporations, and even some people in the government. Never, in fact, had a recession been so widely predicted in advance. Alan Greenspan, for example, head of Ford's Council of Economic Advisers predicted a moderate recession in 1979 lasting into 1980.[81] The Bank of America predicted a "mild and short recession" in 1979, its seriousness depending upon success in dealing with inflation.[82] Wall Street "money managers" were "convinced" a recession was coming.[83] Even the Carter administration was reported to have "quietly" joined in these forecasts of a mild recession.[84]

In opting for a recession and at least some additional unemployment added to the six million already out of work (according to greatly understated official figures), Carter again shows where he and his Administration stand. Union leaders, as well as the average worker, much prefer wage, price, interest, profit, and rent controls over the prospect of increased unemployment and have made this plain.[85] Business sees such controls as a step towards socialism and much prefer increased unemployment and risking recession. As Irving Shapiro, chairman of DuPont, put it at a Business Council meeting in December 1978, "We can live with slower economic growth in 1979 and 1980 — even with a mild recession, but we cannot afford the consequences of a reversal of the policies now in place."[86] "Slower growth," Shapiro later added, "isn't bad news," but is "exactly the medicine our economists have said the country needs at this time."[87] Thus business and the federal government are prepared to take the "downside risk," as one individual expressed it, in order to prevent what are from their point of view worse alternatives, continued high inflation or economic controls.

The timing of Carter's economic moves indicates that there were political as well as economic motives involved. They came too late to have much negative economic effect upon the November 1978 elections, yet hopefully in time to allow a brief economic upswing during the 1980 election year. Carter's actions were considered by one Republican business observer, Washington Forum president Edward Garlich, to be "a stroke of genius. . . perhaps even the makings of a two term presidency. If Carter gets the economic slowdown early, then a pickup in late '79 and '80 and he brings inflation down, he'll look terrific in an election year."[88] The real question is if the mild recession which Carter's program aims for can bring inflation down very much. Before this question is considered, the final element of Carter's new economic policy, his budget cutting program, should be considered.

In his first state of the union address in January 1978, President Carter talked of the importance of budgets for indicating the government's priorities and policies for meeting national needs.[89] This is certainly true, and the outline of Carter's 1979-80 budget indicates again that his priorities are against the interests of the average American. In peacetime and during a period of economic distress — high inflation and unemployment — Carter's budget increases military spending while drastically cutting social welfare spending. The Pentagon budget will be raised from about $114.5 billion to about $126 billion in the 1980 budget. The biggest items are the Trident submarine, several new Navy ships, new airplanes and the MX missile. The Trident and MX are particularly dangerous new weapons systems and could give the U.S. a first-strike capability in the 1980s, resulting in new instabilities in the nuclear arms race. At the same time Carter will cut the overall budget deficit to about $30 billion to help control inflation. This means a reduction of about $15-$18 billion in already inadequately funded domestic programs. Such an overall reduction in federal spending is now politically popular in America because of the way inflation has hurt people's pocketbooks. But no one wants to have his or her own program cut, and thus infighting, acrimony, and bitterness are occurring at all levels of the federal government.

As mentioned above, the Office of Management and Budget (OMB) is the central organ planning these cuts, as part of Carter's program to increase control over the party politics/ special interest process. It is clear that the losers in the process will be those who depend on federal social welfare, health, employment, housing, and education programs. This means the sick, aged, poor, and minorities in particular. That these people are the ones most powerless to affect decisions in Washington only makes it more certain that they will be the primary victims of Carter's domestic budget reductions. A look at the specific programs which will be reduced or even eliminated illustrates this fact. Among those slated for serious cuts include the Comprehensive Employment and Training Act (CETA), which places unemployed low-income people in public service jobs; federal summer job programs for young people; federal health programs, such as preventive health care, health education, drug and alcohol abuse and basic health research. Included would be "drastic slashes" in programs like hypertension, immunization, medic-aid-medicare, venereal disease treatment, and preventive health care for Indians. Senator Edward Kennedy (D-Mass.), the chairman of the Senate's Health subcommittee, called these cuts "unacceptable and unprecedented," adding that "the American people would pay for these reduction with their health."[90]

OMB plans additional cuts in Social Security and disability insurance programs — current rules will be changed to give smaller benefits. Reductions in construction of subsidized housing for the poor are also planned, a fact which led Patricia Harris, Housing and Urban Development secretary, to complain that such cuts were "socially regressive" and resulted in an "unprecedentedly low" housing program, even compared to previous Republican administrations.[91] Cuts are also planned in subsidies to urban rapid transit systems — something which will further automobile and gasoline use — as well as in environmental programs, such as waste water treatment (sewer) construction programs, water and air quality planning, and the new Urban Parks Program.[92]

Carter's 1979-1980 budget proposals clearly indicate that federal government spending has, in part, come down to a question of guns or butter. Whereas previous administrations could offer a large measure of both, current circumstances demand a partial sacrificing of one or the other. The cold war policies of the Carter Administration abroad, policies designed primarily to serve the multinational corporations, have led to a rise in the already grossly swollen military budget, while eliminating or reducing programs for the needy. The net effect is a program aimed at rolling back the social welfare gains of the 1960s under the guise of the need for "defense" and controlling inflation. Carter has now clearly accepted the Republican perspective that government expenditures on "non-productive" activities (excluding, of course, military spending) are inflationary. He has agreed with businessmen that welfare spending undermines work incentives and squeezes corporations out of money markets. Labor discipline — allowing factory speedup and thus productivity increases — had to be increased by a low minimum wage, a high level of unemployment, a scarcity of good public sector jobs, and low levels of welfare.

These practices introduce the important question of the status of human rights in the United States. If the rights to health care, adequate clothing, food, and shelter are included with political and civil rights, as Carter himself correctly does, we could accurately say that Carter Administration programs have resulted in a deterioration of human rights in the United States. The numbers of people at or just above the poverty level stood in 1975, according to conservative government figures, at 37 million people (those with incomes at $6900 a year or lower). Due to administration economic policies, this is now increasing. [93] Rates of imprisonment are very high in America, second in per capita only to South Africa in the Western world. Experts estimate that over one-half million people are in American jails, 60 percent of whom earned less than $6000 in the year prior to their arrest. [94] Many of these individuals, white and minority, are "political prisoners" in the sense that racism, discrimination, or poverty led them to a life of crime and assured they would not receive adequate defense in court. These social factors prompted Andrew Young to say that many "are in prison much more because they are poor than because they are bad. . . Our system . . . sends intelligent, aggressive poor people to jail and [rewards] intelligent, aggressive rich people." [95] The lack of a national health care system leaves only the United States and South Africa among the Western world's nations without such a system. The lack of such a system, something the Carter administration has done virtually nothing about, has serious effects on the lives of poor people in particular. Scholarly studies conducted by health care professionals show that blacks in America have markedly higher rates of hypertension, cancer, mental illness, and infant mortality than whites. These higher rates result in an overall death rate for American blacks nearly twice that of whites in the same age groups.[96]

CONCLUSION: WILL THE CARTER ECONOMIC PROGRAM SUCCEED?

Whatever moral judgments are justified in regard to Carter's economic plans, an analysis of the program questions whether it can succeed in even its limited aims. Assuming the 96th Congress accepts the program during its 1979 session, will a majority of the American people? And, if the entire program is successfully implemented, will it significantly reduce inflation and encourage investment and a return of prosperity during the 1980s?

The Carter economic program has been extremely successful in its central aim: it has raised corporate profits to record high levels. While most Americans are tightening their belts under the impact of inflation and recession, corporations and their stockholders are enjoying a string of prosperous years. Citibank, one of the world's biggest banks, reported in its March, 1979 *Monthly Economic Letter* for example, that 1978 was a "banner year" for stockholders and corporate treasurers, with new records set in several earnings catagories.[97] In one of these areas, the rate of profit on equity, Citibank reported in April that "for all corporations in the survey, the rate of return jumped from 14.1% in 1977 to 14.9% in 1978, *the highest return on equity in the more than 50 years Citibank has compiled these figures*"[98] (emphasis added). Early profit reports for 1979 show that this trend has continued into the first quarter of 1979, with net profit after taxes for all manufacturing corporations up 41 percent over the (already high) first quarter of 1978, and the profit rate on stockholders' equity 3.3 percent higher than the first quarter of 1978.[99]

The result is less the high saving and investment which Carter and his economic advisers hope to encourage by catering to corporate needs, than a strengthening of corporate power and development priorities, the same priorities which created current economic problems in the first place. The ruling class will continue to be able to decide, with little public influence, what our nation's development agenda should be, and if the past is any guide, this will not correspond to the actual needs of the American people in the 1980s. More of the same, only worse, is thus likely during the next few years: an unstable economy with high inflation and unemployment, since corporate control of the economy, the main structural source of both, is not being altered. Given these realities, the Carter Administration's management of the economy is unlikely to succeed in its other aims, even in the short run.

First of all and in the short term, the program is internally contradictory. There are numerous inflationary aspects to the program: a high arms budget, high interest rates, continued expansion of the money supply, permissiveness toward corporate mergers (allowing prices to rise), and energy deregulation which also has ensured price rises.

Second, the program is unjust and so will stimulate resistance and class struggle within the United States. The 1980s are thus likely to experience strikes and sharp conflict between government and business on the one hand and an organized working class trying to preserve its standard of living on the other. Since the cities and minorities, especially blacks, will be particularly hard hit in the 1980s by this program, the danger of urban disturbances exist. Conservative blacks like Vernon Jordan, head of the National Urban League, warned that unless blacks and poor people "are given relief, it will be impossible to contain their despair or for them to sublimate their anger to the political process."[100]

The higher unemployment created by Carter's economic policy will probably more than wipe out the $15-18 billion saved by slashing domestic social welfare spending. Even a 1 percent rise in unemployment increases federal costs for unemployment insurance by many billions of dollars. There are also numerous other unknowns, such as the possibility of instability in key raw material-producing areas of the globe, a continued decline of confidence in the dollar abroad, higher world oil prices, a continued negative balance of trade, and reduced consumer spending due to high levels of consumer debt and the possibility of reduced consumer confidence in the future. There also promise to be serious fights in the Congress, conflicts which could torpedo key parts of Carter's program. These facts made the short-run prospects of complete success rather dim, although partial success, a small reduction in the rate of inflation, for example, is possible.

Third and more fundamentally, Carter's economic program fails to deal with the basic long-range problems which created inflation and the current crisis to begin with. As mentioned above, inflation is deeply rooted in the fabric of advanced capitalist political economy. The very deficit spending and monetary policies necessary to stimulate the economy and prevent depressions also help cause inflation. Carter's proposed budget cuts, while severe in the area of social welfare, are inadequate to seriously affect inflation because inflationary military spending is being boosted. The monopoly pricing structures in the heart of the economy — oil, steel, interest rates, automobiles, rubber, and electricity in particular — are largely unaffected by Carter's new programs. Monopoly pricing — based on the fact that most significant industries arc dominated by a few major corporations — is the major source of inflation. Since profit is the basic motive and reason for existence of these companies and little control over them presently exists, higher prices are inevitable. In addition, a new wave of mergers is creating larger, even more dominant economic units at the heights of the American economy, strengthening the remaining monopoly corporations. International factors, largely out of the control of any single nation, also increase inflation and instability in present circumstances. The cartelization and price hikes of some raw materials like oil constitute one example of such a factor.

Another is the class struggle in wealthy nations like France or Italy which stimulates a capital flight to the United States. The rich who bring their money to America make many kinds of investments, but primary among them is land, and such speculative investments drive up the price of scarce land and thus housing as well. The present high cost of housing is largely due to higher land costs, since on-site labor costs have actually declined during the last twenty years.[101] America's very high negative balance of trade during 1977 and 1978 has also created inflation by driving down the value of the dollar.[102] The basic causes are several. First, heightened international economic competition (over the past fifteen years especially) due to increasing world industrial capacity and relative free trade conditions has occurred.[103] Second, prices of some monopolized raw materials like oil have greatly increased during the past five years. Third, the American foreign policy of informal empire has resulted in high military spending abroad, on foreign bases and troops stationed around the world. Finally, the high levels of unemployment in Europe have also kept American exports below what they might otherwise be.[104]

All these factors point out the obvious — economic and political structures of the current system are increasingly inadequate to deal with the problems now emerging. Carter's economic recovery program is much too limited to begin to solve present contradictions. In the short run (that is, during 1980 and 1981), the Carter Administration will have to move to either economic controls or an actual depression to significantly reduce inflation, the latter being the only real "solution" to inflation in a capitalist economy. In the long run, it is unlikely that the problems of the current system can be solved by either real recession or real controls since both cause other problems. Much more fundamental change is required to do that, including first and foremost democratic control of the investment, price and profit system.

Whether or not such fundamental change takes place largely depends on the response of those Americans with a stake in full employment and social justice, equal opportunity, and urban regeneration — the majority of America's working people. To challenge Carter's program demands that they formulate one of their own, since corporate liberalism offers less and less to working people. To take this course there must be a challenge to the fundamental premises of American foreign policy and a willingness to fight for a basic change in the social and economic system at home. Labor must increasingly realize that as long as the present system exists, the structural imperatives of that system will demand that labor's place remain subordinate. As long as the economy is operating under capitalist rules and depends upon capitalist confidence and investment for its prosperity, anything that threatens the capitalist class' interest in profitability becomes a threat to the prosperity of the entire system, a danger which must be curbed to preserve capitalism. As long as no real alternative is posed to a privately owned economy, the state and capitalist class will curb worker power.

The new era of capitalist austerity and the current stage of the corporate state have cracked, if not shattered, the New Deal coalition and long-standing alliance between corporate liberalism and the labor movement leadership. Old alliances arc likely to increasingly collapse and the mass of Americans become more disenchanted with the system. What has Carter done to try to minimize thcsc trends and both maintain the legitimacy of the system and preserve his own popularity and reelection chances in 1980? The next chapter will discuss these questions.

Notes

1. *Dun's Review*, December, 1976, p. 69.

2. *Fortune*, March 27, 1978, p. 53.

3. *Business Week*, December 20, 1976, p. 60.

4. *Los Angeles Times*, September 7, 1975, p. IV 1.

5. *Business Week*, November 29, 1976, p. 23.

6. *New York Times*, February 5, 1978, p. III 1; *Newsweek*, January 9, 1978, p. 52.

7. *New York Times*, July 28, 1978, p. D1; Februrary 5, 1978, III p. 1.

8. *The Nation*, October 29, 1977, pp. 419-420.

9. *New York Times*, February 5, 1978, p. III 1.

10. Jimmy Carter, *Weekly Compilation of Presidential Documents* (Washington, D.C.: U.S. Government Printing Office, 1977) XIII, p. 1858.

11. Ibid., pp. 1861, 1866.

12. Ibid., pp. 1861, 1863.

13. Ibid., p. 1866.

14. *New York Times Magazine*, January 8, 1978, p. 42.

15. *Congressional Quarterly Weekly Review*, September 2, 1978, p. 2304.

16. See for example the comments on lobbying for the end to the arms embargo on Turkey in *Congressional Quarterly Weekly Review* (CQWR), August 5, 1978, p. 2041; on natural gas deregulation, *CQWR*, September 16, 1978, pp. 2452-2454; on the Panama Canal *CQWR*, October 21, 1978, p. 2999.

17. *CQWR*, October 7, 1978, p. 2721.

18. *CQWR*, August 19, 1978, p. 2171; *Guardian*, September 6, 1978, p. 5.

19. *CQWR*, March 11, 1978, p. 655.

20. *CQWR*, July 22, 1978, p. 1839.

21. *CQWR*, August 15, 1978, p. 1777; *New York Times*, April 12, 1978, p. 1; *San Francisco Examiner*, October 7, 1978, p. 2.

22. David Rockefeller's article is reprinted in *San Francisco Sunday Examiner and Chronicle*, November 26, 1978, p. B3.

23. Quoted in *The Progressive*, November, 1978, p. 44.

24. *San Francisco Chronicle,* November 27, 1978, p. 5.

25. *Dollars and Sense,* July-August, 1978, p. 13.

26. *Business Week,* October 24, 1977, p. 32.

27. Ibid.

28. *Wall Street Journal,* July 28, 1978. Patrick E. Haggerty, now general director of Texas Instruments, was a founding member of the Trilateral Commission. When he left, Mark Shepherd, Jr., now the corporation's chairman, joined the Commission. Both men are members of the Business Council, and Shepherd is also a member of the Conference Board and CED.

29. Larry is on the membership committee of the CFR, and a trustee of both the Conference Board and CED.

30. *Guardian,* December 13, 1978, p. 2.

31. *In These Times,* August 16-22, 1978, p. 3.

32. Fraser's statement is reprinted in *In These Times,* August 9-15, 1978, p. 4.

33. According to a Labor Department source quoted by *In These Times,* March 30-April 5, 1977, p. 5.

34. *Seven Days,* May 23, 1977, p. 9.

35. Ibid., and *In These Times,* May 3-9, 1977, p. 2.

36. *Wall Street Journal,* March 7, 1978.

37. Ibid.

38. *Dollars and Sense,* September, 1978, p. 6.

39. *CQWR,* October 21, 1978, p. 3002.

40. *In These Times,* March 8-14, 1978, p. 2.

41. *Guardian,* July 5, 1978, p. 3.

42. *CQWR,* September 16, 1978, p. 2452.

43. Ibid., p. 2453.

44. *CQWR,* October 7, 1978, p. 2721.

45. *CQWR,* October 21, 1978, p. 2999 and *CQWR,* August 5, 1978, p. 2041.

46. *In These Times,* March 8-14, 1978, p. 2.

47. *CQWR,* August 5, 1978, pp. 2035-2036.

48. Ibid., p. 2036.

49. *In These Times,* August 24-30, 1977, pp. 6-7.

50. *CQWR,* December 24, 1977, p. 2641.

51. *CQWR,* May 6, 1978, p. 1097.

52. *CQWR,* October 21, 1978, p. 3000.

53. The Three other Senate members of the Commission — Alan Cranston (D-Calif.); John C. Culver (D-Iowa); and John H. Glenn Jr. (D-Ohio) — did vote for cloture however.

54. *Seven Days,* January, 1978, p. 9.

55. *Seven Days*, May 5, 1978, p. 11.

56. Ibid.

57. Jimmy Carter, *Weekly Compilation of Presidential Documents* (Washington, D.C.: U.S. Government Printing Office, 1977) XIII, p. 1864.

58. *CQWR*, June 10, 1978, p. 1437.

59. Quoted in *Seven Days*, November 10, 1978, p. 7.

60. *San Francisco Sunday Examiner and Chronicle World*, August 20, 1978, p. 9.

61. *In These Times*, August 9-15, 1978, p. 14; *Dollars and Sense*, November, 1978, p. 17.

62. *The Progressive*, December, 1978, p. 8; *Seven Days*, November 10, 1978, p. 7.

63. *CQWR*, October 21, 1978, p. 3001.

64. *San Francisco Sunday Examiner and Chronicle World*, December 17, 1978, p. 12.

65. See *New York Times*, July 24, 1977.

66. *Trialogue*, Summer 1978, p. 3.

67. Ibid.

68. *San Francisco Sunday Examiner and Chronicle World*, May 27, 1979, p. 7; *Guardian*, May 23, 1979, p. 3.

69. *San Francisco Chronicle*, April 27, 1979, pp. 1, 16; *San Francisco Sunday Examiner and Chronicle World*, May 20, 1979, p. 7.

70. *San Francisco Chronicle*, July 17, 1979, p. 16.

71. *Business Week*, April 10, 1978, p. 126.

72. *New York Times*, May 13, 1978, p. 29.

73. Ibid.

74. *New York Times*, May 26, 1978, p. D1.

75. *Dollars and Sense*, July-August, 1978, p. 5.

76. Quoted in *In These Times*, July 12-18, 1978, p. 4.

77. *New York Times*, May 24, 1978, p. D1; *Guardian*, December 20, 1978, p. 5.

78. *San Francisco Chronicle*, December 4, 1978, p. 28; *Newsweek*, November 6, 1978, pp. 33-34; *Guardian*, December 13, 1978, p. 2.

79. *Guardian*, December 27, 1978, p. 3.

80. *CQWR*, November 4, 1978, pp. 3182-3183.

81. *San Francisco Sunday Examiner and Chronicle World*, November 19, 1978, p. 7.

82. *San Francisco Chronicle*, November 30, 1978, p. 29.

83. *San Francisco Sunday Examiner and Chronicle*, November 12, 1978, p. C13.

84. *San Francisco Sunday Examiner and Chronicle World*, November 19, 1978, p. 7.

85. *In These Times*, November 8-14, 1978, p. 3; *CQWR*, October 28, 1978, p. 3182.

86. *San Francisco Chronicle*, December 15, 1978, p. 41.

87. *Guardian*, December 27, 1978, p. 3.

88. *San Francisco Sunday Examiner and Chronicle*, November 26, 1978, p. C12.

89. *New York Times*, January 24, 1978, p. 1.

90. *San Francisco Chronicle*, December 4, 1978, p. 11.

91. *Time*, December 4, 1978, p. 34.

92. *San Francisco Sunday Examiner and Chronicle*, December 17, 1978, p. 12A.

93. U.S. Bureau of Census, *Statistical Abstract of the United States, 1978* (Washington, D.C.: U.S. Government Printing Office, 1978), p. 465.

94. *In These Times*, September 13-19, 1978, p. 19.

95. *Seven Days*, September 8, 1978, p. 22.

96. See Ailon Shiloh and Ida Cohen, *Ethnic Groups in America: Their Morbidity, Mortality and Behavior Disorders* (Springfield, Illinois: C.C. Thomas, 1974).

97. Citibank, *Monthly Economic Letter,* March 1979, p. 3.

98. Citibank, *Monthly Economic Letter,* April 1979, p. 7.

99. United States Federal Trade Commission, *Quarterly Financial Report for Manufacturing, Mining and Trade Corporations, First Quarter, 1979,* (Washington, D.C.: U. S. Government Printing Office, 1979), pp. 11, 16.

100. *New York Times,* December 5, 1978, pp. 1, 20.

101. *In These Times,* May 17-23, 1978, p. 16.

102. The trade deficit was $26.5 billion in 1977 and about $28 billion for 1978. *San Francisco Chronicle,* December 29, 1978, p. 57.

103. *Time,* December 4, 1978, pp. 64-65.

104. Ibid.

6

The 1980 Election and Beyond

The same model of power which has been used to explain Jimmy Carter's rise to the presidency and his particular policies can also be used to investigate the strategies, programs, and potential of the candidates for the 1980 campaign, and examine how the alternatives which will face the voter in November 1980 are now being determined.

In summary, three factors are involved. First, access to a high level of wealth — preferably personal wealth as well as political donations — is a prerequisite for running for any high political office, especially the presidency. A candidate with close ties to a sector of the capitalist class has a tremendous advantage in the race for the White House. Wealth gives a candidate the opportunity to campaign full time, as well as the funds needed to make the campaign a success.

Second, in current circumstances, no candidate is likely to get very far without favorable coverage in the mass media, especially the more prominent and influential media corporations mentioned in Chapter 3. These are the same corporations which are heavily interlocked with the Trilateral

Commission, Business Roundtable, Council on Foreign Relations, Business Council, and the other key policy-planning organizations of the Eastern Establishment. The way to gain such support is for a candidate to demonstrate over a period of years that he or she is "responsible" and is a domestic and foreign-policy "moderate" from the point of view of the establishment.

A final element, although not as critical as the first two, is best labeled charisma or salability. This is often important at the point in the selection process where the voters have some input. Voters essentially choose a favorite among a pre-selected list of acceptable candidates. This process preserves the illusion of democratic control of American politics and gives the winner at least a temporary mandate for carrying out or advocating certain policies. In this respect the outsider-versus-insider and "new face" image-making has some influence as do some of the more individualistic aspects of each campaign, such as better staff, more campaign time, etc. These personal factors must, however, be seen in their secondary context.

The potential of the candidates who are likely to challenge Carter for the presidency in 1980 can be examined, to the extent known, by looking at their ties to two main sectors of the ruling class, their actual and potential sources of financial and media support, and such factors as personal charisma, strategy, staff, amount of campaign time, and so on. The best way to group the candidates is not only as Republicans and Democrats, but also as centrists, with ties to the biggest multinational corporate capitalists, and rightists, with links to the smaller, more regionally and domestically oriented capitalists. All of the widely mentioned 1980 presidential candidates fit into one of these last two basic groups. Two additional potential candidates, and one new political party representing the liberal-labor grouping in America, will also be discussed (see Table 6-1).

Each of these three groups has general characteristics which can be summarized before moving to a discussion of

Table 6-1
PRESIDENTIAL CANDIDATES MENTIONED FOR 1980

Left ──────────── Policy Perspective ──────────── Right

Liberal Labor	Liberal Center	Centrists	Right Center	Rightists
Welfare State Liberals		*Corporate State Conservatives*		*Laissez Faire Ultra-Conservatives*
Harrington	Kennedy	Carter	Connally	Reagan Crane
Dellums	Mondale	Bush	Dole	Kemp
	Stevenson	Baker		Haig
	Culver	Brown	Moynihan	
	Church	Anderson	Ford	
	Weicker	Richardson		
	Hart	Thompson		

Table 6-2

Eastern Establishment Policy Group Connections of Possible 1980 Presidential Candidates

Council on Foreign Relations	*Trilateral Commission*
Anderson	Anderson
Baker	Bush
Church (former)	Carter (former)
Culver	Culver
Bush	Mondale (former)
Mondale	Richardson (former)
Moynihan	Thompson
Richardson	
Stevenson	
Haig	

Atlantic Council Directors	*Conference Board Trustees*
Bush	Connally (former)

The Commitee on the Present Danger

Connally

specific candidates. The right, as was briefly mentioned in Chapter 2, is supported by newer money and medium- and small-sized corporations and is stronger in the southern and western United States and the Congress. It tends to be more special-interest conscious and to define the national interest in a narrower way. It is more "isolationist" in foreign policy; generally opposes the welfare state; and favors a hard line in dealing with unions.* It plans to solve economic problems by weakening and destroying labor unions, cutting the money supply feeding inflation, ending government subsidies to business and other groups, and cutting taxes and government spending sharply.

The center, whose candidates the great majority of the biggest businessmen of America support, is where the old-line, aristocratic upper class, the dominant sector of the ruling class, holds sway. The center is strongest in the East and Midwest, but has representatives and allies all around the nation. It generally controls the executive branch of the federal government. In terms of policy this group is internationalist and interventionist in foreign policy; supports a limited welfare state; and has a de facto alliance with labor leaders in order to use unions as a stabilizing force to prevent the rise of socialist consciousness and help management control the work force. It generally favors using various forms of "incomes policy" (wage and price guidelines) to persuade workers to moderate their economic demands in order to hold down inflation.

The liberal-labor power grouping in America consists of most of the major unions, as well as liberal, women's, and minority organizations. It has only a secondary influence in Congress and the executive branch, and this level of influence has only been achieved through an alliance with the center, an alliance going back many decades. Some in this coalition

---

*Despite the rhetorical excesses of the political right in America, their smaller business backers tend to be less involved in and therefore less interested in foreign markets and investments — and hence less interventionist in practice than liberal Democrats.

are socialist-minded and see the transformation of capitalism
as the only way out of the nation's economic problems, but
feel the only realistic way to influence American society is
through the Democratic party. This group is the most hetero-
geneous and internally divided of the three, with its con-
stituent elements uniting only around the necessity for the
federal government to intervene in economic and social life
in order to extend the general welfare and aid those most
powerless in the country.

Looked at another way, each of these groupings can be
described as mainly representing these constituencies and
ideologies:

The right — smaller businesses and *laissez faire;*
The center — the biggest multinational corporations and
    banks and the corporate state;
The liberal-labor coalition — the working class, its allies and
    the welfare state.

THE RIGHT

Ronald Reagan: The New "Mr. Republican"

Ronald Reagan is far and away the favorite of most political
observers and Republican party leaders to win the 1980
Republican nomination. His candidacy has a number of
strengths, but faces some obstacles as well. On the plus side,
his personal and political finances are in a very healthy state.
While born into the family of a "down at the heels" Illinois
shoe salesman, Reagan worked his way through college and
became a successful Hollywood actor.[1] In 1952 he married
Nancy Davis, the daughter of a wealthy Chicago neurosurgeon,
who shared and reinforced his conservative political views.
By 1976, after nearly forty years in the movies and working
for General Electric Corporation (TV's *Death Valley Days*),
Reagan estimated his net worth at nearly $1.5 million.[2] His
yearly income during the 1970-75 period ranged from a low

of $73,000 to a high of $252,000.[3] Besides the personal wealth, which places him in the top half of 1 percent of American wealth-holders, Reagan has numerous professional and medium- and small-business supporters, giving him an extensive and solid financial base for a run for the presidency. This financial base has been manifested over the past few years primarily in the success of Reagan's political action committee, Citizens for the Republic. Citizens for the Republic raised more money ($2.1 million) during 1977 and the first half of 1978 than any other non-party political action committee in the nation.

Added to his financial advantage is Reagan's charismatic appeal. Few politicians can match his style and glamour on the podium. In an age of television and the politician as actor, Reagan has the professional's advantage. His campaign organization is well staffed and experienced and unlikely to make the mistakes that allowed Ford to win in 1976. The Californian's ultraconservative message is also more in tune than ever with today's smaller, more hard-core Republican party. As the party has shrunk over the past twenty years it has become so influenced by rightists that even a man as conservative as Gerald Ford has found himself positioned in, of all places, the more "liberal" half of his party. These ultraconservatives of the "new right" find their hero in Ronald Reagan, and he represents their best chance to wrest presidential power from the centrists in 1980.

At the same time, these ultraconservatives advocate policies based on their socio-economic interests. Inevitably, their candidate will clash with the dominant sector of the ruling class positioned in and defining the center of the political spectrum. This clash is one of the profound negatives that tends to block a Reagan rise to power — the hostility of the dominant corporations and the national media, the same mass communications corporations which helped bring down Goldwater, McGovern, and Nixon. The "new rightists," including Senator Paul Laxalt (R.-Nev.), Reagan's 1976

campaign chairman, openly state their hostility to the nation's
big business leadership. Their ties with the large corporations
are "just about gone," reports *Congressional Quarterly.*[4]
Laxalt reportedly advised a local chamber of commerce
meeting in Ogden, Utah, to "thumb your noses at big
business. . . you can't count on this sector. . . to represent
. . . free enterprise."[5] He added that the true constituency of
the new conservatives was not the Fortune 500 who are
"playing both sides" (sometimes supporting liberal Democrats
for example), but the "taxpayers and producers in the middle,"
small farmers and businessmen.[6] This orientation is indicated
by the kind of businessmen who have advised and supported
Reagan, men like Holmes Tuttle, a wealthy Los Angeles car
dealer. Also indicative are the audiences to whom Reagan
has been speaking over the past several years, as well as the
messages he has been sending. Reagan, as could be expected,
is especially popular in the more conservative South and
West, where he addresses gatherings of smaller business
groups like the National Association of Truck Stop Operators
or the National Turkey Federation and special interest groups
like dentists, chiropractors, or gun owners.[7] At such meetings
Reagan quips about being "honored to be here with an
endangered species — small businessmen."[8] Then he makes
a set domestic speech about the over-regulation and over-
taxation of the federal government, spiced up with punch
lines like "when you get in bed with the federal government
you're going to get a lot more than a good night's sleep."[9]
On foreign policy matters Reagan rails against America's
"betrayal" of a "friend and ally" like Taiwan, calling for "a
detailed program of specific guarantees to our friends and
allies on Taiwan."[10] A typical foreign-policy theme is that
Carter has not been tough enough on human rights violations
in the USSR and too hard on "friends and allies" like the
governments of Chile and Rhodesia. He favors a large defense
budget, saying that the "foreign scene necessitates our
spending."[11] Reagan's campaign approach is summed up by

his statement that he wants an America of "limited government and unlimited freedom," yet so strong that it would not fear "foreign tyrants or domestic agitators."[12]

Such policy views make Reagan anathema to most centrist big business leaders, including the great majority of Eastern Establishment Republicans as well as the most influential media corporations. Reagan has few ties to these two important groups, so they will be busy during the entire 1980 election period thinking of ways and means of blocking Reagan's nomination and election. The Californian's liabilities are numerous enough to give his enemies lots to talk about. First of all, his right-wing image and past — he actively campaigned for Goldwater and John Birch Society member John Rousselot — will give him problems. His tendency to make extreme statements before thinking them through is also likely to create serious difficulties. For example, Reagan has been quoted as saying during the Vietnam War that the U.S. should "declare war on North Vietnam. We could pave the whole place over by noon and be home for dinner." On student demonstrations he said that "if it is necessary to have a blood bath, let's have it." On the poor looking for free food after the Patty Hearst kidnaping, he said, "It's too bad we can't have an epidemic of botulism."[13]

Reagan is trying to moderate his rightist image, saying that he no longer opposes friendship, trade, and diplomatic relations with China, but only opposes this at the expense of Taiwan.[14] Prior to Carter's decision to grant China full diplomatic recognition some of Reagan's aides, led by lawyer John Sears, were talking about a possible trip to China by the candidate, signaling a more flexible approach to international communism. Sears, one of the less dogmatic of Reagan's advisers, pointed out in his July 1978 discussion with the *New York Times* that Reagan's image as an ultraconservative was his biggest handicap and emphasized that "events may erase that impression."[15] Sears's concern with moving toward the center is especially aimed at making

Reagan a viable presidential candidate once he has secured the nomination. The problem is that this strategy entails the risk of losing part of Reagan's ultraconservative base. For this reason, plus ideological concerns, other Reagan advisers, such as Lyn Nofziger, have opposed watering down the rightist theology, resulting in staff bickering within the Reagan team, and Nofziger's exit from the Reagan campaign staff during the summer of 1979.

Reagan's ties to the dominant centrist sector of the ruling class are limited but hardly nonexistent. One of his longtime supporters is Justin Dart of Dart Industries, who is a member of the Business Roundtable's policy committee. Reagan is also trying very hard to broaden his links to this key power grouping, dispatching supporter Maxwell Rabb, a prominent New York lawyer and a member of the Eisenhower administration, to host an affair at New York's posh 21 Club to try to bring in elements of the Republican center.

It is highly unlikely, however, that Reagan, even if he gains some centrist support, will be able to gain the backing of the key media corporations so important in making and breaking presidents. These guardians of American consciousness are not all-powerful, but they will be able to make an issue of many things in order to undermine Reagan. First of all, the Californian's enemies will make an issue of his age. He will be sixty-nine in 1980. This would make him the oldest man elected president since William Henry Harrison in 1840, who delivered his inaugural address in a driving rainstorm, caught pneumonia, and died a month later. The media can be expected to seize upon any illness or off-day to portray the candidate as too old for the demanding character of the job.

Reagan's acting background and the well-known fact that he writes few of his own speeches will also allow many to argue that he is merely a script-reading actor without the intellect or judgment necessary for the presidency. Furthermore, the Los Angeles speechwriting firm which writes Reagan's

Taiwan lobby

speeches is paid $5000 a month to represent the Taiwanese government in the United States and is registered with the United States government as a foreign agent. The firm, Deaver and Hannaford, Inc., is owned by Michael K. Deaver and Peter D. Hannaford, both of whom worked for Reagan when he was governor of California and have been closely associated with him ever since. The firm writes most of Reagan's speeches, including the scripts for his radio shows and newspaper column. Since it is, at the same time, being paid to create a favorable public image for Taiwan, a conflict of interest is evident. In addition, since under the Foreign Agents Registration Act it is illegal for foreign agents to contribute to American political campaigns — and Reagan is obviously running — Deaver and Hannaford may be in violation of the law.[16] The potential for a widely exposed scandal which could hurt Reagan politically is obvious here and additional investigative reporting might disclose other unsavory details.

The establishment media will stress Reagan's right-wing political perspective in order to discredit him. The *New York Times*, for example, recently editorialized that he has expended his political career on "unworthy causes" and now wants to change his image by cynically making a China trip. The *Times* sarcastically suggested that Reagan should "practice for Peking with a visit to Harlem. And after he has mastered the art of Presidential travel, but only then, he might ask someone to show him the sovereign state of Panama."[17] Reagan's past support of Richard Nixon could also become a general election issue, since Reagan defended Nixon during 1973 and 1974, saying that the President should be believed when he said "I am not a crook."[18] A Reagan also faces other problems in his run for the White House. His control of his own home state of California seems to be slipping, with some of his long-time big business financers defecting to John Connally and George Bush.[19]

Reagan faces another possible problem as the early frontrunner. It is an interesting fact that since 1964 every one of the early leaders for the presidential nomination of the non-incumbent party has failed to be nominated. Nelson Rockefeller in 1964, George Romney in 1968, Edmund Muskie in 1972, and several Democrats in 1976 stood higher in the polls when the campaign began than the eventual nominee. The expectations are high for the frontrunner. He must win in the early primaries to remain a credible candidate, whereas others can place second or third and be promoted as the "surprise" of the year. So the dangers of being the frontrunner — especially in the early caucus in Iowa and primaries in New Hampshire and Massachusetts, where Reagan's greatest strength does not lie — are high. Since at least some Republicans want to win in 1980 and the influential media are sure to play up any faltering on Reagan's part, his candidacy could collapse early, before the Florida and other southern and western primaries where his real strength lies. Finally, there is the danger that another right-wing candidate, Congressman Philip M. Crane (R.-Ill.), will undercut Reagan among his right-wing supporters, splitting the rightist vote and opening the way for a "new face" centrist to win the nomination.

Philip M. Crane — The New Darling of the Far Right

At forty-nine, Congressman Crane is young compared to Reagan. The son of an ultraconservative Illinois psychiatrist, Crane is well educated, with a Ph.D. in history from Indiana University, and is a former history professor at Bradley University. His early political experience included work for both Goldwater and Nixon before he was elected to Congress from a very conservative suburban area north of Chicago. As chairman of the American Conservative Union, Crane has built a small following on the far right of the political spectrum. He is definitely to the right of Reagan and attracts those who feel Reagan has become too moderate, those whom one of Reagan's advisers called "real nuts," adding that "we're better off without them."[20] Crane is apparently an ideological purist, speaking and voting against anything and everything that would involve the federal government in the lives of the people, such as aid to education, welfare spending, consumer protection, busing, and so one. His campaign theme is to free people from excessive government and unreasonable taxation and regulation. He stresses family, religion, and super patriotism. Crane is also, of course, against the Panama Canal Treaty and full U.S. recognition of China.

Crane is not afraid, as Reagan apparently is, to speak out on the so-called "social issues" like crime, drugs, busing, abortion, homosexuality, and the "permissive society" generally. These questions especially interest the far right, since it believes it can gain working-class votes with these issues. Republican centrists criticize the use of social issues to build a stronger party and win power. They feel that economic issues must be the basis because social issues are dangerous and transitory. Republican National Committee chairman and Trilateral Commission member William Brock III, for example, argues that stressing specific social issues is "hazardous for the political system."[21]

What Crane may or may not realize is that he is apparently being used by the centrist Republicans in order to try to deny Reagan the nomination. Former President Ford, currently the de facto leader of the centrist Republicans and a man who very much wants to block Reagan, admitted that he "encouraged Phil Crane to run."[22] Such a strategy may explain why Crane received favorable coverage in *People* magazine in September 1978, which called his family "the cornbelt Kennedys."[23] *People* is owned by Time, Inc., and the editor-in-chief until he retired early in 1979 was Hedley Donovan, a Trilateral Commission member and CFR director. Donovan and *Time* obviously do not want Crane as President and his fringe candidacy is not especially newsworthy. The more likely explanation for the attractive picture and portrait is to build up Crane enough to seriously undermine Reagan.

Initial reports from New Hampshire, where Crane began campaigning in the summer of 1978, the earliest beginning ever, indicate that he has a "strong organization," "substantial support," and is a real threat to Reagan in the state. Even so, Crane's comparative lack of financial backing and the probable long-term hostility of the influential media make it highly unlikely that he will turn out to be more than a "pawn in their game."

Robert Dole

Senator Robert Dole (R.-Kansas), while a man of the right wing, stands closer to the center of the political spectrum than Reagan, one of his main allies. He, like John Connally, stands in roughly the same place in the spectrum as Richard Nixon did. His intense Republican partisanship has made him the darling of many on the right, but a hated figure among Democrats. His alley-fighter style has drawn words of praise from Senator Barry Goldwater, who says he likes Dole because he "will grab the other side by the hair and drag them down the hill."[24]

Dole, the son of a grain elevator worker who operated a cream and egg station, rose to national prominence as a first-term senator when he served as the Nixon administration's "unshakably loyal partisan" during the 1969-71 years.[25] During these years Dole fought for every Nixon policy or appointment, no matter how ill-advised or unpopular. One of Dole's favorite lines was coined by a newspaperman who said, "if you like Richard Nixon, you'll love Bob Dole."[26] His "abrasive style" and "patent ambition" were first noticed during those years. *Time* called him the "new Agnew" and the "administration's No. 1 gunslinger. . . zapping Democrats with Agnewesque zeal."[27] A White House aide said Dole was like a "hungry Doberman pinscher," and one of Dole's Senate colleagues added that "he's the kind of guy I'd like to stand back-to-back with in a knife fight."[28] These kinds of characteristics endeared Dole to both Nixon and Reagan; and these two men, more than any other, have been responsible for Dole's present prominence. Nixon chose Dole to be the chairman of the Republican National Committee, where he served from 1971 to 1973.

As chairman of the Republican National Committee, Dole met and worked with Lyn Nofziger, who had been a Reagan secretary prior to joining the Nixon White House. Nofziger became Dole's top aide and "communications director." According to *Time*, he share's Dole's "instinct for the jugular and the groin."[29] Dole's connections with Nofziger and Reagan got Dole the Republican vice presidential nomination in 1976 when Ford, seeking to unite the party, allowed Reagan to choose among six names submitted to him by Ford.[30]

Dole speaks well of Republicans on the right and center right, saying as early as spring 1973, for example, that Connally, who "represents the broad middle ground" was a "strong contender" for the 1976 Republican presidential nomination.[31] But Dole, unlike some members of the right wing, is also tolerant of centrist Republicans. He supported Rockefeller, for example, for Vice President and said in 1974 that a Ford-Rockefeller ticket in 1976 would be "strong" and "balanced."[32] Dole's fierce ambition leads to a pragmatism that is close to complete opportunism. While every politician changes position in order to take advantage of shifts in the political weather, Dole's changes in position and alliances have sometimes been extremely rapid. Dole stopped defending and abandoned Nixon once it was clear that the President had become unpopular in Kansas. He also halted Kansas speaking invitations to men like Spiro Agnew and Connally, substituting centrists like Eliot Richardson, Edward Brooke, and Lowell Weicker.[33]

While voting with the Republican-Southern Democrat Conservative Coalition the vast majority of the time, Dole is also ideologically more flexible than most rightists, having co-sponsored — with George McGovern no less — food stamp legislation because it was economically beneficial to the farmers of his home state.[34] He also helped sponsor a bill to establish a consumer protection agency and criticized President Ford in 1975 for advocating tax reductions and spending cuts.[35] Thus, when Dole describes himself as a "fiscal conservative" and drapes himself in conservative rhetorical garb, it is within the context of a very pragmatic ideological stance, since, as one observer put it, "Bob Dole would rather be President, period."[36]

Dole's chances for the presidency are not great. He can probably raise enough money to enter the race — although not as much as several other Republican candidates — but his unstatesmanlike public stance in the past makes it certain that he will not be the establishment media's favorite. Dole's Nixon ties and past anti-press statements — in 1972 he labeled the *Washington Post* a "political instrument" of George McGovern which therefore "should expect appropriate treatment" — make sure that there will be much to criticize.[37] The fact that Dole took (and later returned) $15,600 in campaign contributions from the same dairy cooperatives which were accused of bribing John Connally could also be widely publicized as evidence of corruption. It is typical of Dole's pragmatic attitude that when he returned the contribution he admitted no conflict of interest. He likewise did not admit that it was wrong for the chairman of the Republican National Committee with strong White House ties to take contributions from groups under investigation for trying to influence milk price supports set by the administration. Instead, he returned the contribution because it was "bad publicity" and "why take any chances?"[38] He might well have added, "especially for only $15,600." In short, Dole is largely a man in search of a convincing platform and committed constituency. Only if Reagan dropped out of the race would he have much of a chance to gain even the Republican nomination.

THE REPUBLICAN CENTRISTS

John B. Connally, Jr. The *Tribune* of the Corporate State

Former Texas governor and Secretary of the Treasury John Connally stands with one foot on the political center and the other on the right. Although more of a centrist than Dole, Connally also occupies a place similar to Richard Nixon in the political spectrum in that he has tendencies to be a hard line anticommunist, a tough supernationalist, and (more so than Dole) a supporter of an intensified version of the American corporate state. Connally was close to Nixon and in fact was the President's first choice for vice president when Agnew was ousted in the fall of 1973. [39]

The son of a one-time tenant farmer who founded a bus line, Connally got his political start in the late 1930s as Congressman Lyndon B. Johnson's secretary and all-purpose aide. Over the years he became extremely close to Johnson, serving as president and general manager of Johnson's Austin, Texas, radio station and as administrative assistant to Senator Johnson in charge of business contacts. He helped LBJ take over the Texas Democratic party in the mid-1950s and became President Johnson's representative as governor of Texas from 1963 to 1969. In between his political activities, Connally has pursued a successful legal and business career. After obtaining his law degree in 1941, he became the attorney for two independent Texas oil operators, Sid W. Richardson and Perry R. Bass from 1952 to 1961. Since 1969, with time off to serve as Nixon's Treasury Secretary, Connally has been the senior partner in the Vinson and Elkins corporate law firm in Houston and a director of numerous southern and western based corporations, along with a few which are based in New York. He has important international interests and contacts, having invested in land in Monaco and in a Houston bank with two wealthy Saudi Arabian businessmen. At sixty-two years old, Connally now has a net worth conservatively estimated at $2 to $4 million, mostly in Texas ranchland, putting him in the top half of 1 percent of American wealth-holders.[40]

yes

Connally's experience near the top of the American business establishment and at the very top of the political one has made him a nearly unique politician who knows and operates well in both worlds. With his extensive contacts he will be able to raise large amounts of money for his presidential campaign. As early as March 1979 it was reported that Connally's campaign bank account was already loaded with money due to his hard-sell fundraising among businessmen. *Newsweek* quoted one officer of a major corporation as saying, "There is unbelievable pressure to kick in for Connally."[41] Connally's campaign, like Nixon's in 1972, looks like it will be the very best money can buy. Several years ago he also founded the John Connally Citizens Forum to raise funds for Republican candidates and build up political IOUs, and he, like Reagan, Ford, Dole, Bush, Crane, and other Republican hopefuls, spent much time on the road during 1978 speaking for Republican congressional candidates and building up support for the 1980 campaign.

Connally can be labeled the "tribune of the corporate state" because he combines bellicose anti-Russian and anti-communist views with a kind of full-blown corporate statism at home. Unlike the Republicans to his right, he has little use for even verbal laissez-faire, but has a deep and abiding concern for the welfare of the largest corporations and their owners and therefore advocates getting "a partnership going between government and private industry."[42] What this would mean in practice is indicated by a review of some of the programs Connally has promoted during the Nixon administration — federal loan guarantees in the hundreds of millions of dollars for Lockheed and Penn Central, a new Reconstruction Finance Corporation to provide "seed money" for new business and support for oil exploration to move toward energy self-sufficiency. He also supported wage and price controls which zapped labor by holding down wages and allowing prices to rise, as well as a "get tough" nationalistic approach in dealing with America's trade partners and allies.[43] Other Connally ideas have been called "totalitarian" by observers as diverse as Milton Friedman and Nicholas von Hoffman.[44] His current campaign speeches continue to stress the need for government help to business, the need for a hard line on the Soviet Union, and the necessity for effective leadership to "overcome the crisis of the spirit which is assaulting our national resolve."[45] Since Connally's only chance for the nomination lies with attracting conservative voters, he has of late also spoken out for less federal spending, lower taxes, and restraint on social programs.[46]

Centrist Republicans dislike Connally's <u>ultranationalist</u> foreign policy views, especially the protectionist and go-it-alone tendencies in his trade policies as Nixon's Treasury Secretary. <u>These policies were background events in the founding of the Trilateral Commmission</u> which has tried to *yes* <u>reverse the damage</u> which these policies have done. The centrist, Eastern Establishment media are thus likely to view Connally's candidacy negatively. Some signs of this hostility already exist. Nearly every news article on Connally mentions his "wheeler dealer" image and his close association with Nixon and the Watergate scandals of 1973-74. Even though Connally was acquitted of charges of taking a $10,000 bribe as Secretary of the Treasury to support milk price supports, the issue will keep being raised. The *Christian Science Monitor* says his background is such that the question has been raised "in political circles as to whether Mr. Connally may have been irreparably damaged in terms of a presidential bid."[47] James Reston of the *New York Times* warns that, while Connally could be a "formidable candidate," he "is not going to have an easy or very pleasant time."[48] Reston, whose White House contacts are excellent, also reports that no one in the White House is worried by Connally. The kind of coverage that Connally can expect from the Eastern media is perhaps typified by a *Newsweek* article which appeared in late January 1979. The article quotes Congressman John B. Anderson (R.-Ill.), a Trilateral Commissioner and Connally opponent, as saying that Connally's past association with Watergate and Nixon "will inevitably come up. He was very close to Nixon."[49] *Newsweek* also compares Connally to a riverboat gambler, hardly a favorable or positive image for a presidential candidate:

> Like the riverboat gambler he so much resembles, John Bowden Connally goes to Washington this week to enter the biggest poker game of his career. . . . It is the first time in nearly a decade of shadow candidacies that Connally has opened a campaign with his cards face up.[50]

Newsweek, as one of the most liberal of the Establishment media, may be atypically hostile however. Connally, like Reagan, Crane, and others. does have some media support. *Fortune* had a friendly article on him in mid-1978, and *Time* gave him mixed reviews in a long September, 1979 cover story.[51] The *Saturday Evening Post* and the *Country Gentleman*, two magazines owned by the conservative Ser Vaas family of Indianapolis, both have published cover stories on Connally, endorsing him for president. The Ser Vaas operations have close ties to the John Connally Citizens Forum in Houston, and the senior member of the family is a strong Connally supporter.[52] Connally thus has some influential and wealthy supporters. In addition he has such a high level of charisma, the ability to convince and lead people, that one "sage political pro" is quoted as saying he is "like a snake charmer."[53]

Connally's ties with the Eastern Establishment, while stronger than Reagan's, Cranc's, or Dole's, are weaker than the centrist Republicans who will be discussed next. Connally was once a member of the Conference Board. and was a founding board member of the establishment's anti-Soviet organization, the Committee on the Present Danger. This again puts him on the right wing of the centrist corporate state establishment. The Committee on the Present Danger's 141 members include many powerful upper class cold warriors, like Richard Mellon Scaife (the Mellon family), Mary Pillsbury Lord (the Pillsbury family), C. Douglas Dillon, and John M. Cabot; cold war intellectuals like Paul H. Nitze, Norman Podhoretz, Eugene V. Rostow, Dean Rusk, and Bayard Rustin; former military leaders like Elmo R. Zumwalt, Maxwell D. Taylor, and Lyman L. Lemnitzer; wealthy business leaders such as David Packard, John T. Connor, and Henry H. Fowler; and also Lane Kirkland, Secretary-Treasurer of the AFL-CIO.* Packard, whose business contacts are wide — he is also a member of the Business Council, Business Roundtable, Trilateral Commission and Atlantic Council — has in fact agreed to be a fundraiser for the Texan. A list of twenty-four of Connally's corporate supporters published in *Time* magazine included twelve members of the Business Council, five members of the Business Roundtable's policy committee, four Committee for Economic Development trustees, three Council on Foreign Relations members and business leaders like John deButts of ATT, Walter Wriston of Citicorp, and Donald Kendall of Pepsico.[54] While this still leaves plenty of big businessmen outside the Connally camp for Carter, Bush, Baker and others to collect from for their campaigns, it does illustrate that Connally is one of the favorites of a sector of the Eastern Establishment.

George H.W. Bush: The Jimmy Carter of the 1980 Election?

There are several reasons to compare fifty-five-year-old George Herbert Walker Bush's run for the presidency with Jimmy Carter's. His is a relatively obscure "new face," not widely known by the public, and he is not presently holding public office. His campaign strategy involves using these facts to his advantage, both by allowing him to run as an outsider and

*See Appendix 1-F for complete list of Committee on the Present Danger members.

by giving him more time to campaign. Like Carter, he plans to win early in the Iowa caucuses and the New Hampshire and Massachusetts primaries or lose everything, since his main opponents — Reagan, Connally, and Baker — are at the same time potentially weaker in New England and stronger in the later primaries. Most importantly, Bush, like Carter, has both Southern and Eastern Establishment connections. He is, as Carter was when first running for President, a member of the Trilateral Commission.

Bush was born into an aristocratic New England family, the son of Prescott S. Bush, a director of CBS, Dresser Industries, and Prudential Insurance Company, and a partner in the Brown Brothers Harriman and Company investment banking firm. The elder Bush later became active in Republican politics, first as a fundraiser, then as a United States Senator from Connecticut (1952-63). George Bush went to the correct New England schools (Greenwich Country Day School, Andover, and Yale) and made the right contacts. After Bush served in World War II as a pilot, his father got him a position with Dresser Industries to work in the boom days of the Texas offshore oilfields. In Texas, Bush helped found the Zapata Petroleum Corporation, becoming its president and a Texas oil millionaire at an early age.[55]

His financial position secure, Bush turned to politics in the mid-1960s, running a losing campaign for the U.S. Senate in 1964, then succeeding in becoming a Congressman from Houston from 1966 to 1970 and a close ally of Richard Nixon during those years. Nixon, the master of reconciling the two main factions within the Republican party, recognized at an early date the uniqueness and usefulness of George Bush. Bush combined Eastern Establishment refinement and business connections with the expansive outlook and ties of a Texas oil operator. He was thus in a perfect position to satisfy both the Southern and Western ultraconservatives and the Eastern Establishment centrists within the party.

During the 1970-74 years, first Nixon and later Ford

tapped a loyal Bush for a number of important posts — first United Nations ambassador, then chairman of the Republican National Committee, chief of the U.S. Liaison office in Peking, and finally head of the CIA in charge of restoring its image in the aftermath of the exposés of CIA misdeeds. These appointed positions gave Bush the chance to make good contacts and receive exposure among national and international political leaders. Since leaving office, he has been a director of First International Bancshares of Houston, the largest bank holding company in the South and Southwest. It also has a London subsidiary.[56] As could be expected, this bank has wide business connections. Its directors (although not Bush himself) sit on the boards of several small banks, oil and life insurance companies, as well as Braniff Airways, Dr. Pepper, and Pepsi Cola companies.

Bush's background and political and business connections have served him well, putting him in touch with those who can help his run for the presidency. He has been a member of the Council on Foreign Relations since the early 1970s and a director since 1977. Bush was invited to join and became a member of the Trilateral Commission in 1977.[57] During the past few years Bush has also been active in the American Enterprise Institute for Public Policy Research, a rapidly growing Establishment think-tank with a more conservative slant than either the CFR or Trilateral Commission. The leadership of the Institute includes top corporate officials and has interlocks with all of the key policy planning organizations with the exception of the Brookings Institution (see Appendix). These ties make him the Republican presidential candidate best connected to the dominant sector of the ruling class, the Eastern Establishment. Bush is reported to be the "current early favorite" of the Eastern wing of the party.[58]

Bush's personal wealth and ruling-class connections will help him raise enough money to enter the race for the presidency, and these close links will assure that he gets favorable media coverage as a certified centrist, guaranteed to follow the wishes of the Establishment once in high office. Such friendly media coverage has already become noticeable. *Newsweek* reported in August 1978 that Bush was doing "surprisingly" well, "wowing New Hampshire on a first scouting trip," and "has shown the best early foot" there.[59] This immediately reminds one of media's 1975 buildup of Carter. *Newsweek* went on to say that Bush "has a portfolio of imposing credentials" — as well as "a Texas-accented Yankee civility with appeal across ideological lines." *Newsweek* added that the other Republicans have problems:

> Baker, 52, offended the right by supporting the Panama Canal treaties and has lit few fires elsewhere. Connally is bucking advancing age at 61, his *arriviste* standing in the party and the residue of his brush with Watergate — his indictment, trial and acquittal on a charge of bribery. Dole, 55, is in an awkward position of courting the favor of a party that widely blames him and his cut-and-slash campaigning for bringing Ford low in 1976.[60]

Newsweek is not the only Establishment media outlet to begin a buildup of Bush. Jack Germond and Jules Witcover of the *Washington Star* — owned by Time, Inc. — wrote a very favorable article on Bush as early as January 1979. The article was distributed around the nation, appearing in the *Chicago Tribune*, *New York News*, the *Arizona Daily Star*, and other newspapers. The Germond-Witcover article, entitled "George Bush Takes on Reagan," has a large photo of a presidential-looking Bush and begins by saying:

> It is a crisp Saturday morning and a tall, earnest man stands before a crackling fire in an old farmhouse telling why he wants to be president of the United States. It is a scene familiar to his listeners. They remember Kefauver in a similar setting in 1952, Kennedy in '60, Goldwater in '64, Carter and Reagan in '76. This time the man is George Bush . . .[61]

Bush is thus compared to the successful New Hampshire candidates of the past and put in a presidential context.

Calling Bush a "tall earnest man" and putting him in front of a "crackling fire in an old farmhouse" is quite a contrast to Connally as "riverboat gambler." The article goes on to call Bush experienced, a "man of the world" and quotes a local voter as saying that Bush is "great."[62]

There is some evidence that Bush is being backed, in a de facto fashion, by ex-president Gerald Ford. Ford has let Bush have his 1976 general election campaign chairman, Houston lawyer James Baker III.[63] Many former Ford supporters in New Hampshire also now back Bush. Ford's former pollster, Robert Teeter, called one of "the best in the business," has also joined the Bush camp.[64] Other Republican centrists, like Governor William Milliken of Michigan, have been saying positive things about Bush. Bush is also said to have charm. Even well-known right-winger William F. Buckley Jr. said Bush has a "genius for making friends."[65]

A final similarity between Bush and Carter is the relative paucity of information on their past policy positions, stands taken on the nation's domestic and foreign policy dilemmas over the years. The relative lack of a clear and full record — due to neither having held high elected political office on the national level — gave candidate Carter and now gives Bush the opportunity to slant their issue rhetoric to conform with the political imperatives of the moment. In Carter's case, his views were slanted to the liberal side in the 1976 Democratic primaries in order to pick up enough of the liberal-labor vote to win the nomination. Bush is listing to the right in order to gain enough of the conservative vote in the Republican primaries to win the nomination. Bush, for example, says he opposes the Panama Canal Treaties. In actuality, both Bush and Carter are the ultimate in pragmatic centrists, men dedicated to serving the interests of the largest multinational corporations and banks. A Bush presidency would probably be only marginally different from Carter's.

Howard Baker: The 'Great Compromiser' of 1980?

Howard H. Baker, Jr., of Tennessee, the Senate's minority leader and thus currently the highest Republican elected official in the United States, is attempting to put himself, often with success, in the political center of the Republican party. In this position, he is trying to become the bridge between the party's two major factions, the "great compromiser" who can win the nomination and unify the party enough to win in 1980. In major party debates, such as at the "tidewater Conference" in early 1979, Baker succeeded in putting himself at the center of the debate and got consensus on the major issue — the Republicans will no longer support the tradition of bipartisanship in foreign policy. This potential healer of the party, although at the political center of the GOP, sometimes takes right-wing policy positions in order to appeal to the ultraconservative sector of the Republicans.

Baker is a native of Huntsville, Tennessee, a town, according to a neighbor of Baker quoted by *People* magazine, "built around the Bakers. It's like a feudal setting, and Howard was raised very much the lord of the manor."[66] Baker's father and two grandfathers were all politically prominent as lawyers, judges, and sheriffs. His father was a member of the United States House of Representatives from 1950 to 1964. Young Howard was educated at private schools and became a lawyer himself. As an attorney he obtained light sentences for his criminal clients and represented several major coal corporations in legal actions against the United Mine Workers. He was also active in business, becoming part owner of a local bank and making large real estate investments.[67] In 1951 he married Joy Dirksen, the daughter of the late Senator Everett Dirksen (R.-Ill.).

This background has assured that Howard Baker, Jr., was "financially well-off," as the *New York Times* put it, and had enough money and support to get elected to public office as a Senator in 1966.[68] That he can command reasonably large amounts of political money is indicated by the fact that he raised nearly $2 million for his reelection effort in 1978.[69] Since becoming a Senator he has joined the Council on Foreign Relations (in 1974); and Henry Kissinger, now a CFR director and an executive committee member of the Trilateral Commission, is one of Baker's advisers.[70] Baker can thus be said partially to represent, in the area of foreign policy especially, the views of the Eastern Establishment and Kissinger. (Baker voted for the Panama Canal treaties.) The current hard line-soft line division within that establishment and the CFR over the SALT II treaty has allowed Baker to oppose it, pleasing the right wing of the Republican Party, while not alienating the centrists of the Eastern Establishment. Baker had angered the rightists by voting yes on the Panama Canal issue, but by doing so he signaled his stature as a "statesman" to the establishment media, which duly rewarded him with favorable coverage. James Reston of the *New York Times* said, while the Panama Canal debate was still on, that Baker faced his "first major test" as a presidential hopeful on the Canal issue, adding that "so far he has handled it with admirable care and skill."[71] Tom Wicker of the *Times* argued that the heavy pressure on Baker to vote no served him well, since it showed that Baker will not knuckle under to transient moods and movements.[72] Baker gambled that he could get establishment media support with a yes vote on Panama and recover enough of the right wing to win nomination by taking a hard line on other issues. So far this strategy appears to be working. Certainly, the *New York Times* likes Baker, calling him "articulate," "witty," "urbane," "easygoing," "dapper," "youthful looking," and "polished" all in one article.[73] *People* magazine, owned by Time, Inc., called him "very possibly" the Republicans' "best hope for President in 1980," and included several big Carteresque pictures of a toothy, smiling Baker with his family in folksy settings in its April 3, 1978 issue.[74] This favorable coverage, along with Baker's CFR ties, indicate that the establishment media will probably give him the support he needs to make a serious run for the presidency.

Some of Baker's more recent actions, such as his "no" vote on labor law revision, his hard-line stance on SALT II, and his support for a constitutional amendment to balance the federal budget, suggest that he is now focusing more on gaining the confidence of the rightists. If he can succeed moderately well in this, he might win the nomination from a faltering frontrunner and possibly even the election.

Some negatives working against Baker include his friendship with Nixon and the fact that, as Senate Minority Leader, Baker does not have the free time for a full time campaign schedule, which Reagan, Connally, and Bush do. Baker may have to play a waiting game, hoping that none of the numerous Republican primary candidates emerges as a clear winner. He would then be in an excellent position to use his parliamentary skills and fence-mender image and reputation to win the nomination at the convention.

Republican Dark Horses: Kemp, Haig, Ford, Thompson, Anderson, and Richardson

These rightist and centrist Republicans hope to have some influence in 1980, but almost no one expects them to gain the nomination. The most that any of them can hope for is a kingmaker role at the convention or behind the scenes in the primaries or a vice presidential bid.

The only far right-winger in this group is Jack Kemp, the upstate New York Congressman. He gained prominence by co-sponsoring (with Senator William V. Roth of Delaware, a rightist member of the Trilateral Commission) a tax reduction measure that would cut federal taxes by one-third. As a Reaganite, Kemp is pledged to support Reagan if he runs, but if the former California governor loses the nomination to a centrist, Kemp could be the vice presidential choice to unite the party. He is maintaining a high profile with speaking engagements for this reason as well as because he has Senate ambitions.

General Alexander Haig, a CFR member, is another vice presidential possibility. He has resigned his post as NATO commander and is getting publicity by speaking out on what he perceives as the Soviet threat to the West.

Former President Gerald R. Ford hopes to be 1980's kingmaker and has allowed most of his campaign apparatus to go to George Bush. If Bush and the other centrist Republicans fail to defeat Reagan in the early primaries, Ford may enter the race as the only hope to defeat Reagan. Ford fears that the Reaganites would destroy the party and holds a grudge against Reagan since he believes that the Californian's 1976 challenge cost him reelection. He is therefore likely to go all out to sabotage the former governor.

Illinois governor and Trilateral Commissioner James R. Thompson clearly wants to be President, but apparently has decided that 1980 is not the best year for him to make a full-scale effort. He is probably open to a vice presidential slot, of course, but can otherwise be expected to try in 1984 or 1988.

Congressman John B. Anderson of Illinois, a CFR member and Trilateral Commissioner, also has presidential ambitions and has been exploring the possibility of running to try to gain higher office and end the danger of right-wing control of the Republican party. His close Eastern Establishment connections give him favorable media exposure, but the most that he can hope for is a vice presidential bid.

Elliot L. Richardson, now an Ambassador-at-Large for Carter, has been called the GOP's "other George Bush." He, like Bush, is a New England aristocrat, has held numerous appointive positions in the federal government, and is a certified centrist — a former CFR director and Trilateral

Commissioner. He is frequently mentioned by the media as a potentially attractive candidate and may get his chance as a vice presidential selection.

THE DEMOCRATIC CENTRISTS

Edmund G. Brown, Jr.: Out-Cartering Carter

Governor Edmund G. "Jerry" Brown of California is only one of two Democratic politicians that White House politicos are afraid of. Patrick Caddell, the president's pollster and pollster and political operative called Brown as early as December 1976 the "largest single threat" to Carter's re-election.[75] *Business Week,* quoting an unnamed insider, reported in mid-1978 that White House fear of Brown "borders on paranoia." The reason is not difficult to find. Brown is one of the best politicians in America, is actively running for President, and is trying, with some success, to present himself, as Carter did, as an unorthodox, pragmatic, and ideologically neutral political outsider. In short, Brown is attempting to tap, as Carter did, support from all sides of the political spectrum — liberal, center, and right. The problem, from Carter's perspective, is that Brown can, in Brown's words, "go left and right at the same time" better than Carter can.[76]

Brown has some advantages over Carter in the 1980 presidential duel now shaping up. First of all, Brown is the one running as the outsider this time. As someone unconnected and opposed to the Washington establishment, he can speak about national questions without the responsibilities of national power. Second, Brown is very bright, articulate, and convincing in the give and take of debate. Brown has studied the use of media in politics extensively, taking pains to be "cool" when on television and paying close attention not only to the actual messages he projects, but the subliminal ones as well. Third, he is also trying to build on symbols, on an image as a man even more fiscally conservative and personally frugal than Jimmy Carter. He supports constitutional action to balance the federal budget, criticizes too much government regulation, lives in a modest two-bedroom apartment, and rides to work in a Plymouth instead of a Cadillac limousine as Carter does. Finally, Brown's record as governor has a something-for-everyone quality that will, Brown hopes, allow him to gain support from across the political spectrum — left, right, and everything in between. He has accomplished this in California, becoming quite popular in a large and economically, socially, and politically diverse state. Some examples of Brown's policy inconsistencies and the political results include:

1. A strong stand against the death penalty. Brown vetoed legislative efforts to reinstate capital punishment. Even though the veto was later overridden by a two-thirds vote, it prompted liberal support. At the same time, however, Brown supported increased prison construction, longer prison sentences for repeating offenders, and improvements in police technology. The latter programs gained him the support of conservative police officer associations in California.

2. Brown gained liberal and labor support for helping California farmworkers and public employees gain collective bargaining rights, as well as appointing labor leaders, women, and minorities to high state posts. State AFL-CIO head John Henning became a University of California Regent, Rose Bird became Chief Justice of the State Supreme Court, and blacks and Chicanos gained judicial posts in unprecedented numbers. At the same time, Brown said he would limit government regulation of business, slapped a pay freeze on California's public employees, and advocated tax cuts and constitutional changes to insure a balanced budget at both the state and federal levels, as favored by conservatives.

Brown, like Carter, is thus a man of the "new breed" of Democrat, inconsistent and therefore impossible to easily categorize ideologically. This inconsistency can, of course, be an asset or a handicap depending on how the candidate is perceived by the mass of voting Americans. Is the man seen mainly as merely an unprincipled opportunist or as a statesman bending to the will of the people? Both interpretations are possible; which one wins depends on objective circumstances and the candidate's ability to convince business, political leaders, the media and voters.

Jerry Brown, forty-one, is no newcomer to politics. His father, Edmund G. "Pat" Brown, rose through the political ranks from San Francisco's District Attorney to State Attorney General, then to Governor of California from 1958 to 1966. Jerry experimented with the counter-culture movement; participated on the fringes of the civil rights, farm workers, and antiwar movements in the 1960s; and went to Yale law school, receiving his degree in 1964. He ran for Secretary of State in 1970, trading, as fellow Catholic Edward M. Kennedy did in his early political career, on the fame of the family name. Supported by the liberal-labor-minority coalition of the California Democratic party, Brown ran and won the governor's chair in 1974 and was reelected in 1978. He made a brief bid for the presidency in 1976, entering late, but beating Carter and the other candidates in several primaries, giving him exposure and increasing Brown's confidence about his ability to win on the national level.

While his personal net worth is "only" in the hundreds of thousands, in past campaigns Brown has shown an ability to raise large amounts of money from corporate leaders, individual businessmen, labor unions, and the entertainment industry centered in Hollywood and Los Angeles.[77] In the 1978 state election, for example, Brown was able to raise over $3 million, with large contributions coming from sources as diverse as Best Chevrolet of Modesto, California, and Tiger Oil of Houston (over $30,000 each); the Teamsters Union ($15,000); Bank of America ($11,600); the Hollywood Turf Club ($10,000); Western Airlines ($5,000); Jane Fonda ($1,300); and a $45,000 bank loan guaranteed by singer Helen Reddy and her husband Jeff Wald.[78] These last two contributions reflect

Brown's support from Jane Fonda and Tom Hayden's Campaign for Economic Democracy, a grassroots California political organization, and the Los Angeles music industry where Brown has good connections as a close friend of singer Linda Ronstadt. Other supporters include Music Corporation of America's board chairman Lew Wasserman, who also helped Carter in the early stages of his run for the presidency, as well as Richard Silberman, Brown's finance chairman and former banker and top executive of the Jack-in-the-Box fast food chain. These kinds of connections and the additional contacts they can bring assure that Brown will have adequate, if not substantial, funds for a run for the White House. On a spring 1979 trip east for the National Governors' Conference, Brown proved his access to campaign financiers by meeting with numerous important political fundraisers, such as Howard Stein, president of Dreyfus Corporation, General Motors chairman Thomas Murphy, Ford chairman Henry Ford II, the top executives of fifteen major corporations which do business in California, United Auto Workers president Douglas Fraser, AFL-CIO leaders, Manhattan Borough president Andrew Stein, and the presidents of six national Jewish organizations representing millions of American Jews.[79]

Brown's ties with the Eastern Establishment are, however, apparently minimal. Brown and his key advisers do not belong to any of the major policy organizations of the dominant sector of the ruling class. A leader of at least one of these organizations, Joseph A. Pechman, the director of economic studies at the Brookings Institution, one of the more liberal of the policy organizations, has taken a hardline anti-Brown stance. He has argued in regard to Brown's balanced budget position that "Jerry Brown is being counterproductive in our economic system — he is an opportunist. I hope this proves to be his political deathknell."[80] Brown does, however, have some indirect Eastern Establishment ties through some of his appointments, campaign contributors, and his father's legal and political connections. Brown has appointed at least one member of the Committee for Economic Development to a state advisory board, for example. As previously mentioned, leaders of the Bank of America donated heavily to his 1978 reelection campaign and the chairman of that bank was a founding member of the Trilateral Commission. Brown's father has, as a Los Angeles lawyer, legal ties with O'Melveny and Meyers, a corporate law firm with close big business and policy group ties. One member of that firm, Warren Christopher, was one of the Trilateral Commission members who joined the Carter Administration's State Department. The lack of close ties to the Eastern Establishment and its media outlets, together with his lack of political principle (and thus the inability to predict what he would do once in office), mean that Brown's shortcomings, faults, and style will come under attack in the establishment media.

Some signs of media hostility already exist. It is no accident, for example, that it was the pro-Carter *New York Times* which sent an investigative reporter to probe Brown's campaign contributions for material that could be damaging to the governor's reputation and campaign efforts. Not surprisingly, information about Brown's connections to shady characters and questionable deals made by the state on behalf of these interests were uncovered and reported by the *Times* and then picked up by other newspapers.[81] The details of the case — it involved a wealthy Mexican oil family with business dealings with California state and local government which may have made unreported donations to the Brown campaign — are less important than the fact that in the corrupt world of American politics there are unreported scandals behind nearly every campaign but the *Times* made a special effort to uncover and publicize the scandals behind Brown's to raise questions about the Governor's integrity.

A more subtle put-down of Brown was the January 1978 article which *Time* ran on Brown's energy plans. Under a drawing of Brown on a horse tilting at a windmill, *Time* made Brown's desire to turn to alternative energy sources like wind, solar, wood chips, and walnut shells seem ridiculous, quoting the governor as saying "walnut shells actually work."[82] The article then recounts Brown's plan for a state space program with a space academy and ends the article by quoting a Brown detractor as saying, "Jerry has always been a little spaced-out, but this is carrying things too far."[83]

Less subtle were the questions Joseph Kraft asked Brown in an early 1979 interview. He and James Reston of the *New York Times* are probably the two journalists most closely tied to the Eastern Establishment. Kraft asked Brown if he were not simply an opportunist and, in the wake of the People's Temple and Moscone-Milk killings, "just the most prominent political example of the California flake?"[84] Brown handled Kraft's questions well enough for the journalist to conclude that if Brown doesn't have all the answers he "usually has most of the comebacks." Kraft concluded that ". . . Brown remains to me the most interesting figure in American politics. He is smart and adroit and quick. If he enters the presidential primaries, as he almost certainly will, he will be coming at Jimmy Carter not from the right, but from all directions."[85] After interviewing Brown, James Reston came to a similar conclusion, saying that Brown ". . . is still the most interesting, if the most unpredictable, personality in American politics today, and win or lose, he will at least bring some new and arresting questions into the presidential campaign of 1980."[86] Such grudging respect for Brown indicates that, despite Brown's opportunistic stance and weak ties to the Eastern Establishment, he could become acceptable to it with more contact. The very fact that Brown has received extensive media attention indicates that he is at least marginally acceptable to the establishment, in contrast to black Congressman Ronald Dellums, for example, who is also considering a run for the presidency, but is receiving almost no media coverage.

There are not yet any other definite signs of this acceptability, however. *Business Week* says Brown has recently "discovered" business and is making an effort to increase his ties. But the magazine also says that Brown's effort has "flopped" and quotes the president of the California Manufacturers Association as saying "most business people still view him with suspicion."[87] However, the California Manufacturers Association is part of the more conservative segment of the California business community, and, as noted, Brown received a big campaign contribution from the Bank of America, a central institution in the California business scene. Brown has proved willing to cater to business in the past, as part of his "go with the flow" style — adjusting to existing power forces. His firing of James Lorenz, director of the state's Employment Development Department, during his first term is most instructive in this regard. In order to reduce the state's high unemployment levels, Lorenz proposed a program of public service employment, a state bank and development corporation, and disclosure regulations for the loan policies of insurance companies and banks. Lorenz rapidly came under attack from the right wing and the California business establishment, so Brown fired him. Brown replaced Lorenz's program with an advisory committee from the leadership of California's corporate giants, including Bank of America, Pacific Telephone and Standard Oil of California.[88]

A final element in any assessment of Jerry Brown and his 1980 presidential chances must include judgments about his chances for gaining the support of the liberal-labor coalition, the sector of the Democratic party most disaffected from Jimmy Carter. Here the evidence is again mixed; some segments of the coalition still speak highly of and support Brown, others blast him and some do both. The ambivalence about Brown in the labor movement is perhaps typical. The California state labor movement was basically in the Brown camp until the last six months of 1978, when Brown changed position on key economic questions, supporting lowered property tax rates and a national balanced budget and opposing pay raises for state employees. Until then Brown's ties with the state and national AFL-CIO were better and stronger than Carter's. As one top AFL-CIO official put it in mid-1978, "Brown's paid his debts to us."[89] The president of one large national union, the Service Employees, said in early 1979 that he will support Brown against Carter, adding that his first choice is Edward M. Kennedy.[90] Brown is also wooing leading anti-Carter labor leaders (like George Meany and Douglas Fraser, president of the UAW), meeting with them, exchanging ideas, and building support.

On the other hand, Brown's support for a constitutional amendment and, if necessary, a constitutional convention to insure a balanced federal budget has angered many labor leaders, who call it a right-wing proposal. Jack Henning, state AFL-CIO head, said, "it's Herbert Hoover all over again."[91] Still, on balance, labor's disillusionment with Carter is so great that many will probably back Brown as the only effective way to "send a message" to the White House. One liberal grassroots California group, Tom Hayden and Jane Fonda's Campaign for Economic Democracy, has supported Brown in the past because he has allowed them some small level of access to state power. Hayden says,

> I would prefer for us to deal with Jerry Brown, who represents an alternative energy path and entry into political power for groups like CED [Campaign for Economic Democracy] and the UFW [United Farm Workers], than with Younger [Brown's opponent in the 1978 governor's race], who would exclude us and probably try to repress us.[92]

Following his 1978 election victory Brown appointed Hayden California's representative on the Southwest Border Regional Commission, an inter-state body designed to promote economic development along the Mexican border.[93] Brown's ties with Hayden and Fonda help him with anti-war, anti-nuclear power constituencies, and the governor has also acquired former Vietnam war critic Daniel Ellsberg as a foreign policy adviser.[94]

At least some other liberal groups who are anti-Carter,

such as the Americans for Democratic Action, definitely will not be supporting Brown. An ADA leader denounced him in February 1979 as a Joseph McCarthy kind of figure, "a pandering demagogue," who is "catering to baser mob instincts," a man who "will do or say anything — even risk the destruction of the Bill of Rights — in his pursuit of power."[95] Brown's quick shifts of position may lead more people to label him an opportunist and demagogue, destroying the trust needed to get votes, let alone rule. In this respect he is a gambler and maverick. Brown does see himself as the only man raising certain questions and putting certain issues on the agenda for discussion. On the balanced budget issue, for example, Brown says his call for a constitutional convention will open up a debate on priorities, with military spending, the health, education, and welfare budget and others open to new scrutiny. Interestingly enough, he is the only candidate talking about the possibility of a more intense level of class struggle emerging in the near future — he wants to head it off — as well as the strong possibility of "hard times ahead."[96] The way to avoid these serious problems, Brown argues, is to cut government spending in order to reduce inflation and free private money for investment, technological development, and increases in productivity. According to Brown, these changes in turn would create long-run prosperity. Brown believes that controlling inflation is the "historic role" of the Democratic party. Just as Nixon had to be the one to go to China, big spending Democrats must stop inflation. Brown's other proposals include a cut in foreign aid to dictatorships, a stress on investment in new energy sources like solar, wind, and geothermal, and the creation of Common Market type arrangements among Canada, Mexico and the United States. Such an arrangement would create a very strong economic unit and give the United States more easy access to key raw materials like oil. It is safe to say, however, that the problems of late capitalism in America are too serious to be solved by Brown's approach.

Denying a sitting President renomination is very difficult and, in fact, has not been done in this century. Brown is also unpopular with party leaders and the political establishment generally, but he has seized on a very popular issue in the balanced budget idea. Over 70 percent of Americans agree with it. In this time of crisis and relative political fluidity, it is possible, but not likely, that Brown could ride the issue to the White House.

Edward M. Kennedy: The Next President?

Edward M. Kennedy, 47, the last of the Kennedy brothers, took a long time to decide that he really wanted to be President, resisting temptation to become an active candidate in 1968, 1972, and 1976. That 1980 will be different is indicated by the establishment of an official campaign committee, the active campaign role now played by members of his immediate family, and the increasingly sharp attacks on Jimmy Carter's Presidential failings. Kennedy's opposition to Carter's policies on national health insurance, social welfare budget cuts and sale of advanced U.S. jet airplanes to Saudi Arabia has been well publicized. Less well known is the fact that Kennedy has been one of the President's strongest Senate supporters, with only one senator having a more pro-administration voting record during Carter's first two years in office. In actuality, then, there would probably be little difference between a Kennedy and a Carter presidency. Kennedy would offer a little more social welfare, perhaps slightly less defense spending, but the real thrust and content of domestic and foreign policy would be essentially the same. Unless popular pressure could push him to act against corporate power, the only thing different about a Kennedy presidency might well be the ability to sell those policies at home and abroad. Kennedy's superior speaking ability, style, and charm could give Carter's policies a new lease on life.

Personally a member of the American aristocracy with inherited wealth in the millions, Kennedy has close ties to key figures of the Eastern Establishment. He can raise large amounts of campaign money very quickly and he generally receives favorable coverage from the central organs of the establishment media. He has good connections to the most important policy organizations of the dominant sector of the ruling class. For example, of his five current advisers in the key area of national economic policy, one, Walter W. Heller of the University of Minnesota, is a member of the Trilateral Commission and the other four — Joseph A. Pechman, Arthur M. Okun, Alice M. Rivlin, and George L. Perry — are present or former leaders of the Brookings Institution's economic studies program, the same organization which supplied Charles L. Schultze, Barry Bosworth and other Carter Administration economic planners. In addition, Okun and Rivlin are members of the Council on Foreign Relations, and Perry is a member (as Schultze was) of the Committee for Economic Development's Research Advisory Board.[97]

Furthermore, his close Senate allies, John Culver (D.-Iowa) and Alan Cranston (D.-Calif.) are both Trilateral Commission members and Culver is also in the CFR. Culver is very close to Kennedy, his college roommate at Harvard. Culver served as Kennedy's legislative assistant, and in turn received help from Kennedy in his Senate race in Iowa. Another close family friend, Theodore Sorensen, is a very active CFR member. At least some of Kennedy's old establishment friends from the days of Camelot, men like Robert S. McNamara, McGeorge Bundy, and others, who felt they were "the best and the brightest," are now likely to rally to a Kennedy candidacy now that the Senator has decided to run.

Two interconnected circumstances, concerning both the ruling class and party politics levels of American politics, have convinced Kennedy to end his long flirtation with the presidency. First, serious economic problems, together with President Carter's inability to rally the American people behind him and his programs, have created a crisis of confidence which threatens to undermine the political stability which has been taken for granted for so long by America's rulers. Connected with this is the fact that incumbent Democratic politicians are increasingly in danger of being blamed for the crisis and voted out of office. Since twenty-four Democratic Senators are up for reelection in 1980, it is quite possible that, with Carter at the head of the ticket, the party could lose control of the Senate, depriving Kennedy of his own position as head of the powerful Judiciary Committee. Therefore the Draft Kennedy movement included many Democratic Senators along with prominent labor leaders, Hollywood entertainers and representatives of the old aristocracy (the Draft Kennedy movement in New Hampshire, for example, was headed by a woman named Dudley Webster Dudley, whose ancesters include Daniel Webster and Thomas Dudley, Deputy Governor of Massachusetts while John Winthrop ruled that colony in the 1630s).

Polls show that Kennedy has more charisma than any other possible candidate in 1980, much more than Carter; he can inspire and mobilize people rapidly. Certainly the Republicans fear him more than any other Democrat. The reasons for Kennedy's popularity are clear. His family connection, as the last of the fabled Kennedy brothers, men who are now part of the heroic folklore of American politics, makes him an instant celebrity and a kind of president in exile. He is the inheritor of the myth of Camelot, snatched from the American people by gunfire in November 1963 and June 1968. Although Kennedy rarely, if ever, refers to this connection in his speeches, should he decide to, it would be powerfully persuasive. Kennedy is also the last big-name liberal, a man who probably could reconstruct and perhaps even maintain for a time the old Roosevelt New Deal coalition. Changes in the American political economy make such a coalition impossible in the long run, but Kennedy could probably achieve a short run success in resurrection.

Kennedy's entry means that there will be a bitter fight over the Democratic presidential nomination, a fight which could well leave the party seriously divided for the Fall confrontation with the Republicans. Kennedy's strategy is to try and minimize the dissension and damage by steamrolling Carter early in the primaries, proving his contention that Carter can not lead, then reunite the party in time for the general election. Since he has excellent contacts in Iowa, New Hampshire and Massachusetts, where the first caucuses and primaries are held, his strategy is sound. Whatever the outcome, his race for the Presidency will make the 1980 election year one of the most dramatic ever.

Darkest Democratic Horses — Moynihan, Hart, Mondale, Church, Stevenson, and Culver

These center right, centrist, and center left Democrats may have some influence in 1980, but it is unlikely any of them will gain the nomination. These men have both connections and high ambitions, however, so they are men to watch in the 1980s.

The most conservative is Senator Daniel P. Moynihan (New York), who is a Council on Foreign Relations member. He is a favorite of the "neo-conservative" movement and has enough support from the Jewish community and hard-line cold warriors in the labor movement to give him a solid financial and organizational base. In the future he is likely to inherit many of the political supporters of Senator Henry Jackson of Washington, a fellow cold warrior. Moynihan will not challenge Carter in 1980, however, unless the political maverick Jerry Brown defeats Carter first and other factors look good.

Senator Gary Hart of Colorado ran George McGovern's 1972 presidential campaign, but has moved to the right politically since then. Hart is young, attractive, and ambitious, and could be influential in future Democratic politics.

Vice President Walter Mondale will almost certainly enter the campaign if, for some reason, Carter withdraws. He has good Eastern Establishment connections as a CFR member and former Trilateral Commissioner and close ties with many traditional Democratic constituencies as well — the Jewish community, black leaders, organized labor, farmers, and liberal activists. If Carter withdrew, Mondale would have to finesse the fact that he was the President's man for so long. Such maneuvering might prove to be impossible.

Senator Frank Church (Idaho), a former member of the CFR, beat Carter in several late primaries in 1976, showing he has ability and presidential interest. As the new chairman of the Senate Foreign Relations Committee, Church will be in the public eye and has a forum to criticize Carter should the President blunder. He is not likely to enter the race, but given the fluidity of events, he cannot be counted out.

Senator Adlai Stevenson III (Illinois), a CFR member, announced in early 1979 that he was considering a run for the presidency. With his father's nationally known name (his father was Illinois governor and two-time Democratic presidential nominee), he has the advantage of instant ballot recognition. He is a liberal and can expect to attract many Democratic liberals disillusioned with Carter. He can probably get minimally adequate funding and some media support. Stevenson's sincerity has been questioned, however, since the first person to let reporters know that Stevenson was considering the race was Robert Strauss, one of Carter's most trusted advisers. Carter himself could use Stevenson (or someone else for that matter) as a stalking horse to divide the anti-Carter vote in some key primaries, allowing the President to emerge victorious against Brown and Kennedy.[98]

Senator John C. Culver (Iowa) is another CFR member who, once he was named to the Trilateral Commission, began to be mentioned as a possible future President. Culver is a very close Kennedy ally and would probably play an important role in a future Kennedy administration. His chances in 1980 are limited, except as a possible vice presidential candidate for a nominee who needs Kennedy and Eastern Establishment connections.

The Liberal-Labor Grouping: Harrington, Dellums and the Citizen's Party

Finally, there are two possible candidates and one newly established third party at the liberal-left end of the American political spectrum who should be mentioned. Michael Harrington and Congressman Ronald Dellums (D.-California) are both members of the Democratic Socialist Organizing Committee (DSOC) and Harrington is also its chairman. It is a mildly socialist organization dedicated to change through work in the Democratic party and with liberals, academics, and labor leaders. DSOC hopes to turn the liberal-labor grouping on the left side of the existing political spectrum into a socialist coalition for change. Since the American political spectrum is skewed to the right, the left wing of the Democratic party, as represented by DSOC, is no further left than the mainstream of the British Labor Party, the German Social Democratic Party, or the French, Spanish, Portuguese, or Swedish socialist parties, several of whom have been ruling parties in their respective countries.

Both Harrington and Dellums have been discussing the possibility of running an "educational" campaign to challenge Carter on fundamental issues. Neither has yet decided to definitely run, but both agree that Carter must have a challenger on the left. Harrington, who supported Carter in 1976, is part of the waiting-for-Kennedy crowd, saying that the Massachusetts senator is the "optimum" candidate because he could win in 1980, ignoring the fact that Kennedy's policy approach is nearly identical to Carter's. Harrington also states that if he ran, he would run basically as a liberal and not raise socialist issues. [99]

A leader of the congressional black caucus, Dellums was first elected as an anti-Vietnam war spokesman. He appears to be more ready to raise explicitly socialist issues like worker control of corporations, socialized medicine and national ownership of the railroads within the context of what he calls "economic democracy."[100] Dellums has not yet decided to enter the race, but in any case his outline of a program does not address the basic issue of how to solve the economic crisis facing the United States and much of the world. For that a more fundamentally radical approach is needed. To enter the campaign seriously, Harrington and Dellums would also need a large amount of money. Dellums estimates $5 million to start and the potential for raising $20-35 million.[101] There is no sign yet that he or any other representative of the labor-liberal coalition can raise such sums. If a Dellums or Harrington campaign organization started early and carried out mass mailings, however, enough money might be gathered to at least run an educational campaign and raise issues which desperately need to be part of America's public debate.

With Dellums and Harrington still weighing a run for the presidency within the Democratic party, a new organization, calling itself the Citizen's Party, has decided to break with both major parties, and declare its intention to field a presidential candidate in 1980. The new party has the long-range goal, over the next decade, of regenerating American democracy by replacing one of the two major parties, much as the Republican replaced the Whig party in the 1850s.

Its immediate goals are to begin by running a candidate, probably environmentalist Barry Commoner, and to raise many of the key issues which both major parties now ignore: the need for public control of the energy industries, a halt to the development of nuclear power, a push for energy conservation and solar energy, a sharp cut in military spending, an end to support to repressive foreign governments, guaranteed full employment, stable prices for the basic necessities of life, and citizen control of the giant corporations which dominate the American economy.[102] While raising these fundamental issues they hope to get 5 percent of the 1980 vote and lay the basis for future gains. Since most of the labor, minority, women's, environmental and citizen's organizations which make up the liberal-labor grouping are still tied to the Democratic party, they face a difficult task. They will have additional problems now that Kennedy is running and they will have more if a rightist Republican is nominated because many rank and file Americans will want to vote for a Democrat in order to block the rise to power of an extreme conservative.

Whatever the outcome of their initial effort, the attempt to break with the Democrats and form a new party is important. It illustrates the growing disillusionment with the Democratic party and the search for alternatives. Unless Democratic politicians become more responsive to popular needs, the Citizen's Party or another insurgent party may take its place.

JIMMY CARTER: THE PRESIDENT'S 1980 RE-ELECTION STRATEGY

What does the chief executive intend to do to retain the presidency through 1984? While the exact details of implementation will depend on as yet unknown factors — particularly world and national political and economic trends and events and the policy positions, strategy, and tactics of rival candidates — the general outline of Carter's strategy is clear. It has three main aspects: try to create a new dominant coalition with symbolic populism; fully use the advantages of incumbency; and continue to play up to big business, the Eastern Establishment and its media.

Symbolic populism — the fervent condemnation of forces which seem to threaten the "average American" — has long been a mainstay of American politics. Its use in elections is as predictable as the subsequent lack of effective action against the "special interests" and situations that were railed against. Carter used symbolic populism heavily during his first campaign, frequently being careful to be ambiguous about exactly who the "special interests" were and what he would do about them once in office. This allowed people to read their own meanings into Carter's rhetoric. As President, Carter has continued to use symbolic populist talk, while acting in concrete ways to help special interests. Thus the President critized the "ripoff" of big oil companies, while deregulating natural gas and removing gasoline price controls, allowing even higher profits for these corporations. He verbally attacked the tax breaks for millionaires given by Congress, then signed the legislation into law instead of vetoing it. And, as we have seen, "human rights" rhetoric is excellent for showing the nation and the world the sincerely humane goals of the President, while in actual practice it has had little or no effect on either American policy or the actions of other nations. The President tells us that legal skills are "wastefully" and "unfairly" distributed and "nearly all" prison inmates "are drawn from the ranks of the powerless and poor," but does nothing about it.[103] Carter also allowed his Health, Education and Welfare Secretary to speak out against smoking as a health hazard, while he himself told an audience of tobacco producers that the federal government and tobacco industry "ought to have an accurate and enlightened education program and research program to make the smoking of tobacco even more safe than it is today."[104]

Carter has also tried to bring symbolic and stylistic politics into the White House by cutting certain frills and reducing the formality of ceremonialism of the presidency, as well as using townhall meetings, "fireside chats," visits to people's homes and other techniques to try to create the populist image he wants people to have of him. These approaches will be a key part of Carter's 1980 campaign.

Connected with symbolic populism is Carter's apparent intention, as contradictory as it may sound, to run again as an outsider — the foe of extravagance and waste, the terror of bureaucrats, the champion of a government as good as its people — against the special interests. Carter strategist Patrick Caddell argued that "it is crucial that President Carter keep the image that he is not part of the traditional political establishment."[105] Ironically, Carter's own ineptness and failures as President will, to some extent, allow him to run against the Washington Establishment, the lobbyists, those in Congress, and the media who oppose him and have blocked his programs. He plans to argue that he is still an outsider, a scrapper fighting for the little guy against vague "insiders." His press secretary Jody Powell has said, "this particular President has come to Washington and done battle with the powers that be."[106] Whether or not this approach will succeed in building a winning coalition is an open question, especially since people tend to want competence. But if Carter can blame others, he might again capture the public's mood. So far, he has seemed to succeed in gaining a public image as a sincere, concerned, honest, hardworking man doing a difficult job. Such an image, together with symbolic populism and the "New Foundation" slogan, helps create a passive attitude among the mass of Americans. After all, so the argument goes, the President is on our side and is doing the best he can in tough circumstances.

A second aspect of Carter's 1980 strategy is to use to the fullest extent possible the power and advantages of incumbency. Carter plans to time foreign and domestic policy initiatives for maximum political benefit. He has already done this with the economy, tightening the economic screws in late 1978, so as not to hurt Democratic congressional election chances. The President hopes to be able to reflate the economy in time to insure a pre-election boom to carry him to vicotry.

The Carter Administration's reorganization of July 1979 is an additional example of how a President can order actions which can command headlines and, potentially at least, improve his chances for re-election. In what was called a "Cabinet shakeup," Carter purged several Cabinet members who were actually or potentially not "team players" politically (i.e. not strong enough supporters of Carter's re-election campaign) or seen as a political liability for the 1980 election. Joseph A. Califano Jr. (HEW), W. Michael Blumenthal (Treasury) and Brock Adams (Transportation) fit into the first category and James Schlesinger (Energy) into the second. As part of the changes, trusted aide Hamilton Jordan was installed as Chief of the White House Staff with greatly increased powers, including control (with only two known exceptions among the White House Staff) over access to the President. Given Jordan's historic role as Carter's principal campaign strategist, a role he will also play in the 1980 campaign, it is obvious that his new position is aimed at improving the President's re-election chances by making sure all administration decisions are made with political goals in mind.

The reorganization therefore marked an initial step in Carter's re-election campaign, a conclusion strengthened by Carter's active travel and speech-making schedule since the changes. Reinforcing this view is the fact that Carter reportedly told Califano that he "had to get the Cabinet and the Administration ready for the 1980 election," and therefore could not afford to have relatively independent men like Califano — who angered politically potent Southern tobacco growers, among others, with anti-smoking campaigns and other actions — in his administration.[107] As *Time* put it "everywhere loyalty had become the watchword."[108] And upon entering office, Califano's successor, Patricia Harris, reportedly told HEW's civil rights staff to keep in mind political considerations when it pursues controversial cases such as school desgregation.[109]

The strengthening of the role of the Georgians and others deemed fully reliable politically by Carter set off a minor crisis of business confidence, however — some apparently feared he might actually begin to act on some of his populist rhetoric in order to try to raise his popularity and assure re-election — causing the President to reassure business by quickly replacing Blumenthal at Treasury with former Textron Corporation, Business Council and Conference Board leader G. William Miller. Then Carter installed CFR member and Trilateral Commissioner Paul A. Volcker in Miller's former position as Chairman of the Federal Reserve Board. Both Miller and Volcker are fiscal conservatives who intend to try to slow inflation with recession and higher unemployment. The *New York Times* reported that Wall Street bankers and Trilateral Commissioners Robert V. Roosa and David Rockefeller were "strong influences" in Carter's decision to name Volcker, who is a former employee of Rockefeller's Chase Manhattan Bank.[110] To try to shore up relations with the media, Carter also tapped Hedley Donovan, *Time*'s recently retired editor-in-chief, and, as previously pointed out, another Trilateral Commissioner (and a CFR director as well) to be one of Carter's senior advisers, with direct access to the President and advisory responsibilities so broad that they include "special missions," in both domestic and foreign policy as well as media relations.[111]

Similarly, a trip to China, the Middle East, or other foreign policy extravaganzas could be orchestrated at the appropriate moment, (during, say, January of 1980) giving the President needed publicity and pushing his rivals out of the limelight. The ability of a President to take decisive action abroad in moments of political crisis should not be underestimated, especially in light of the timing of similar crises in the past. Decisive presidential action was not foreordained, but did come, in the Cuban Missile Crisis just prior to the 1962 elections, at the Gulf of Tonkin during the 1964 election campaign, and in Vietnam during the 1968 and 1972 presidential races. In every case, and not accidentally, the opposition's campaign was undercut by the actions of an incumbent President. Carter's sudden recognition of China and his role in the Egypt-Israeli peace agreements show again how a President can act in foreign policy to prop up his popularity. The President does, of course, also get blamed if something goes wrong. In the present era of economic crisis at home and a tendency toward radical change undermining U.S. influence abroad, events could turn out to be uncontrollable at a critical moment and seriously hurt Carter's chances. However, as long as the President takes some kind of decisive action in foreign policy, feelings of nationalism will encourage Americans to rally around "our" leader.

Another area where the incumbency is decidedly advantageous is in the area of patronage. A President always has high-paying jobs for individuals who are important enough politically to warrant them. Federal judgeships, high- level bureaucratic jobs, ambassador's posts and so on are "political plums" dispensed to those who can and will help the President politically. The White House can also be opened up to grass roots leaders for lunches or dinners and a pep talk with the President. Carter has in fact been doing the latter, inviting "hundreds" of local officials, businessmen, labor and Democratic party leaders "almost every week" to the White House for a visit.[112] Close personal ties with these leaders gives the President an added advantage in political help when election day comes.

Carter also controls the Democratic party apparatus and John C. White, the head of the Democratic National Committee (DNC). The Carter forces intend to use their control of the party structure to make it an operating arm of the President. As Carter adviser Patrick Caddell put it, the DNC must be "Carterized," made "an active vibrant political arm of the Carter White House. . . the DNC should serve as a patronage center in working with the White House in the staffing of not only the government in Washington, but the regional offices and also the rewarding of projects. . . . "[113] In addition the DNC should also be used to undercut potential adversaries, especially Senator Edward Kennedy and Governor

Jerry Brown, as well as liberals in Congress. Writing in December 1976 Caddell felt that, since Carter planned to move right and co-opt Republican issues, more opposition to the President would come from Democrats than Republicans, and therefore potential adversaries had to be identified and controlled.[114] When the DNC adopted rules for the 1980 primaries, the changes made it more difficult for challengers to win delegates to the 1980 convention. These rules were, in the words of *Congressional Quarterly,* "expected to aid President Carter's renomination drive in 1980."[115] A participant concluded that the new rules were "designed to make it a little more difficult for anyone to challenge Jimmy Carter in 1980," and a big city mayor said, "there's no way you can interpret it except as favoring the incumbent."[116]

The handling of the 1978 Democratic mid-term convention in Memphis is another example of how the DNC now works to support Carter. A dissident coalition of liberals and unionists, led by Douglas Fraser, President of the UAW, tried to challenge Carter's budget priorities at the convention and had trouble even getting their resolution on the agenda. They did well to get nearly 40 percent of the vote after DNC chairman White used parliamentary and other forms of manipulation to try to weaken opposition forces.[117] The nearly 40 percent which they did receive illustrates the high level of opposition Carter does face in the Democratic party, but with the organizational muscle of the party apparatus in the President's hands it will be very difficult for Carter's opponents to win in primary states and at the 1980 Convention, as they discovered at Memphis. White House forces had a trial run for the 1980 Democratic Convention and clearly won.

It is evident that Carter and his advisers have concluded that the appeal of liberalism is illusory, that the American people have decisively shifted to the right, and that Carter should try for a center-right coalition rather than the traditional Democratic center-liberal coalition. Just to be sure, however,

Carter's planners think that the liberal-labor grouping should be left as much as possible with no alternative and nowhere to go. In regard to the black vote, for example, administration sources said in early 1979 that they were not worried because no Republican can take the black vote from Carter and potential Democratic challengers (excluding Kennedy, who they did not expect to enter) are no more attractive to blacks than Carter. As one Carter man put it: "Where can the blacks go?"[118] The same could be said for labor, liberals, and much of the women's movement. Carter has appointed a few of their number to lesser posts, but has appointed far more centrist Republicans and Democrats to high level posts than the liberal-labor grouping. As the Democratic party shifts right, partly due to actions by the President, more centrist Republicans and independents can find a home there, so Carter's reasoning goes, and a new winning political coalition can be constructed. Some have thus remarked that there are now two business-controlled Republican parties, or, as one Washington joke put it, ". . . big business owns the Republican party outright and now has leased the Democrats with an option to buy."

A final element of Carter's 1980 strategy is maintaining good relations with the media establishment. At the most general level, as we have seen in previous chapters, Carter has tried to please the media by bringing its representatives into policy-making positions and following policies which they approve. More specifically, Carter has been relatively open and accessible to reporters (especially compared to Richard Nixon), has held a long series of little publicized White House dinners with media leaders, and has frequently taken actions recommended by the *New York Times*, the leading news organ of the Eastern Establishment.

White House dinners with different groups of journalists and their spouses have the obvious aim of making them grateful and sympathetic to the President and of allowing him to talk personally with reporters, building up support.

The full influence of the dinners is difficult to determine, especially since Carter has forbidden White House staff to announce or confirm that the dinners even occur or to say who is invited. Despite this desire for secrecy, two separate reports confirm that such intimate dinners are part of Carter's re-election strategy. A very fragmentary list of those attending these dinners include reporters and columnists like Joseph Kraft; Hedrick Smith of the *New York Times*; Barbara Walters of ABC; Tom Brokaw of NBC; Elizabeth Drew of the *New Yorker*; Marquis Childs; Richard Stroudt of the *Christain Science Monitor* and the *New Republic;* and others.[119]

Carter also has in several cases responded quickly to recommendations contained in the *New York Times'* editorials. In March 1978, for example, the *Times* editorially called for Carter to revoke Bert Lance's diplomatic passport since the shady former banker and ousted Office of Management and Budget head was traveling around the world billing himself as the "Special Envoy of the President." The very next day Lance's passport was revoked by the Carter administration.[120] The administration acted just as quickly on a May 12, 1978 *Times* editorial recommendation to delay Carter's planned $25 billion tax cut due to increased inflation. The very next day Carter announced a smaller tax cut and a three month delay in implementation, citing inflationary pressures.[121]

Several *New York Times* editorials have defended or praised the President, although a few have been critical. A December 1978 editorial supporting Carter's economic policy said that the nation's economic situation demands the medicine Carter is applying and that Kennedy, Douglas Fraser, and other liberal critics are wrong.[122] An earlier editorial expressed concern over excessive criticism of Carter, saying his goals and willingness to address national problems are laudable, and his agenda the correct one.[123] The *Times* has also criticized Carter occasionally for being too cautious and conservative. After his first State of the Union address, for example, it called him "a sensible President, but not yet a leader or a teacher, even for a quiet time."[124] Even this mild critique was moderated by James Reston, the *Times* Washington Bureau Chief, who praised Carter's message as "quietly eloquent."[125] Reston has been Carter's biggest booster in the pages of the *Times*, lauding the President again and again. Carter's hiring of Reston's son as a State Department spokesman no doubt did not hurt, nor does the fact that Reston sees the President in private frequently and is one of the few reporters regularly invited to the meetings of the Trilateral Commission. Even in areas where the general conclusion is that Carter failed, such as the President's trip to Mexico in early 1979, Reston mentioned the President's "personal successes," such as Carter's addressing the Mexican President in Spanish, the effect of which "would be hard to overestimate.[126]

Reston lauds Carter's foreign policy, saying that it "will probably bear comparison with the record of any American President since the Second World War."[127] Reston even goes so far as to blame the American people for turning against Carter, arguing in his April 15, 1979 column, for example, that Carter came to Washington "promising to produce a 'Government as good and generous and unselfish as our people' and, on the whole he has kept his promise. Maybe the trouble is that 'the people' are not quite as good and generous and unselfish as he thought."[128]

Other *Times* reporters also continue to say positive things about the President. Hedrick Smith reported in April 1979, for example, that Carter "still has plenty of the political magic that worked so well for him in 1976," and Tom Wicker added that same month that Carter "still has the 1976 campaigner's touch with the plain people."[129]

Not surprisingly, *Time* magazine, the other main Carter backer among the media during 1975 and 1976, also still gives Carter very high marks. Their presidential observer, Hugh Sidey, has praised Carter's courage for not overreacting to domestic and world events, saying that "even while suffering dramatic domestic political losses, Carter comes down on the side of patience — the essence of courage for these hours."[130] In news stories *Time* is still openly pro-Carter, defending him as a victim of events out of any nation's control, as in its March 5, 1979 issue with its headline "Carter: Black and Blue." Carter's critics argue that he should act, said *Time*, yet when challenged "to explain what he should be doing differently, the rhetoric is strong, but the answers are far from persuasive."[131] None of the Republican presidential challengers now opportunistically attacking "what now seemed their best immediate target, Carter's foreign policy. . . bears any responsibility for the commitment of American lives to distant causes."[132]

If *Time* and the *New York Times* still seem solidly behind Carter, other representatives of the establishment media are clearly taking a somewhat more critical stance, although hardly unambiguously anti-Carter. The reasons for criticism are not difficult to find. While the *New York Times* and *Time* stress how difficult Carter's job is and how intractable the problems he faces are, other media are stressing Carter's weaknesses and failures. The critique comes from the center-right, the Hearst press and the *Wall Street Journal* as the prime examples. The *Journal*, for example, feels that Carter could have done much more to preserve imperial interests in situations like Panama, Ethiopia, or Iran and argues that both the Administration and the *New York Times* are complacent about the global significance of such setbacks.[133] The *Journal* stresses that Soviet power is waxing and the United States power is waning and demands that the Carter administration "show some backbone somewhere."[134] The *Times* responded to the unusual attack — newspapers usually do not mention each other in print — by defending Carter's restrained approach, arguing that it is not indifference "to recognize that the power to preserve or install American-sponsored regimes belongs to another era, and that the Soviet Union does not manufacture all turmoil, even if it seeks to profit from it. . . Americans have to shake the habit of mistaking every difficulty as a sign that Moscow is snatching the world from their grasp."[135] The *Journal*'s hard line on Carter's foreign policy is tempered by the fact that Norman C. Miller, one of their key political commentators, argues that the President looks good compared to the Republican and Democratic alternatives.[136]

Thus opinion leaders within the media establishment are still mostly pro-Carter, but there is some disagreement on the question of how well Carter has done in defense of ruling class interests. This fact, combined with Carter's low poll ratings — one local newspaper publisher has lamented Carter's "inability to rally the people behind him" — clearly indicate his inability to completely fool the people with symbolic populism and other theatrics.[137] Carter's unpopularity worries ruling class leaders who, after all, depend upon the President to sell their policies to the people. If a centrist candiate like Bush, Baker, or Connally appears to have significantly greater crowd appeal, that candidate will rapidly gain substantial ruling class support, and Carter will be dumped as counterproductive to long-range corporate interests. A factor supporting this interpretation is the fact that presidential election contests are often a reaction to the current or a recent occupant of the White House. Thus Carter, the man with an image of honesty, integrity and trustworthiness ran against Richard Nixon and his surrogate Gerald Ford. Therefore the 1980 election may be a contest between Carter, now perceived as weak and barely competent, and a man like Connally, Kennedy, Reagan, Baker or Bush whose image may be that of a much more forceful leader. The American people appear to be hungry for a strong President who will tell them what to do to solve their problems.

Despite Carter's incumbency advantage and still fairly high level of media support, he is less well positioned even within his own party than any sitting President in the last half century. This fact reflects the fluidity of current American politics. The reason for this is less Carter's incompetency, although that is involved, than the structural problems of the system Carter inherited and refuses to change, highlighted by the rise of newly powerful nations in the world arena and systemic economic crisis at home. These problems cannot be solved through the kind of timid measures Carter and his ruling class supporters have espoused. The *New York Times*, *Time*, and other ruling class opinion-makers are still Carter supporters in part because they recognize the difficulties he faces in trying to manage an unmanageable system, akin to putting square pegs in round holes. They also recognize Carter's real successes, especially in helping to restore trust in the integrity and humaneness of the system at the top. They also recognize the value of having a Democratic President implement an austerity program on the working class, since this makes mass protest and disaffection less likely.

To sum up, Carter, while in a better position to achieve re-election than most Republicans think, does nevertheless face real problems and political obstacles in his re-election bid. The constituency which elected him, particularly minorities and working people, is the hardest hit by Carter's austerity program — making it likely that they will not turn out for him next election day. On the other hand, while his poll ratings are currently low, Carter has been successful in maintaining a middle-of-the-road political image and a close match exists between Carter's political philosophy as perceived by the public and how the American people position themselves on a left-right continuum.[138] The outcome of the 1980 race will be determined by these factors, as well as by Carter's opposition and the existing political trends, both of which can be briefly evaluated.

THE CANDIDATES SUMMED UP

In 1980 there will be many behind-the-scenes power brokers — wealthy political financiers, media leaders, and political strategists. The candidates with the best connections to the strongest of these power brokers are Carter himself; George Bush, a Trilateral Commission member and director of both the CFR and Atlantic Council; Vice President Mondale, still a CFR member and a former Trilateral Commissioner; John Culver and John B. Anderson, both CFR members and Trilateral Commissioners; Elliot L. Richardson, a former CFR director and a Trilateral Commissioner; and John B. Connally, a director of the Committee on the Present Danger and former Conference Board Trustee. Other candidates have various ties and policy orientations as shown in Tables 6-1 and 6-2.

A total of fourteen, over one-half of those often mentioned or openly running for President, thus have direct membership in one of the major policy planning groups, with fully ten belonging to the Council on Foreign Relations and seven current or past members of the Trilateral Commission. Even those having no direct ties, such as Kennedy, Brown, or even Reagan, have indirect links through close political allies, large contributors, friends, or appointees. Only a few of the candidates on the left or right edges of the American political spectrum — men like Crane or Dellums — are possibly unlinked to the dominant sector of the ruling class. Whether one of those with direct or indirect ties to the ruling class emerges as the next President of the United States depends partly upon the kind of support he can muster among the voters — as previously mentioned the primaries are partly to find out who can best implement ruling class policies through personal popularity — and partly on how successful the Establishment media are in selling their favorite candidates. Above all the ruling class wants to be enough in control to have several options available no matter which way the political winds blow and they clearly have that power.

TRENDS FOR THE 1980S

Certain political trends could influence the electoral winds in the 1980s. American politics tends to be cyclical in nature, going through periods of change, then reaction. The forces behind these shifts are complex, but they are tied in with larger world and national economic and political events, as well as the responses of the ruling class and the majority of Americans to these events — in short, wars, revolutions, depressions, and the class struggle. Outlining these shifts over time since the First World War we can see a rough pattern.

The 1920s (1917-1929) — a conservative period with a fairly high level of repression, ended with the onset of the great depression. Harding, Coolidge, and Hoover were the typical political leaders.

The Depression-World War II period (1930-1945) — a period of change marked by a relatively high level of mass action. Roosevelt was the dominant political leader.

Cold War-1950s (1945-1960) — repression, "McCarthyism" comes again; a quiet time for conservative Republicans like Eisenhower.

The 1960s — the decade of mass movements: civil rights, antiwar, student rights, and counterculture reinvigorate America's traditions of mass actions and egalitarianism.

The 1970s — again a quiet time, Nixonian repression and the "me decade." Nixon and conservative Democrat Carter are typical political leaders.

Thus, if past trends hold true, we are presently probably near the high tide of the conservative phase of the cycle. The most likely event to touch off the shift to the left — which will come sooner or later because conservative "solutions" to the problems facing America are grossly inadequate — is mass unemployment resulting from a deep recession or depression. The timing of such an economic downturn cannot be predicted with any accuracy, but the signs of its approach are quite evident, as pointed out earlier. The right wing in America is now working through both of the main political parties and is stressing its traditional messages — conservatism on cultural and personal issues, hard-line anticommunism in foreign policy, laissez-faire capitalist economics, anti-unionism, deregulation, budget and tax cutting, and a general decrease in the federal government's role in the political economy. Carter is clearly trying to gain the conservative votes which have grown in the wake of this rightward trend. The Trilateral Commission's own publication, *Crisis of Democracy*, with its emphasis on the need to limit and restrict democracy, is but one example of this rightward drift. It argues that the United States and much of the Trilateral World suffer from the "democratic distemper," a societal sickness from too much democracy. The cure stresses the need to curtail the press, higher education, and mass movements.[139] Other examples include the increase in anti-union policies among the biggest corporations and the hard-line anti-Soviet position taken by many ruling class leaders.

The growing strength of the organized right might delay the coming shift to the left and impose even more reactionary policies on the nation for a time, but in the long run this program will fail because it will not halt the inflation and economic decline which are rooted in the very structure of contemporary capitalist economics, or the relative decline of American power abroad since the events in the communist and Third Worlds are ultimately beyond the control of the United States and its trilateral allies. Rapid and at times spectacular change abroad will inevitably influence change at home. Conservatives and liberals alike fail to identify the real sources of inflation and economic crisis in America and decline abroad. The first grows out of an oligopolistic ownership and pricing structure in the domestic economy and the latter out of an international class struggle between rich and poor nations. Since the disease is falsely diagnosed, the medicine will clearly be the wrong kind. In short, the left will have a resurgence as the only force addressing the real problems of this nation.

When the left does regain its strength it may not be in the liberal-social democratic form characteristic of the post-New Deal era. There are clear signs that liberalism as a coherent and convincing ideology is dying and preliminary indications are that it is being replaced with forms of socialist thinking in some unions, and in some feminist, minority, and other organizations. It is still too early to predict how fundamental the shift is. Liberal habits of thinking, such as the desire for mere government regulation of the private corporations which control America — instead of an insistence on public enterprise and social control over the production, price, and investment system — are still strong in these organizations and their leaders.

While the American people are hardly convinced about the need for an American form of socialism — defined here as an economic and political system democratically owned and managed by the people themselves — they are angry and want change. It is therefore likely that the 1980s will be a time of struggle and change, of party and ideological realignment. There has been discussion of a new party or parties developing and one or both of the old dominant parties collapsing, just as the Whig party disintegrated in the period of intense political crisis in the 1850s prior to the American Civil War. It is clear, for example, that party loyalty and party-wide ideological consistency are at a low ebb and fully one-third of all voters now label themselves "independents." People are also greatly dissatisfied with the political and economic choices they face. Continuing inflation and unemployment with soaring corporate profits will both label the real cause of the problem and suggest changes needed.

CONCLUSION: BEYOND THE CARTER PRESIDENCY

This book has shown how corporate leaders control the political process and render American democracy a mere formality with no meaningful content because real choices are lacking. It is clear that we are now in a new stage of ruling class control of American politics. Such control is increasing as corporations and policy-planning groups like the Trilateral Commission take a more direct role in selecting, financing, and selling candidates of both parties at the highest levels of American politics, shaping the alternatives that the public are given on election day. Jimmy Carter thus represents an intensified form of the long familiar corporate President. His is the first Democratic presidency and cabinet to be so devoid of party complexion and so free from popular constituencies. The party politics level of American politics has little influence on this President. He is tied to corporate power, and the American people are increasingly aware of this fact. Carter's policies have demonstrated the growing conflict between big business capitalism and a democratic politics serving the general welfare.

This conflict is now the main contradiction of both the Carter Administration and contemporary American politics. As we have seen, the President's policies have been very successful in one key area, that of profits, the "bottom line" and end result of most interest to corporate leaders. With profits at record levels, they have every reason to be pleased with the Carter Administration's economic performance. But this very fact is the main source of Carter's broader unpopularity with the American people, because by planning and implementing economic policies which redistribute income and wealth upward to the rich, he has taken from those at the middle and lower end of the socio-economic class structure. Carter is finding that the reality of people's day to day lives and the struggle to make ends meet is more real than media

manipulation, symbolic populism, foreign policy extravaganzas and the other tools in the President's political kit. Thus,
Carter's unpopularity will remain into the 1980s even if he is
re-elected due to the lack of positive choices offered the
American people.

Ruling class control of the government is thus becoming
more transparent as corporate interests are aided while the
interests of working people are ignored. One result has been
some labor leaders becoming sharply critical of the corporate
state consensus, most notably William Winpisinger of the
Machinists and Douglas Fraser of the United Auto Workers.
Both have made strong statements about the need for fundamental change — Winpisinger has even argued that the
American corporate state is now acquiring many of the
attributes of fascism — although their actions (as distinct
from talk) are as yet still timid.

Another result has been an ever decreasing percentage of
eligible voters going to the polls as more and more Americans
correctly conclude that the politicians vying for their votes
will either ignore them, or more probably, actively abet the
powerful corporate interests that dominate America. In 1976
only 28 percent of the electorate voted for Jimmy Carter, but
this was enough for him to win, as only 54.4 percent voted at
all. In mid-term elections the turnout is now only about one-
third of the electorate. These figures represent historic lows
and show that the American people increasingly demand real
choices or they will not vote.

The political system is in disarray because the current
political economy is less and less functional for the American
people. A central problem with the existing American political
economy is that public influence and authority are almost
totally excluded from the economic sphere; yet the great
majority of Americans must rely upon private business to
make and implement decisions — on investment, technological
development, location of industry, production, and so on —
that are, in effect, public policies. The interdependence of

people means that these private decisions must be subject to public control.

Several national and world trends indicate that the American people will increasingly demand a greater share of authority over economic decision making. One is the ecological-energy crisis. Since the earth's resources are finite, the ownership, exploitation, and use of these limited resources, such as oil and gas, must be better regulated. The profit motive has proved to be an extremely poor form of regulation. The reality of worsening economic problems under capitalism will also result in increased support for a reasonable alternative.

A final aspect is the fact that the logic of democratic public control of the economy is convincing once carefully examined. One of the clearest and best argued short statements on this question was written by one of the most brilliant individuals of the Twentieth Century, a man who few realize was also a socialist — Albert Einstein. Einstein wrote in 1949 that:

> The economic anarchy of capitalist society as it exists today is, in my opinion, the real source of the evil. . . .
>
> Private capital tends to become concentrated in few hands, partly because of competition among the capitalists, and partly because technological development and the increasing division of labor encourage the formation of larger units of production at the expense of the smaller ones. The result of these developments is an oligarchy of private capital the enormous power of which cannot be effectively checked even by a democratically organized political society. This is true since the members of legislative bodies are selected by political parties, largely financed or otherwise influenced by private capitalists who, for all practical purposes, separate the electorate from the legislature.
>
> Moreover, under existing conditions, private capitalists inevitably control, directly or indirectly, the main sources of information (press, radio, education). It is thus extremely difficult, and indeed in most cases quite impossible, for the individual citizen to come to objective conclusions and to make intelligent use of his political rights.
>
> Production is carried out for a profit, not for use. There is

no provision that all those able and willing to work will always be in a position to find employment; an "army of unemployed" almost always exists. Since unemployed and poorly paid workers do not provide a profitable market, the production of consumer's goods is restricted, and great hardship is the consequence. Technological progress frequently results in more unemployment rather than in an easing of the work for all. Unlimited competition leads to a huge waste of labor, and to that crippling of the social consciousness of individuals I mentioned before.

This crippling of individuals I consider the worst evil of capitalism. Our whole educational system suffers from this evil. An exaggerated competitive attitude is inculcated into the student, who is trained to worship acquisitive success as a preparation for his future career.

I am convinced there is only *one* way to eliminate these grave evils, namely through the establishment of a socialist economy, accompanied by an educational system that would be oriented toward socialist goals. In such an economy, the means of production are owned by society itself and are utilized in a planned fashion. A planned economy, which adjusts production to the needs of the community, would distribute work to be done among all those able to work and would guarantee a livelihood to every man, woman and child. The education of the individual, in addition to promoting his own innate abilities, would attempt to develop in him a sense of responsibility for his fellow men in the place of the glorification of power and success in our present society.[140]

This book has shown that the power of the American ruling class and its political representatives is indeed immense, but stronger still is the potential power of an organized, aroused and active people. One aim of this book has been to try to expose the way the political system actually operates at its highest level, to help mobilize Americans to end an era of control of our nation by the corporations and for the corporations. The results of that control are more and more obviously detrimental to the great majority of Americans. They include such depressing items in the daily news as the danger to humanity posed by nuclear weapons and nuclear power, the militarization of our society, and social inequality and crisis reflected in the high levels of crime, family breakdown, child abuse, poverty, unemployment, imprisonment, and drug and alcohol abuse. As long as the existing undemocratic corporate order is preserved, the need to build a healthy and happy society cannot be addressed. The real issue is thus the fundamental one of power and control over American society. Since the two major political parties are systematically avoiding this basic issue, and refusing to face up to the capitalist roots of the current economic instability and social problem, the nation is in a serious political and economic crisis. To solve the crisis, the American system of representative democracy must become really meaningful by extending it to the workplace and investment process and thereby become a more direct, comprehensive, participatory democracy characterized by socio-economic equality and an end to privileged classes. A new party will have to come into being to put this fundamental issue of economic and political control on the agenda for debate, struggle and resolution. The reality of corporate power and misrule is the great issue of our time. It must be brought into public debate as the central question of the 1980s: who shall rule America, the corporate ruling class or the people?

Notes

1. *New York Times Magazine,* February 22, 1976, p. 13.
2. *New York Times,* February 26, 1976, p. 1.
3. *New York Times,* May 16, 1976, pp. 1, 30.
4. *Congressional Quarterly Weekly Review,* (CQWR), August 5, 1978, p. 2025.
5. Ibid.
6. Ibid., pp. 2025-2026.
7. *San Francisco Chronicle,* February 7, 1979, p. 6; *San Francisco Sunday Examiner and Chronicle,* January 14, 1979, p. A9.

8. *San Francisco Sunday Examiner and Chronicle,* February 4, 1979, p. B6.
9. *San Francisco Chronicle,* February 7, 1979, p. 6.
10. *San Francisco Sunday Examiner and Chronicle,* February 11, 1979, p. A21.
11. *United States News and World Report,* August 14, 1978, pp. 24-25.
12. *New York Times,* June 25, 1978, p. 27.
13. *New York Times,* August 15, 1976, VII, pp. 4-5.
14. *San Francisco Sunday Examiner and Chronicle,* February 11, 1979, p. A21.
15. *New York Times,* July 20, 1978, p. A13.
16. *San Francisco Chronicle,* February 5, 1979, p. 10.
17. *New York Times,* July 23, 1978, IV, p. 8.
18. *New York Times,* January 26, 1975, p. 38.
19. *San Francisco Examiner,* August 11, 1979, p. 3.
20. *Esquire,* August 29, 1978, p. 33.
21. *CQWR,* August 5, 1978, p. 2027.
22. *Newsweek,* August 14, 1978, p. 18.
23. *People,* September 11, 1978, p. 29.
24. *New York Times,* August 20, 1976, p. 1.
25. *Newsweek,* January 18, 1971, pp. 17-18.
26. *New York Times,* August 20, 1976, p. 1.
27. *Time,* May 3, 1971, p. 20.
28. *Ibid., Newseeek,* January 18, 1971, pp. 17-18.
29. *Time,* May 31, 1971, p. 20.
30. *New York Times,* August 20, 1976, p. 1.
31. *New York Times,* May 7, 1973, p. 21.
32. *New York Times,* November 11, 1974, p. 21; *New York Times Magazine,* October 20, 1974, p. 101.
33. *New York Times Magazine,* October 20, 1974, pp. 37, 102.
34. *Esquire,* August 29, 1978, p. 35.
35. *New York Times,* November 11, 1974, p. 21; *New York Times,* October 26, 1975, IV, p. 2.
36. *Esquire,* August 29, 1978, p. 35.
37. *New York Times Magazine,* October 20, 1974, p. 101.
38. *New York Times,* June 15, 1974, p. 16.
39. *New York Times,* August 10, 1974, p. 3.
40. *Fortune,* July 31, 1978, pp. 87-92.
41. *Newsweek,* March 12, 1979, p. 23.
42. *The New Republic,* November 11, 1978, pp. 20-23.
43. Ibid.
44. *Inquiry,* January 8 and 22, 1979, p. 11.
45. *San Francisco Examiner,* January 24, 1979, p. 10.
46. *Christian Science Monitor,* January 10, 1979, p. 7.
47. Ibid.
48. *San Francisco Chronicle,* January 31, 1979, p. 45.
49. *Newsweek,* January 29, 1979, p. 36.
50. Ibid.

51. *Fortune,* July 31, 1978, p. 87; *Time,* September 10, 1979, pp. 12-21.

52. *Inquiry,* January 8 and 22, 1979, pp. 9-10.

53. Ibid.

54. *Time,* July 16, 1979, p. 58; Appendix I.

55. *New York Times,* November 25, 1976, p. 1.

56. *New York Times,* February 23, 1977, p. D3.

57. See Appendix for January, 1978 Commission membership.

58. *Politics Today,* November/December, 1978, p. 26.

59. *Newsweek,* August 14, 1978, p. 17.

60. Ibid.

61. *The Arizona Daily Star* (Tucson, Arizona), January 20, 1979, p. 14A.

62. *San Francisco Chronicle,* January 6, 1979, p. 6.

63. *San Francisco Chronicle,* January 31, 1979, p. A4; *New York Times,* December 23, 1978, p. 7.

64. *Esquire,* August 29, 1978, p. 34; ABC Evening News, February 18, 1979.

65. *National Review,* September 1, 1978, pp. 1102-1103.

66. *People,* April 3, 1978, pp. 22-25.

67. Charles Moritz (ed.), *Current Biography Yearbook* 1974 (New York: H.W. Wilson, 1974), p. 20.

68. *New York Times,* January 5, 1977, p. 14.

69. *New York Times,* January 4, 1979, p. A16.

70. CFR Annual Report, 1973, 1974; *The New Republic,* January 21, 1978, p. 13; *Newsweek,* July 4, 1977, pp. 14-15.

71. *New York Times,* January 8, 1978, IV, p. 19.

72. *New York Times,* November 20, 1977, p. 15.

73. *New York Times,* January 5, 1977, p. 14.

74. *People,* April 3, 1978, pp. 22-25.

75. *Newsweek,* March 13, 1978, p. 30; "Initial Working Paper on Political Strategy," Memorandum by Patrick H. Caddell, December 1976, reprinted in *Congressional Record,* Senate, June 21, 1977, p. S10350.

76. *In These Times,* October 25-31, 1978, p. 3.

77. Brown owns land worth more than $100,000 in Nevada County, California, a home in Los Angeles, and bonds. *San Francisco Chronicle,* March 3, 1979, p. 8.

78. *San Francisco Chronicle,* February 2, 1979, p. 21.

79. *San Francisco Chronicle,* March 1, 1979, p. 12; *San Francisco Examiner,* March 2, 1979, p. 20.

80. *San Francisco Sunday Examiner and Chronicle,* January 28, 1979, p. C10.

81. See for example *San Francisco Sunday Examiner and Chronicle World,* March 18, 1979, p. 6.

82. *Time,* January 30, 1978, p. 28.

83. Ibid.

84. *San Francisco Chronicle,* February 7, 1979, p. 41.

85. Ibid.

86. *San Francisco Sunday Examiner and Chronicle Sunday Punch,* March 11, 1979, p. 3.

87. *Business Week,* July 17, 1978, pp. 58-59.

88. *The New Republic,* January 28, 1978, p. 21.

89. *Business Week,* July 17, 1978, pp. 58-59.

90. *San Francisco Chronicle,* January 31, 1979, p. 7.

91. *Guardian,* January 31, 1979, p. 6.

92. *In These Times,* October 25-31, 1978, p. 3.

93. *San Francisco Sunday Examiner and Chronicle World,* March 4, 1979, p. 25.

94. *Time,* July 30, 1979, p. 31.

95. *San Francisco Chronicle,* February 14, 1979, p. 8.

96. ABC Television, *Issues and Answers,* February 25, 1979; *San Francisco Sunday Examiner and Chronicle,* February 25, 1979, p. 4A.

97. *Newsweek,* September 24, 1979, p. 29; and membership list and Annual Report of the Brookings Institution, Trilateral Commission and Committee for Economic Development.

98. *San Francisco Sunday Examiner and Chronicle,* February 11, 1979, p. 2B.

99. *In These Times,* December 27, 1978-January 2, 1979, p. 4.

100. *In These Times,* February 21-27, 1979, p. 17.

101. Ibid.

102. Working Paper of The Citizens Committee, reprinted in *In These Times,* August 22-28, 1979, p. 15.

103. *CQWR,* May 13, 1978, p. 1202.

104. *San Francisco Sunday Examiner and Chronicle,* August 6, 1978, p. 1.

105. *Congressional Record,* Senate, June 21, 1977, p. S10351.

106. *New York Times,* June 25, 1978, p. IV2.

107. *San Francisco Examiner and Chronicle World,* July 29, 1979, p. 7.

108. *Time,* July 30, 1979, p. 11.

109. *San Francisco Chronicle,* August 3, 1979, p. 6.

110. *New York Times,* July 26, 1979, p. A16.

111. Ibid., pp. A1, A15, A16.

112. *The Atlantic,* March, 1979, p. 44; *Newsweek,* October 23, 1978, p. 41.

113. Caddell's December, 1976 memorandum to Carter is reprinted in the *Congressional Record,* Senate, June 21, 1977, p. S10350.

114. Ibid., pp. S10349-10350.

115. *CQWR,* June 17, 1978, pp. 1571-1572.

116. *The New Republic,* February 4, 1978, p. 11;   *New York Times,* June 10, 1977, p. 7.

117. See *The New Yorker,* January 15, 1979, pp. 49-87.

118. *Christian Science Moniter,* January 24, 1979, p. 10.

119. *The New Republic,* October 21, 1978, p. 8; Tom Brocaw, NBC Television *Today Show,* October 9, 1978.

120. *New York Times,* March 22, 1978, p. A24; *New York Times,* March 23, 1978, p. 1.

121. *New York Times,* May 12, 1978, p. 28; *New York Times,* May 13, 1978, p. 1.

122. *New York Times,* December 13, 1978, p. A26.

123. *New York Times,* April 9, 1978, IV p. 18.

124. *New York Times,* January 22, 1978, IV p. 18.

125. *New York Times,* January 20, 1978, p. 23.

126. *San Francisco Sunday Examiner and Chronicle, Sunday Punch,* February 25, 1979, p. 3.

127. *New York Times,* April 15, 1979, IV p. 17.

128. Ibid.

129. *New York Times,* April 27, 1979, p. 1; *New York Times,* April 29, 1979, IV p. 19.

130. *Time,* March 5, 1979, p. 13.

131. Ibid., p. 10.

132. Ibid.

133. *Wall Street Journal,* January 19, 1979, p. 10.

134. *Newsweek,* February 26, 1979, pp. 22-23.

135. *Guardian,* February 28, 1979, p. 21; see also *New York Times* editorials of February 18, 20 and 21, 1979.

136. *Guardian,* March 21, 1979, p. 21.

137. *San Francisco Sunday Examiner and Chronicle,* January 7, 1979, p. B2.

138. *San Francisco Chronicle,* March 19, 1979, p. 8.

139. Michael J. Crozier, Samuel P. Huntington, and Joji Watanuki, *The Crisis of Democracy: Report on the Governability of Democracies to the Trilateral Commission* (New York: New York University Press, 1975), pp. 64, 102, 105-106; *Trialogue,* Spring 1976, pp. 10-11.

140. *Monthly Review,* May 1949. Reprinted in *In These Times,* March 21-27, 1979, p. 24.

Appendix I

Behind-the-Scenes Rulers of the United States: Leaders of Core Policy-Planning Organizations

A. The Trilateral Commission (founded 1973)
   1. 1975 North American Membership list
   2. 1978 North American Membership list
B. The Council on Foreign Relations (founded 1921)
   1. 1976 Officers and Directors
   2. 1978 Officers and Directors
C. The Business Council (founded 1933)
   1. 1977 Officers and Members
D. The Business Roundtable (founded 1972)
   1. 1978 Policy Committee Members
E. The Brookings Institution (founded 1927)
   1. 1976 Trustees
   2. 1979 Trustees
F. The Committee on the Present Danger (founded 1976)
   1. 1976 Officers and Directors
G. The Atlantic Council of the United States (founded 1961)
   1. 1978 Officers and Directors

Note on Appendix

An examination of the following lists of leaders of the seven most important policy planning organizations shows the central role played by big businessmen. The individuals belonging to four or more of these seven organizations are all top corporate leaders, for example:

David Rockefeller — Chairman of Chase Manhattan Bank
Frank Cary — Chairman of International Business Machines
David Packard — Chairman of Hewlett-Packard
Mark Shepard Jr. — Chairman of Texas Instruments
Robert Roosa — Partner Brown Brothers Harriman
Douglas Dillon — Chairman U.S. and Foreign Securities

There are numerous interlocks between these seven organizations, these six men alone interconnect all seven for example.

THE TRILATERAL COMMISSION
1975 Officers and North American Members

Gerard C. Smith, North American chairman
Max Kohnstamm, European chairman
Takeshi Watanabe, Japanese chairman
François Duchëne, European deputy chairman
Zbigniew Brzezinski, Director
George S. Franklin, North American secretary
Christopher J. Makins, Deputy director
Tadashi Yamamoto, Japanese secretary

North American Members

*I.W. Abel, *President,* United Steelworkers of America
David M. Abshire, *Chairman, Georgetown University Center for Strategic and International Studies*
Graham Allison, *Professor of Politics, Harvard*
Doris Anderson, *Editor,* Chatelaine *Magazine*
John B. Anderson, *House of Representatives*
Ernest C. Arbuckle, *Chairman, Wells Fargo Bank*
J. Paul Austin, *Chairman, The Coca-Cola Company*
George W. Ball, *Senior Partner, Lehman Brothers*
Russell Bell, *Research Director, Canadian Labour Congress*
Lucy Wilson Benson, *Former President, League of Women Voters*
W. Michael Blumenthal, *Chairman, Bendix Corp.*
*Robert W. Bonner, Q.C., *Bonner and Foulks, Vancouver*
Robert R. Bowie, *Clarence Dillon Professor of Internat'l Affairs, Harvard*
John Brademas, *House of Representatives*
*Harold Brown, *President, California Institute of Technology*
James E. Carter, Jr., *Former Governor of Georgia*
Lawton Chiles, *United States Senate*
Warren Christopher, *Partner, O'Melveny and Myers*
†William T. Coleman, Jr., *Secretary, Dept. of Transportation*
Barber B. Conable, Jr., *House of Representatives*
Richard N. Cooper, *Frank Altschul Prof. of Internat'l Economics, Yale*
John C. Culver, *United States Senate*
Gerald L. Curtis, *Director, East Asian Institute, Columbia University*
Lloyd N. Cutler, *Partner, Wilmer, Cutler and Pickering*
Archibald K. Davis, *Chairman, Wachovia Bank and Trust Company*
Emmett Dedmon, *Vic-President and Editorial Dor., Field Enterprises, Inc.*
Louis A. Desrochers, *Partner, McCuaig and Desrochers*
Peter Dobell, *Dir., Parliamentary Ctr. for Foreign Affairs and Foreign Trade*
Hedley Donovan, *Editor-in-Chief, Time, Inc.*
Daniel J. Evans, *Governor of Washington*

---

*Executive Committee
†In Government Service in 1975

Gordon Fairweather, *Member of Parliament*
Donald M. Fraser, *House of Representatives*
Richard N. Gardner, *Henry L. Moses Professor of Law and International Organization, Columbia University*
*Patrick E. Haggerty, *Chairman, Texas Instruments*
William A. Hewitt, *Chairman, Deere and Company*
Alan Hockin, *Executive Vice-President, Toronto-Dominion Bank*
Richard Holbrooke, *Managing Editor,* Foreign Policy
Thomas L. Hughes, *Pres., Carnegie Endowment for Internat'l Peace*
J.K. Jamieson, *Chairman, Exxon Corporation*
Lane Kirkland, *Secretary-Treasurer, AFL-CIO*
Sol M. Linowitz, *Senior Partner, Coudert Brothers*
Bruce K. MacLaury, *President, Federal Reserve Bank of Minneapolis*
Claude Masson, *Professor of Economics, Laval University*
Paul W. McCracken, *Edmund Ezra Day Prof. of Business Admin., Univ. of Mich.*
Walter F. Mondale, *United States Senate*
Lee L. Morgan, *President, Caterpillar Tractor Company*
Kenneth D. Naden, *President, National Council of Farmer Cooperatives*
Henry D. Owen, *Dir. Foreign Policy Studies Program, The Brookings Institution*
David Packard, *Chairman, Hewlett-Packard Company*
*Jean-Luc Pepin, P.C., *President, Interimco, Ltd.*
John H. Perkins, *Pres., Continental Illinois National Bank and Trust Company*
Peter G. Peterson, *Chairman, Lehman Brothers*
*Edwin O. Reischauer, *Professor, Harvard; former U.S. Ambassador to Japan*
†Elliot L. Richardson, *U.S. Ambassador to the United Kingdom*
*David Rockefeller, *Chairman, Chase Manhattan Bank*
Robert V. Roosa, *Partner, Brown Brothers Harriman and Company*
*William M. Roth, *Roth Properties*
William V. Roth, Jr., *United States Senate*
Carl T. Rowan, *Columnist*
*William W. Scranton, *Former Governor of Pennsylvania*
*Gerard C. Smith, *Counsel, Wilmer, Cutler and Pickering*
Anthony Solomon, *Consultant*
Robert Taft, Jr., *United States Senate*
Arthur R. Taylor, *President, Columbia Broadcasting System, Inc.*
Cyrus R. Vance, *Partner, Simpson, Thacher and Bartlett*
*Paul C. Warnke, *Partner, Clifford, Warnke, Glass, McIlwain and Finney*
Marina von N. Whitman, *Distinguished Public Service Professor of Economics, University of Pittsburgh*
Carroll L. Wilson, *Prof. of Managem't., Alfred P. Sloan School of Managem't. MIT*
Arthur M. Wood, *Chairman, Sears Roebuck and Company*
Leonard Woodcock, *President, United Automobile Workers*

THE TRILATERAL COMMISSION
1978 Officers and North American Members

David Rockefeller, North American Chairman
Mitchell Sharp, North American Deputy Chairman
Georges Berthoin, European Chairman
Egidio Ortona, European Deputy Chairman
Takeshi Watanabe, Japanese Chairman
George S. Franklin, Coordinator
Charles B. Heck, North American Secretary
Hanns W. Maull, European Secretary
Tadashi Yamamoto, Japanese Secretary

North American Members

*I. W. Abel, *Former President, United Steelworkers of America*
David M. Abshire, *Chairman, Georgetown University Center for Strategic and International Studies*
Gardner Ackley, *Henry Carter Adams Prof. of Political Economy, Univ. of Mich.*
Graham Allison, *Dean, Public Policy Program, John F. Kennedy School of Government, Harvard*
Doris Anderson, *Former Editor,* Chatelaine *Magazine*
John B. Anderson, *House of Representatives*
Anne Armstrong, *Former U.S. Ambassador to Great Britain*
J. Paul Austin, *Chairman, The Coca-Cola Company*
George W. Ball, *Senior Partner, Lehman Brothers*
Michel Belanger, *President, Provincial Bank of Canada*
*Robert W. Bonner, Q.C., *Chairman, British Columbia Hydro*
John Brademas, *House of Representatives*
Andrew Brimmer, *President, Brimmer & Company, Inc.*
William E. Brock, III, *Chairman, Republican National Committee*
George Bush, *Former Dir. of Central Intelligence; former Chief of U.S. Liaison Office in Peking*
Claude Castonguay, *Pres., Fonds Laurentien; Chairman of the Board, Imperial Life Assurance Co.; former Minister in the Quebec Government*
Sol Chaikin, *President, International Ladies Garment Workers Union*
William S. Cohen, *House of Representatives*
*William T. Coleman, Jr., *Sr. Partner, O'Melveny & Myers; former Secretary of Transportation*
Barber B. Conable, Jr., *House of Representatives*
John Cowles, Jr., *Chairman, Minneapolis Star & Tribune Co.*
Alan Cranston, *United States Senate*
John C. Culver, *United States Senate*
Gerald L. Curtis, *Director, East Asian Institute, Columbia University*
Lloyd N. Cutler, *Partner, Wilmer, Cutler & Pickering*
John C. Danforth, *United States Senate*
Louis A. Desrochers, *Partner, McCuaig and Desrochers, Edmonton*

*Executive Committee

Peter Dobell, *Director, Parliamentary Centre for Foreign Affairs and Foreign Trade, Ottawa*

Hedley Donovan, *Editor-in-Chief, Time Inc.*

Claude A. Edwards, *Member, Public Service Staff Relations Board; former President, Public Service Alliance of Canada*

Daniel J. Evans, *Pres., Evergreen State College; former Governor of Washington*

Gordon Fairweather, *Chief Commissioner, Canadian Human Rights Commission*

Thomas S. Foley, *House of Representatives*

George S. Franklin, *Coordinator, The Trilateral Commission; former Executive Director, Council on Foreign Relations*

Donald M. Fraser, *House of Representatives*

John H. Glenn, Jr., *United States Senate*

Philip M. Hawley, *President, Carter Hawley Hale Stores, Inc.*

Walter W. Heller, *Regents' Prof. of Economics, Univ. of Minnesota*

William A. Hewitt, *Chairman, Deere & Company*

Carla A. Hills, *Cochairman, Alliance to Save Energy; former Secretary of Housing and Urban Development*

Alan Hockin, *Executive Vice President, Toronto-Dominion Bank*

James F. Hoge, Jr., *Chief Editor, Chicago Sun Times*

Hendrik S. Houthakker, *Henry Lee Prof. of Economics, Harvard*

Thomas L. Hughes, *Pres., Carnegie Endowment for Internat'l Peace*

Robert S. Ingersoll, *Deputy Chairman of the Board of Trustees, The University of Chicago; former Deputy Secretary of State*

D. Gale Johnson, *Provost, The University of Chicago*

Edgar F. Kaiser, Jr., *Pres. and Chief Exec. Officer, Kaiser Resources Ltd.*

Michael Kirby, *Pres., Institute for Research on Public Policy, Montreal*

Lane Kirkland, *Secretary-Treasurer, AFL-CIO*

*Henry A. Kissinger, *Former Secretary of State*

Sol M. Linowitz, *Senior Partner, Coudert Brothers; former Ambassador to the Organization of American States*

Winston Lord, *President, Council on Foreign Relations*

*Bruce K. MacLaury, *President, The Brookings Institution*

Paul W. McCracken, *Edmund Ezra Day Prof. of Business Admin., Univ. of Mich.*

Arjay Miller, *Dean, Graduate School of Business, Stanford University*

Lee L. Morgan, *President, Caterpillar Tractor Company*

Kenneth D. Naden, *President, National Council of Farmer Cooperatives*

*Henry Owen, *Dir., Foreign Policy Studies Program, The Brookings Institution*

David Packard, *Chairman, Hewlett-Packard Company*

Gerald L. Parsky, *Partner, Gibson, Dunn & Crutcher; former Assistant Secretary of the Treasury for International Affairs*

William R. Pearce, *Vice President, Cargill Incorporated*

Peter G. Peterson, *Chairman, Lehman Brothers*

Edwin O. Reischauer, *Professor and Director of Japan Institute, Harvard; former U.S. Ambassador to Japan*

*Charles W. Robinson, *Vice Chairman, Blyth Eastman Dillon & Co.; former Deputy Secretary of State*

*David Rockefeller, *Chairman, The Chase Manhattan Bank, N.A.*

John D. Rockefeller, IV, *Governor of West Virginia*

Robert V. Roosa, *Partner, Brown Bros., Harriman & Company*

*William M. Roth, *Roth Properties*
William V. Roth Jr., *United States Senate*
John C. Sawhill, *Pres., NYU; former Administrator, Federal Energy Administration*
Henry B. Schacht, *President, Dummins Engine Company*
*William W. Scranton, *Former Governor of Pennsylvania; former U.S. Ambassador
to the United Nations*
*Mitchell Sharp, *Member of Parliament; former Minister of External Affairs*
Mark Shepherd, Jr., *Chairman, Texas Instruments Incorporated*
Edson W. Spencer, *President and Chief Executive Officer, Honeywell Inc.*
Robert Taft, Jr., *Partner, Taft, Stettinius & Hollister*
Arthur R. Taylor
James R. Thompson, *Governor of Illinois*
Russell E. Train, *Former Administrator, Environmental Protection Agency*
Philip H. Trezise, *Former Assistant Secretary of State for Economic Affairs*
Paul A. Volcker, *President, Federal Reserve Bank of New York*
Martha R. Wallace, *Executive Dir., The Henry Luce Foundation, Inc.*
Martin J. Ward, *Pres., United Assoc. of Journeymen and Apprentices of the
Plumbing and Pipe Fitting Industry of the U.S. and Canada*
Glenn E. Watts, *President, Communications Workers of America*
Caspar W. Weinberger, *Vice Pres. and General Counsel, Bechtel Corporation*
George Weyerhaeuser, *Pres. and Chief Exec. Officer, Weyerhaeuser Company*
Marina v.N. Whitman, *Distinguished Public Service Professor of Economics,
University of Pittsburgh*
Carroll L. Wilson, *Mitsui Prof. in Problems of Contemporary Technology, Sloan
School of Management; Dir., Workshop on Alternative Energy Strategies, MIT*
T.A. Wilson, *Chairman of the Board, The Boeing Company*

Former Members in Public Service

Lucy Wilson Benson, *Under Secretary of State for Security Assistance*
W. Michael Blumenthal, *Secretary of the Treasury*
Robert R. Bowie, *Deputy to the Dir. of Central Intelligence for Nat'l Intelligence*
Harold Brown, *Secretary of Defense*
Zbigniew Brzezinski, *Ass't. to the President for National Security Affairs*
Jimmy Carter, *President of the United States*
Warren Christopher, *Deputy Secretary of State*
Richard N. Cooper, *Under Secretary of State for Economic Affairs*
Richard N. Gardner, *U.S. Ambassador to Italy*
Richard Holbrooke, *Ass't. Secretary of State for East Asian and Pacific Affairs*
Walter F. Mondale, *Vice President of the United States*
Jean-Luc Pepin, P.C., *Cochairman, Task Force on Canadian Unity*
Elliot L. Richardson, *U.S. Ambassador at Large with Responsibility for UN Law of
the Sea Conference*
Gerard C. Smith, *U.S. Ambassador at Large for Non-Proliferation Matters*
Anthony M. Solomon, *Under Secretary of the Treasury for Monetary Affairs*
Cyrus R. Vance, *Secretary of State*
Paul C. Warnke, *Dir., U.S. Arms Control and Disarmament Agency; Chief
Disarmament Negotiator*
Andrew Young, *Former U.S. Ambassador to the United Nations*

B.2   THE COUNCIL ON FOREIGN RELATIONS
1978 Officers and Directors

David Rockefeller, *Chairman of the Board*
Winston Lord, *President*
John Temple Swing, *Vice President and Secretary*
Douglas Dillon, *Vice Chairman of the Board*
Gabriel Hauge, *Treasurer*

DIRECTORS

Robert O. Anderson
George H.W. Bush
Lloyd N. Cutler
Douglas Dillon
Hedley Donovan
George S. Franklin
Philip L. Geyelin
Edward K. Hamilton
Gabriel Hauge
Theodore M. Hesburgh
Nicholas deB. Katzenbach
Lane Kirkland
Henry A. Kissinger

Winston Lord, *ex officio*
James A. Perkins
Peter G. Peterson
Lucian W. Pye
David Rockefeller
Robert V. Roosa
Stephen Stamas*
Paul A. Volcker
Martha R. Wallace
Marina v.N. Whitman
Franklin Hall Williams
Carroll L. Wilson

HONORARY OFFICERS

John J. McCloy, *Honorary Chairman*
Henry M. Wriston, *Honorary President*
Frank Altschul, *Honorary Secretary*

DIRECTORS EMERITI

Frank Altschul
Elliott V. Bell
William A.M. Burden
Arthur H. Dean
Thomas K. Finletter
William C. Foster
Caryl P. Haskins
Joseph E. Johnson

Grayson Kirk
Henry R. Labouisse
John J.McCloy
Walter H. Mallory
Philip D. Reed
Charles M. Spofford
John H. Williams
Henry M. Wriston

*Elected October 7, 1977 to fill the vacancy created by Marshall D. Shulman's resignation, to serve until the Annual Election in 1978.

THE BUSINESS COUNCIL
1977 Officers and Directors

John D. deButts, Chairman

Thomas A. Murphy, Vice Chairman

Benjamin F. Biaggini, Vice Chairman

Irving S. Shapiro, Vice Chairman

Robert S. Hatfield, Vice Chairman

John W. Burke, Jr., Executive Secretary

Executive Committee

*William M. Batten

William O. Beers

Benjamin F. Biaggini

*Fred J. Borch

John D. deButts

E. Mandell de Windt

Robert S. Hatfield

Gilbert W. Humphrey

Reginald H. Jones

*Edmund W. Littlefield

James P. McFarland

Roger Milliken

Thomas A. Murphy

*David Packard

Irving S. Shapiro

Rawleigh Warner, Jr.

F. Perry Wilson

Arthur M. Wood

Walter B. Wriston

*Ex Officio Member

Members

William M. Allen, *Chair. Em., Boeing*

Robert B. Anderson

J. Paul Austin, *Chair. Coca Cola Co.*

Malcolm Baldrige, *Chair. Scovill Mfg. Co.*

William M. Batten, *Chair. N.Y. Stock Exchange*

S.D. Bechtel, *Sr. Dir. Bechtel*

S.D. Bechtel, Jr., *Chair. Bechtel*

William O. Beers, *Chair. Kraft Inc.*

S.C. Beise, *Ex. Pres. Bank of America*

B. F. Biaggini, *Chair. & Pres. S.P RR*

James H. Binger, *Chair. Exec. Com. Honeywell*

Roger M. Blough

W.M. Blount, *Chair. & Pres. Blount, Inc.*

Fred J. Borch

Harllee Branch, Jr.

Ernest R. Breech

Wm. S. Brewster, *V. Chair. Emhart Corp.*

George R. Brown

C.L. Burgess, *Chair. Foreign Pollicy Assn.*

Donald C. Burnham, *Dir-Officer Westinghouse*

Fletcher L. Byrom, *Chair. Koppers Co.*

Louis W. Cabot, *Chair. Cabot Corp.*

Paul C. Cabot, *Chair. State Street Investment Corp.*

Edward W. Carter, *Chair. Carter Hawley Hale Stores*

Frank T. Cary, *Chair. IBM*

W.L. Cisler, *Pres. Overseas Advisory Assn.*

Howard L. Clark, *Chair. Amer. Express*

A.W. Clausen, *Pres. Bank of America*

Lucius D. Clay, *The Continental Group*

John L. Collyer

John T. Connor, *Chair. Allied Chemical*

C.W. Cook, *Chair. Ex. Com. Gen'l. Foods*

John E. Corette, *Chair. Montana Power*

Stewart S. Cort, *Dir. Bethlehem Steel*

John Cowles, *Dir. Minneapolis Star & Tribune Co.*

Bert S. Cross

J.H. Daniels, *Chair. Nat'l City Bancorp.*

Donald K. David

R. Hal Dean, *Chair. Ralston Purina Co.*

John D. deButts, *Chair. AT & T*

Hon. Frederick B. Dent, *Spec. Rep. for Trade Negotiations*

Frank R. Denton, *Ex. V. Chair. & CEO Mellon Nat'l. Bank and Trust*

E. Mandell de Windt, *Chair. Eaton Corp.*

Russell DeYoung

Charles D. Dickey, Jr., *Chair. & Pres. Scott Paper*

C. Douglas Dillon, *Chair. U.S. & Foreign Securities Corp.*

Alphonsus J. Donahue, *Pres. Donahue Sales, Textron*

Frederic G. Donner

W.Y. Elliott

E.H. Evans, Jr., *Pres. McNair Seed Co.*

Walter A. Fallon, *Chair. Eastman Kodak*

Henry Ford II, *Chair. Ford Motor Co.*

William C. Foster

Fred C. Foy

Lewis W. Foy, *Chair. Bethlehem Steel*

C. Francis, *Chair. Francis-Dillard Assoc.*

H.B. Friele

G. Keith Funston

Henry W. Gadsden

A.H. Galloway

Clifton C. Garvin, Jr., *Chair. EXXON*

Thomas S. Gates

F.V. Geier, *Chair. Exec. Com. Cin'ti. Milacron Inc.*

Philip O. Geier, Jr.

Richard L. Gelb, *Chair. Bristol-Myers*

Richard C. Gerstenberg

Carl J. Gilbert

Edwin H. Gott, *Dir. U.S. Steel Corp.*

Elisha Gray II, *Chair. Finance Com. Whirlpool Corp.*

Harry J. Gray, *Chair. & Pres. United Technologies Corp.*

Crawford H. Greenewalt, *Dir. E.I. duPont*

Courtlandt S. Gross, *Dir. Lockheed*

Alfred M. Gruenther

P.E. Haggerty, *Gen. Dir. Texas Instr. Inc.*

Michael L. Haider

Joseph B. Hall, *Cin'ti. Redevelop. Corp.*

John W. Hanley, *Chair. & Pres. Monsanto*

R.V. Hansberger, *Chair. Futura Industr.*

E.G. Harness, *Chair. Procter & Gamble*

John D. Harper, *Chair. Exec. Com. Aluminum Co. of America*

W. Averell Harriman

Shearon Harris, *Chair. & Pres. Carolina Power & Light*

R.S. Hatfield, *Chair. Continental Gp. Inc.*

H.J. Haynes, *Chair. Standard Oil of Calif.*

Ellison L. Hazard

H.H. Henley, Jr., *Pres. Cluett, Peabody*

William A. Hewitt, *Chair Deere & Co.*

Milton P. Higgins

Henry L. Hillman, *Pres. The Hillman Co.*

Jack K. Horton, *Chair. S. Calif. Edison*

Preston Hotchkis, *Chair. Bixby Ranch Co.*

A. Houghton, Jr., *Chair. Corning Glass*

G.W. Humphrey, *Chair. Hanna Mining*

Austin S. Igleheart, *Ex Dir. Gen'l Foods*

Robert S. Ingersoll

J.V. James, *Chair & Pres. Dresser Industr.*

J.K. Jamieson

S.C. Johnson, *Chair. S.C. Johnson & Son*

A. W. Jones, *Chair. Sea Island Co.*

H. C. Jones, *Chair. Burlington Industries.*

Reginald H. Jones, *Chair. Gen'l. Electric*

Edgar F. Kaiser, *Chair. Kaiser Industr.*

F.R. Kappel

George E. Keck, *Pres. Columbia Corp.*

J. Ward Keener

Donald M. Kendall, *Chair. Pepsi Co.*

John R. Kimberly, *Chair. Finance Com. Kimberly-Clark*

Justin Kingson

Joseph L. Lanier

W. F. Laporte, *Chair. Amer. Home Prod.*

Ralph Lazarus, *Chair. Fed. Dept. Stores*

Hon. T.V. Learson, *Ambassador at Large Dept. of State*

James A. Linen, III, *Dir. Time Inc.*

E.W. Littlefield, *Chair. Utah Internat'l.*

A.C. Long, *Chair. Exec. Com. Texaco*

Donold B. Lourie, *Ex Chair. Quaker Oats*

G.H. Love, *Hon. Chair. Consol. Coal Co.*

J. Paul Lyet, *Chair. Sperry Rand*

D.S. MacNaughton, *Chair. Prudential*

M. MacNaughton, *Chair. Castle & Cooke*

George P. MacNichol, Jr.

Deane W. Malott, *Ex Pres. Cornell Univ.*

R. H. Malott, *Chair. & Pres. FMC Corp.*

Barny Mason, Jr., *Chair. Ex. Chm. Union Carbide Corp.*

J.W. McAfee, *Chair. Ex. Com. Union Electric Co.*

S.M. McAshan, Jr., *Dir. Anderson, Clayton & Co.*

Thomas B. McCabe, *Dir. Scott Paper*

John L. McCaffrey

L.F. McCollum, *Ex Chair. Continental Oil*

C. Peter McColough, *Chair. Xerox*
B. McCormick, *Pres. Internat'l. Harvester*
C.B. McCoy, *Chair. Fin. Com. E I duPont*
James P. McFarland, *Chair. Exec. Com. Gen'l. Mills*
Earl M. McGowin
L.W. Menk, *Chair. Burlington Northern*
Gordon M. Metcalf, *Chair. Bd. of Trust., Svngs. & Prof. Shrng. Fnd. Sears Empl.*
Buck Mickel, *Chair. Daniel Internat'l.*
G. William Miller, *Chair. Textron*
Irwin Miller, *Chair. Cummins Engine Co.*
Otto. N. Miller
F.R. Milliken, *Pres. Kennecott Copper*
Roger Milliken, *Pres. Deering Milliken*
H Morgens, *Chair. Ex. Com. Procter & Gamble Co.*
C.G. Mortimer, *Ex Dir. Gen'l Foods*
Thomas A. Murphy, *Chair. Gen'l Motors*
W.B. Murphy
Charles F. Myers, Jr.
Albert L. Nickerson
Aksel Nielsen
Nicholas H. Noyes, *Chair. Fin. Com. Eli Lilly and Co.*
R.S. Oelman, *Chair. Ex. Com. NCR Corp*
David Packard, *Chair. Hewlett-Packard*
T.F. Patton, *Consult. Republic Steel*
Hon. Charles H. Percy, *U.S. Senator*
Donald S. Perkins, *Chair. Jewel Co.*
Thomas I. Phillips, *Chair. Raytheon*
Charles M. Pigott, *Pres. PACCAR Inc.*
C.J. Pilliod, Jr., *Chair. Goodyear Tire*
Gwilym A Price
Philip D. Reed
R.S. Reynolds, Jr., *Chair. Ex. Com. Reynolds Metals*
J.J. Riccardo, *Chair. Chrysler Corp.*
Walter M. Ringer, *Chair. Foley Mfg. Co.*
James M. Roche, *Gen'l. Motors*
D. Rockefeller, *Chair. Chase Manhattan*
W.F. Rockwell, Jr., *Chair. Rockwell International Corp.*
Donald J. Russell
Stuart T. Saunders

Charles Sawyer, *Partner Taft, Stettinius & Hollister*
Emil Schram, *Chair. Valley Farms, Inc.*
D.V. Seibert, *Chair. J.C. Penney Co.*
I.S. Shapiro, *Chair. E.I. duPont*
H.A. Shepard, *Chair. TRW Inc.*
Mark Shepherd, Jr., *Chair. Texas Instr.*
R.R. Shinn, *Pres. Metropolitan Life*
Blackwell Smith
C.R. Smith
J. Stanford Smith, *Chair. & Pres. Internat'l Paper Co.*
L.B. Smith, *Chair. A.O. Smith Corp.*
C.H. Sommer, *Dir. Monsanto Co.*
Edgar B. Speer, *Chair. U.S. Steel Corp.*
Frank Stanton
R.T. Stevens, *Dir. J.P. Stevens & Co.*
Geo. A. Stinson, *Chair. Nat'l Steel Corp.*
Hardwick Stires, *Gen'l. Partner Scudder, Stevens & Clark*
R.D. Stuart, Jr., *Chair. Quaker Oats*
A. T. Taylor, *Chair. Deltec Internat'l. Ltd*
C.A. Thomas, *Chair. Washington Univ.*
E.J. Thomas
C. B. Thornton, *Chair. Litton Industries*
Lynn A. Townsend
Juan T. Trippe, *Hon. Chair. Pan Am Air*
Solon B. Turman
John C. Virden
J. Carlton Ward, Jr.
Rawleigh Warner, Jr., *Chair. Mobil Oil*
Thomas J. Watson Jr., *Chair. Ex. Com. IBM*
G. H. Weyerhaeuser, *Pres. Weyerhaeuser*
J.H. Whitney, *Chair. Whitney Commun.*
Langbourne M. Williams
F. Perry Wilson
T.A. Wilson, *Chair. Boeing Co.*
H. S. Wingate, *Ex Chair. INCO, Ltd.*
A.M. Wood, *Chair. Sears, Roebuck*
R.W. Woodruff, *Chair. Fin. Com. Coca-Cola Co.*
Walter B. Wriston, *Chair. Citicorp*
H.W. Zinmaster, *Chair. Zinmaster Baking Co.*

THE BUSINESS ROUNDTABLE
1978 Policy Committee Members

Thomas A. Murphy, Chairman
Clifton C. Garvin, Jr., Cochairman
Reginald H. Jones, Cochairman
Charles J. Pilliod, Jr., Cochairman

Policy Committee Members

Ray C. Adam, *NL Industries*
Robinson F. Barker, *PPG Industries*
John F. Bookout, *Shell Oil*
Fletcher L. Byrom, *Koppers Co.*
Frank T. Cary, *IBM*
John T. Connor, *Allied Chemical*
Justin Dart, *Dart Industries*
John D. deButts, *A.T.&T.*
James H. Evans, *Union Pacific*
James L. Ferguson, *General Foods*
Lewis W. Foy, *Bethlehem Steel*
Clifton C. Garvin, Jr., *Exxon*
Richard L. Gelb, *Bristol-Myers*
W.H. Krome George, *ALCOA*
John P. Harbin, *Halliburton*
Edward G. Harness, *Procter & Gamble*
Shearon Harris, *Carolina Power & Light*
Robert S. Hatfield, *Continental Group*
Raymond H. Herzog, *3M*
Gilbert W. Humphrey, *Hanna Mining*
Reginald H. Jones, *General Electric*
Ralph Lazarus, *Federated Dept. Stores*
Ruben F. Mettler, *TRW*

Roger Milliken, *Milliken & Co.*
Lee L. Morgan, *Caterpillar Tractor*
Thomas A. Murphy, *General Motors*
David Packard, *Hewlett-Packard*
Donald S. Perkins, *Jewel Companies*
Charles J. Pilliod, Jr., *Goodyear*
Donald T. Regan, *Merrill Lynch*
John J. Riccardo, *Chrysler*
Richard A. Riley, *Firestone*
David Rockefeller, *Chase Manhattan*
Donald V. Seibert, *J.C. Penney*
Irving S. Shapiro, *DuPont*
Richard R. Shinn, *Metropolitan Life*
Geroge P. Shultz, *Bechtel*
William S. Sneath, *Union Carbide*
Edgar B. Speer, *U.S. Steel*
George A. Stinson, *National Steel*
Edward R. Telling, *Sears, Roebuck*
O. Pendleton Thomas, *B.F. Goodrich*
Rawleigh Warner, Jr., *Mobil Oil*
William L. Wearly, *Ingersoll-Rand*
Richard D. Wood, *Eli Lilly*
Walter B. Wriston, *Citibank*

Senior Member
John D. Harper, *ALCOA*

F.1 COMMITTEE ON THE PRESENT DANGER
1976 Officers and Directors

W.V. O'Brien, *Chair. Dept. of Gov. Georgetown University*

G. Olmsted, *Chair. Internat'l Bank, Washington*

David Packard, *Chair of Bd. Hewlett-Packard; ex Deputy Secty Defense*

James L. Payne, *Prof. Texas A&M Univ.*

R.L. Pfaltzgraff, Jr. *Prof. Fletcher School of Law and Diplomacy*

Midge D. Podhoretz, *Author and Editor*

Norman Podhoretz, *Editor, Commentary*

U. Ra'anan, *Prof. Fletcher School*

E.R. Ramey, *Prof. Georgetown Univ.*

Paul Ramsey, *Prof. Princeton University*

M.B. Ridgway, *Gen'l U.S. Army [Ret.]; ex Chief of Staff U.S. Army*

J.P. Roche, *Fletcher School of Law; Spec. Consultant to Pres. Johnson*

Rose H. Chapman, *Ex Under Secty of Treasury*

Peter R. Rosenblatt, *Attorney*

E.V. Rostow, *Prof Yale Law School; ex Under Secty of State*

James H. Rowe, Jr., *Admin Asst to Pres. Roosevelt*

Dean Rusk, *Prof. Univ. of Georgia; ex Secty of State*

B. Rustin, *Pres. A.P. Randolph Institute*

C.E. Saltzman, *Partner, Goldman, Sachs & Co.; ex Under Secty of State*

R.M. Scaife, *Publisher, Tribune-Review*

R. Schifter, *Attorney*

P. Seabury, *Prof. Univ. of California*

A. Shanker, *Pres. Amer. Fed. of Teachers*

M.B. Skacel, *Pres. Chamber of Commerce of Latin Amer. in USA*

Fred Smith, *Chair. Bd. of Trustees, Nat'l Planning Assoc.; ex Asst to Secty of Treasury*

L.H. Smith, *Pres. Paraffine Oil Corp.*

K. Spang, *Int. Bus. Adviser, Citibank*

R,I. Straus, *Dir. Atlantic Council*

H.W. Sweatt, *Ex Chair. Honeywell*

G.K. Tanham, *V. Pres. Rand Corp.*

H. Taylor, Jr., *Ex Dir. Export-Import Bank*

M. D. Taylor, *Gen'l. US Army [Ret.]; ex Chair. Joint Chiefs of Staff and Chief of Staff, US Army*

Edward Teller, *Ex Prof. Univ. of Calif.*

A. Temple, *Chair, Pres., Temple-Eastex*

J.C. Turner, *Pres. Int. Union of Operating Engineers*

C. Tyroler II, *Pres. Quadri-Science Inc; ex Dir. Manp'wr Supply Dept Defense*

W.R. Van Cleave, *Prof. Univ. of S. Calif.*

C.E. Walker, *C.E. Walker Assoc.; ex Deputy Secty of Treasury*

M.J. Ward, *Pres. Plumbers & Pipe Fitters Internat'l Union*

R.E. Ward, *Dir. Ctr for Research in Internat'l Studies, Stanford Univ.*

P.S Weaver, *Pres. Lake Erie College*

R.J. Whalen, *Author and journalist*

E.P. Wigner, *Prof. Princeton Univ.*

F.O. Wilcox, *Dir. Atlantic Council; ex Asst. Secty of State, Chief of Staff, Senate Foreign Relations Com.*

B.D. Wolfe, *Ex Prof. Univ. of Calif; Sr. Res. Fellow Hoover Inst., Stanford*

E.R. Zumwalt, *Admiral USN [Ret.]; ex Chief of Naval Operations*

G.1 THE ATLANTIC COUNCIL of the UNITED STATES
1978 Officers and Directors

Officers and Members of the
Board of Directors

Chairman:
K. Rush, *ex Deputy Secty of State and Ambassador to France and Germany*

Treasurer:
P.F. Brundage, *ex Dir U.S. Budget*

Secretary:
T. Killefer, *Chair U.S. Trust Co.*

Director General:
F.O. Wilcox, *ex Asst Secty of State; Dean SAIS, Johns Hopkins Univ.*

Deputy Dir. General:
J.W. Harned, *U.S. Rep., Atlantic Inst. for Internatl Affairs*

Asst. Dir. General: Martha C. Finley, *ex Admin U.S. Citizen Commiss to NATO*

Vice Chairmen:
H.H. Fowler, *Partner Goldman Sachs & Co., ex Secty Treasury*

W.R. Burgess, *ex Under Secty Treasury Ambassador to NATO and OEEC*

T.C. Achilles, *ex Counselor State Dept & Ambassador to Peru*

Harlan Cleveland, *Dir. Aspen Prog. in Internatl Affairs; ex Ambass to NATO*

E.G. Collado, *ex V Pres. Exxon and Dir. World Bank*

A.J. Goodpaster, *ex Sup. Allied Commander Europe*

W. McC. Martin *ex Char. Bd of Gov. Federal Reserve System*

D. Packard, *Chair Hewlett-Packard; ex Deputy Secty of Defense*

E.V. Rostow, *Prof. Yale Univ.; ex Under Secty of State*

Directors:

D.M. Abshire, *Chair. Ctr for Strategic & Internatl Studies, Georgetown Univ.; ex Asst Secty of State*

D.C. Acheson, *Atty. and ex Counsel, Communications Satellite Corp.*

D.G. Agger, *Pres. DGA Internatl Inc.*

Anne Armstrong, *ex Ambass to Britain & Spec Asst to the President*

W.C. Armstrong, *Consultant,; ex Asst Secty of State*

E.W. Barrett, *Consultant, and ex Asst Secty of State*

A.H. Berding,*ex Asst Secty of State*

J. Blackwelder, *Pres. Environ. Fund*

G. Bradley, *Pres. Internatl Management & Dev. Institute*

W.A.M. Burden, *Partner, W.A.M. Burden & Co.; ex Ambass. to Belgium*

G. Bush, *ex Dir CIA; member Congress*

H.Carter III, *Asst. Secty of State*

W.J. Casey, *ex Under Secty of State and Pres. Export-Import Bank of U.S.*

S.C. Chaikin, *Pres., Genl Secty ILGWU*

G.A. Costanzo, *V Chair. Citicorp & Citibank*

F.L. Deming, *Pres., Natl City Bancorp; ex Under Secty Treasury*

R.L. Dennison, *ex Supreme Allied Commander, Atlantic*

W.D. Eberle, *ex Rep for Trade Negot.*

R.F. Ellsworth, *ex Dep Secty Defense and Ambassador to NATO*

B. Emeny, *ex Pres. Foreign Policy Assoc.*

S.L. Fawcett, *Pres. Battelle Mem. Inst.*

W.H.G. FitzGerald, *V Chair. Financial Genl Bank Shares Inc.*

W.C. Foster, *ex Dir Arms Control & Disarm. Agency; Dep. Secty Defense*

G.S. Franklin Jr., *Coord. Trilateral Commission*

C.J. Gilbert, *ex Spec Rep for Trade Negotiations*

L. Gordon, *Sr. Fellow, Resources for the Future; ex Asst Secty State*

J.E. Gray, *Pres. Internatl Energy Assoc.*
Livingston Hartley, *Author*
C.A. Herter Jr., *ex Dep. Asst Secty State*
J.D. Hickerson, *ex Asst Secty State;
Ambass. to Finland & Phillippines*
M.J. Hillenbrand, *Dir. Genl Atlantic
Inst. for Internatl Affairs; ex Ambass. to
Germany*
C.G. Hoffman, *Dir. Bank of America*
J. Holland, *ex Ambass. to Sweden*
J.A. Hovey Jr., *Supv Auditor, Govt.
Accounting Office*
T.L. Hughes, *Chair. Carnegie Endow.
for Internatl Peace; ex Asst Secty State*
J.N. Irwin II, *ex Dep. Secty of State;
Ambassador to France*
U.A. Johnson, *ex Chief, US Delegation
to SALT; Under Secty of State*
H.A. Kissinger, *ex Secty of State*
P. Krogh, *Dean, Georgetown Univ.*
J.M. Leddy, *ex Asst Secty of State &
the Treasury*
L.L. Lemnitzer, *ex Supreme Allied
Commander, Europe*
Walter J. Levy, *Consultant*
W. Lord, *Pres., Council on Foreign
Relations; ex Asst Secty of State*
J. Lovestone, *ex Dir. of Internatl Affairs
AFL-CIO*
D.W. MacEachron, *Dir. Japan Society*
H.B. Malmgren, *Consultant, ex Dep.
Spec. Rep. for Trade Negotiations*
E.M. Martin, *ex Asst Secty State;
Ambassador to Argentina*
J.S. McDonnell, *Chair. McDonnell
Douglas Corp.*
G.C. McGhee, *ex Under Secty of State;
Ambass. to Germany and Turkey*
R.M. McKinney, *ex Ambass. to Switzer-
land and to Internatl Atomic Energy Ag.*
L.C. McQuade, *V. Pres. WR Grace Co.;
ex Asst Secty of Commerce*
George Meany, *Pres. AFL-CIO*
S.W. Meek, *Chair. Walker Publishing*
M. Muir, *Hon. Chair. Newsweek*
P.H. Nitze, *ex Secty of Navy and Dep.
Secty of Defense*
F.E. Nolting Jr., *Prof. Univ. of Virginia;
ex Ambassador to Viet-Nam*

R. E. Osgood, *Dean, SAIS, Johns
Hopkins Univ.*
H.H. Porter, *Assoc. Dir. Appl. Physics
Lab, Johns Hopkins Univ.*
J.J. Reinstein, *ex Minister for Economic
Affairs, Paris*
E.J. Rice, *V Pres Natl Bank of Wash.*
C.W. Robinson, *V Chair. Blyth Eastman
Dillon & Co; ex Under Secty of State*
R.V. Roosa, *Partner, Brown Bros Harri-
man; ex Under Secty of Treasury*
H.C. Rose, *Lawyer; ex Secty of Treasury*
D. Rumsfeld, *Pres. GD Searle; ex Secty
of Defense and Ambass to NATO*
N. Samuels, *Chair. L. Dreyfus Corp.; ex
Under Secty of State*
J.R. Schaetzel, *Author; ex Ambassador
to the Euro. Communities*
A.W. Schmidt, *ex Ambass. to Canada*
C.v.R. Schuyler, *ex Chief of Staff, Sup-
reme Allied Command Europe*
B. Scowcroft, *ex Asst to Pres. for Natl.
Security Affairs*
J.M. Segel, *Chair. Presidential Airways;
ex US Delegate to UN Genl Assembly*
J.J. Sisco, *Pres. American University;
ex Under Secty of State*
H. Sonnenfeldt, *Vis. Scholar, SAIS,
Johns Hopkins; ex Counselor Dept State*
F.A. Southard Jr., *Consultant; ex US
Dir. Internatl Monetary Fund*
T.W. Stanley, *Pres. Internatl Economic
Policy Assoc.*
R.I. Straus, *Consultant*
R. Strausz-Hupe, *ex Ambass. to NATO,
Sweden, Belgium, Sri Lanka*
E. Tompkins, *Member Amer. Council on
Education*
P.H. Trezise, *Fellow Brookings Inst.; ex
Asst Secty of State; Ambass to OECD.*
W.C. Turner, *ex Ambass to OECD*
J.W. Tuthill, *Pres. Salzburg Seminar; ex
Ambass. to Brazil and OECD*
M.v.N. Whitman, *Prof. Univ. of Pitts-
burgh, ex Member Pres. Council of
Economic Advisers*
W.Wise, *ex US Delegate to UN Genl.
Assembly*

Appendix II

Ownership and Control of the Influential Media

The most influential media corporations of the United States are all controlled by the Eastern Establishment — the dominant sector of the American ruling class — and represent a main source of this Establishment's ideological hegemony over American society. Generally speaking, the more important the media outlet is, the more connections its owners and directors have to the other central institutions of this establishment. Here we will cover the ownership and control of the six most influential media corporations of the Eastern Establishment, in roughly descending order of importance.

THE *NEW YORK TIMES*

The *Times* is owned by the Sulzbergers, an upper-class family of the highest social standing. Family members attend the right schools and colleges, are patrons of the arts and education, and are members of the *Social Register* and clubs like the Century and Metropolitan. As of 1974-75, Sulzberger family members owned about 70 percent of the *Times* Class B stock which controls 70 percent of voting power for the Board of Directors.[1] Another nearly 25 percent of Class B stock is held in the *New York Times'* own Treasury.[2] Family members also hold almost 40 percent of Class A stock, which elects the remaining 30 percent of the Board of Directors.[3] The chairman and president of today's newspaper is Arthur Ochs Sulzberger, who is also a member of the Council on Foreign Relations. As of 1976 three other family members sat on the eleven-person board of directors and several additional family members were employed by the company in top positions. One of the family on the *New York Times* board of directors, Marion Sulzberger Heiskell, is married to Andrew Heiskell, chairman of the board of *Time* magazine, thus linking two of the most fervent of Carter's media supporters.

The board of the *New York Times* during 1975 and 1976 included executives or directors of Morgan Guaranty Trust, Bankers Trust, American Can, and Bristol-Meyers; as well as Cyrus Vance, vice chairman of the CFR and a Trilateral Commissioner; James Reston, a member of the Century and Metropolitan Clubs and active in the Council on Foreign Relations for nearly thirty years; CFR member and CED trustee Richard L. Gelb; and CED trustee and Links Club member William F. May. John B. Oakes, editorial page editor of the *Times* and a member of the owning family, is a member of the CFR and the Century and Cosmos Clubs. All these connections clearly tie the *New York Times* with the dominant element of the American ruling class.

TIME MAGAZINE

Time's ownership structure is more complex than that of the *New York Times*. Several families and New York banks have significant voting rights in the corporation. The key owners of *Time* are the Luce, Larson, Temple and Keeler families and their foundations, trust and funds, which hold over 18 percent of *Time* common stock. All four of these families have direct representation on *Time*'s Board of Directors.[4] In addition, seven banks control 23.5 percent of *Time* stock, led by Morgan Guaranty and Chase Manhattan with 7.4 percent and 5.5 percent respectively.[5] This links *Time* with Carter friend J. Paul Austin (a Morgan director) and, of course, David Rockefeller (chairman of Chase). *Time*, like the *New York Times*, is intimately connected with Eastern Establishment groups like the CFR and Trilateral Commission. As of 1975 two Trilateral commissioners sat on *Time*'s board — *Time*'s editor-in-chief Hedley Donovan, who is also a CFR director, and corporate lawyer Sol M. Linowitz. Kirbo friend, Thomas J. Watson, Jr. of IBM, was also a member of the board. Seven of *Time*'s directors are also members of the Council on Foreign Relations, several are in the *Social Register* or are CED trustees, Links Club members, and university trustees. They direct corporations like Bank of America, Chemical Bank, First National City Bank of Chicago, Colgate-Palmolive, Continental Oil, Standard Oil of California, Kaiser Steel, Mobil Oil, IBM, Bankers Trust, Pan American, Caterpillar Tractor, and others. *Time* is thus very well connected to the Eastern Establishment and is one of its main media outlets.

COLUMBIA BROADCASTING SYSTEM

CBS was created nearly fifty years ago by William S. Paley, who has systematically exercised power of this multibillion dollar corporation up to the present time. As chairman, Paley still rules the company, deciding who will fill the top management positions and even, in some cases, what programs will be aired.[6] As of 1978 Paley and his family owned and voted 6.31 percent of CBS stock, by far the largest single block of stock. Two other CBS directors control 1.67 and 1.18 percent respectively.[7] Paley is, of course, immensely wealthy, with personal assets estimated at over $100 million. He is also intermarried with the Cushing family of Boston, making him an in-law of New York's upper-class Whitney and Astor families.[8] While Paley still controls the biggest individual block of CBS stock, eleven large banks, mostly headquartered in New York, now hold in trusts 38.1 percent of CBS stock.[9] The Rockefeller bank, Chase Manhattan, holds by far the biggest bank block, 14.1 percent and Robert O. Anderson, chairman of Atlantic-Richfield, sits on both boards.[10] An additional Rockefeller-CBS tie is provided by CFR member and *Social Register* listee Roswell L. Gilpatric, who is a director of both Eastern Airlines and CBS. Paley himself is a long-time active member of the Council on Foreign Relations and CFR director William A.M. Burden, a *Social Register* listee, is also on the CBS board. Six additional CFR members are on the CBS board, including, until the fall of 1976, CBS president Arthur R. Taylor, who was additionally a member of the Trilateral Commission. As is the case of the *New York Times* and *Time*, CBS directors sit on a host of other corporate boards, are trustees of CED, American Assembly, and elite universities, and belong to the prestigious clubs and associations of the Eastern Establishment.

LOS ANGELES TIMES

Control of the *Los Angeles Times* has been in the hands of the Chandler family since the nineteenth century. The current publisher, Otis Chandler, is the great-grandson of Harrison Gray Otis, the first publisher of the newspaper.[11] As is the case with CBS and *Time*, eastern and midwestern banks also control voting rights to significant ownership blocks of *Los Angeles Times* stock, amounting to 19.8 percent as of 1974.[12] This percentage does not appear to be high enough, however, given the Chandlers' large stock holdings in the company, to exercise much influence. With one exception, the only individuals included in the official list of stockholders with 1 percent or more of *Times* stock as of September 1977 are the seven trustees of Chandler trusts numbers one and two. These include Otis, Harrison, and Bruce Chandler, all directors of the *Times*, as well as May Chandler Goodan and Ruth Chandler Crocker. Another entry, Chandis Securities, is a Chandler family holding company, with Harrison Chandler as chairman and president. The official list of large stockholders is rounded out by eight banks, three mutual funds, two stock exchanges, one insurance company, and the Mormon Church.[13] None of these latter institutions appears to be represented on the *Times* board of directors.

The *Los Angeles Times* is less well connected to the institutions of the Eastern Establishment than the three media mentioned above, but several of its directors have important ties with it and Jimmy Carter. The key links in 1976 included Trilateral Commissioner and CFR member Harold Brown, a member of the *Los Angeles Times* board, as well as a director of IBM with Watson and Vance. Otis Chandler is also a director of Pan American Airways as was Vance. Another interesting link to Carter is formed by *Los Angeles Times* director Lowell S. Dillingham, chairman of Hawaii's Dillingham Corporation. His daughter Gail is married to William C. Bartholomay, a key Carter contributor and owner of the Atlanta Braves (see Chapter One). *Los Angeles Times* board members are directors of corporations like American Airlines, Ford, Bank of America, and various west coast corporations.

NEWSWEEK

The Washington Post, which owns *Newsweek* magazine, has been in the hands of the Meyer-Graham families since the 1930s when financier Eugene Meyer purchased the newspaper. The two families are united in the person of Katharine Graham, Meyer's daughter and current chairperson of the Washington Post Company. The *Post* has few stockholders outside these two families; banks control only 1 percent for example.[14] The list of owners of 1 percent or more of *Post* stock is dominated by five Grahams and five Meyers, headed by Katharine and Donald F. Graham, both directors of the company.[15] Unlike the media corporations mentioned above, the *Post* had no direct Trilateral Commission connection during 1975. Other Eastern Establishment ties were strong, however, through Katharine Graham, who was a CED trustee, and *Post* directors Nicholas DeB. Katzenbach, a CFR and IBM director, and Arjay Miller, a Wells Fargo Bank director who joined the Trilateral Commission sometime in 1976 or early 1977.

THE WALL STREET JOURNAL

The daily operation of this newspaper is in the hands of professional journalists, but a few families control the ownership and exercise ultimate direction. Available information indicates that control of Dow Jones and Company, the parent corporation of the *Wall Street Journal, Barron's,* and the *National Observer,* is in the hands of the descendants of former Dow Jones president Hugh Bancroft, whose wife was a member of the Barron family, one of the founding families of Dow Jones. The list of owners of 1 percent or more of Dow Jones stock is dominated by the trusts, trustees, and relatives of Jane Bancroft Cook and Jessie Bancroft Cox, both directors of Dow Jones.[16] Another director, James N. White, is a trustee of a Jane Bancroft Cook trust.[17] Three members of the Ottaway family also jointly own 1 percent or more and have a family member on the board, but they are mentioned only once in the official list of large stockholders. In contrast, the Bancroft-Cox-Cook wills, agreements, and trusts add up to seven separate entries on the published list of large stockholders, together making up a complex set of relationships between several banks, lawyers, and beneficial owners.[18]

An official history of the company written in the late 1960s indirectly confirms that the Bancroft family controls Dow Jones by stating that fully two-thirds of the outstanding shares of stock are owned in trusts by the descendants of early owners.[19] The eight remaining directors of Dow Jones include Carter friend and Trilateral commissioner J. Paul Austin, three members of the *Social Register,* two members of the CFR, two members each of the Century Association and Metropolitan Club, a CED trustee, and directors of Mobil Oil, American Express, Caterpillar Tractor, IBM, General Foods, and Royal Dutch Shell, the last five having at least one Trilateral commissioner on each of their boards of directors. Thus the *Wall Street Journal* is almost as closely connected to the same Eastern Establishment network as our other news media.

The ownership and interconnections of these media corporations illustrate how closely intertwined are the elite media in the United States. They are intimately linked with each other and with many leading corporations as well as with the most important policy planning organizations of upper-class America. One example of these interconnections is IBM, a corporation which has common board members with the *New York Times, Time, Los Angeles Times, The Wall Street Journal,* and the *Washington Post/ Newsweek.*

Notes on Appendix II

1. *Moody's Industrial Manual* (New York, 1976), II, pp. 3269-3270.
2. Ibid.
3. Ibid.
4. See Time, Inc., *Joint Property Statement,* September 21, 1978, pp. 52-53.
5. United States Senate, Committee on Government Operations, *Disclosure of Corporate Ownership,* (Washington, D.C.: U.S. Government Printing Office, 1974), p. 170.
6. David Halberstam, "CBS: The Power and the Profits," *Atlantic,* January 1976, p. 36.

7. United States Senate, *Voting Rights in Major Corporations: Staff Study prepared by the Subcommittee on Reports, Accounting and Management of the Committee on Governmental affairs,* (Washington, D.C.: U.S. Government Printing Office, 1978), p. 57.

8. Halberstam, "CBS: The Power and the Profits," p. 36.

9. Senate, *Disclosure of Corporate Ownership,* p. 169.

10. Ibid.

11. *Los Angeles Times,* August 9, 1976, IV, p. 2.

12. U.S. Senate, *Disclosure of Corporate Ownership,* p. 171.

13. Official list taken from *Los Angeles Times,* September 29, 1977, p. I32.

14. U.S. Senate, *Disclosure of Corporate Ownership,* p. 182.

15. *Newsweek,* October 11, 1976, p. 103 and October 10, 1977, p. 115.

16. *Barron's,* October 13, 1975, p. 44.

17. Ibid.

18. Ibid.

19. Dow Jones and Company, Inc., *Well Beyond the Average: The Story of Dow Jones and Company, Inc.,* (New York, n.d.), p. 57.

Index